THE NEXT FORM OF DEMOCRACY

THE NEXT FORM OF DEMOCRACY

How Expert Rule Is Giving Way
to Shared Governance . . .
and Why Politics Will Never Be the Same

Matt Leighninger

Foreword by U.S. Senator Bill Bradley

Vanderbilt University Press
Nashville

© 2006 Vanderbilt University Press
All rights reserved
First edition 2006

10 09 08 07 06   1 2 3 4 5

Printed on acid-free paper.
Manufactured in the United States of America
Designed by Wendy McAnally

Library of Congress Cataloging-in-Publication Data

Leighninger, Matthew.
    The next form of democracy : how expert rule is giving way
    to shared governance-and why politics will never be the same /
    Matt Leighninger, with a foreword by Bill Bradley.—1st ed.
p. cm.
Includes bibliographical references and index.
ISBN 0–8265–1540–1 (cloth : alk. paper)
ISBN 0–8265–1541-X (pbk. : alk. paper)
1. Local government—United States—Citizen participation.
2. Political participation—United States.
3. Democracy—United States. I. Bradley, Bill, 1943- II. Title.
JS391.L45 2006
320.80973—dc22
    2006010591

For Don Lukens and Tom Donnelly,
builders of great institutions

Contents

Acknowledgments

I never intended to write a book. But I found that, in the course of my work, I was being presented with some truly remarkable stories. I began to compile, interpret, and compare these narratives, because that helped me process what I was observing. Eventually, I realized that this was all one story: an account of political change in North America.

So the first group of people I have to acknowledge are the people who have lived this story: the local leaders who are helping their communities navigate the transition from expert rule to shared governance. Some of them are public officials or other kinds of established leaders; others are organizers of temporary projects. Most of them have received very little recognition, even in the midst of their greatest successes.. All of them are extraordinary people, and I have continually been inspired and encouraged by their efforts. I would particularly like to thank Jon Abercrombie, Shakoor Aljuwani, Steve Burkholder, Fran Frazier, Anji Husain, Arnette Johnson, Sandy Robinson, Carol Scott, and Gwen Wright for all they have taught me over the years.

Since I am describing their experiences, some of these local leaders are featured in the book. But there are many others who have helped me understand what their communities are going through, including: Susan Anderson, Faye Bonneau, Bliss Bruen, Sally Campbell, William Carpenter, Melody Ehrlich, Dan Farley, Pat Fruiht, Janet Gendler, Mary Jane Hollis, the Reverend Ernest Jones, John Landesman, Paddy Lane, Kari Lang, Bruce Mallory, Rob Marchiony, Roseann Mason, Carol Munro, Sue Mutchler, Mary Patenaude, Meg Shields, Susan Singh, Ruth Sokolowski, and Judy White.

I would never have had the chance to be inspired by these people if not for the generosity and vision of the late Paul Aicher. As the founder of the Study Circles Resource Center, he ensured that hundreds of communities could have the advice and assistance they needed to launch their own civic experiments. To know Paul was to be in an argument with Paul; he helped to refine the ideas in this book by trying to refute them all. I can still hear the "harrumphs" of his benevolent antagonism.

Martha McCoy and Pat Scully were enthusiastic about my work on this book from the very beginning. They helped me think through my hypotheses, and connected me with other observers of the field. Through their comradeship and their mutual interest in learning from communities, all of my colleagues at the Resource Center—especially Carolyne Abdullah, Molly Barrett, Amy Malick, and Francine Nichols—made great contributions to this book.

My colleagues at the National League of Cities, particularly Gwen Wright, Chris Hoene, and Bill Barnes, provided me with another arena in which to learn. The opportunity to work with them, and with the elected officials on NLC's Democratic Governance Panel, gave me a much greater perspective on what is happening to the relationship between citizens and government. Similarly, Kathy Bailey and NeighborWorks America gave me the chance to learn firsthand from practitioners who are constructing new housing, mobilizing residents, and revitalizing economies at the neighborhood level.

I have also gained a great deal from my contacts with the League of Women Voters' Washington staff and the leaders of its state and local chapters. Cheryl Graeve, Carol Scott, and their tireless, intrepid fellow Leaguers have always inspired and informed my writing.

There is one final organization I must mention: Haverford College, which provided an ideal environment for the development of well-rounded citizenship. Professor Sara Shumer cultivated my interest in democracy, and helped me connect my personal experiences to the political world. Along with Susan Stuard, Paul Jefferson, and Jane Caplan, she gave me the theoretical tools I needed to make sense of my work. Dan O'Flaherty and his colleagues at Columbia's School of International and Public Affairs helped me apply those ideas more specifically to local governance.

Many people were kind enough to review parts of this manuscript — contributing ideas, correcting my mistakes, and providing new information. Peter Adler, Tom Argust, Kathy Bailey, Pamela Beal, Roger Bernier, Carrie Boron, Ruth Ann Bramson, Steve Burkholder, Kiran Cunningham, Ben Eason, Julie Fanselow, Fran Frazier, Archon Fung, Heather Gage-Detherow, Joe Goldman, Sandy Heierbacher, Martin Horn, Jim Hunt, Michael Johnson, Nan Kari, Mark Linder, Amy Malick, Michael McCormick, Harold McDougall, Lyn Menne, Miles Rapoport, Bill Potapchuk, Justin Powell, Brad Rourke, David Ryfe, Lee Serravillo, Carmen Sirianni, Kristina Smock, Clarence Stone, Mary Stone, Paul Thomas, Lars Torres, Katherine Cramer Walsh, and Gwen Wright all gave insights and encouragement. Tim Erickson, Amy Lang, Leanne Nurse, and Martin Rutte took part in an informal title-brainstorming focus group. Meg Shields and Miriam Wyman welcomed me to Canada and gave me a crash course in the recent evolution of Canadian democracy.

Michael Ames at Vanderbilt was always willing to read drafts and provide incisive suggestions. I am very lucky, as my academic colleagues often remind me, to have found an editor who takes such an active role in the writing process.

I write best in quiet crowds, and so most of this book was produced in libraries, coffeehouses, and airplanes. I must thank the staff of the McMaster University Library, the *Staatsbibliothek zu Berlin*, and the Bean Bar of Hamilton, Ontario, for providing working environments that featured books, caffeine, and just enough commotion. My friend Saeed Ahmad always got me to the airport punctually, safely, and amiably.

Molly Barrett has played an integral role in all of my writing for the last twelve years. I have always benefited by her comments on language and ideas, along with her singular strategy of looking at a paragraph and exclaiming, "Oh, that's very nice. But what did you really *mean* to say?"

Bill Barnes and Éva Dömötör have mentored me for even longer, using their dinner table as a convivial training ground for my intellectual development. It took me a long time to conceptualize what I was trying to say in this book, and many of the key breakthroughs came as a result of their friendly, thoughtful interrogations. Jay and Charlene Swett welcomed me into their family and broadened my horizons considerably; they also provided warm hospitality on my frequent trips to New England.

My parents, Bob and Leslie Leighninger, have influenced me in ways that I am only beginning to discover. By their own example, they show how writing and scholarship can be of service to society. In a true test of parental devotion, my father provided feedback on every single chapter. Their parents, Bob and Ruth Leighninger and Paul and Paulette Hartrich, established a legacy of community service and civic activism that I will always strive to uphold.

Jack and Nathaniel Leighninger, my sons, are always eager to hand out flyers about one of "Papa's famous meetings" to their teachers and the parents of their friends. Though they can't yet fathom what I do for a living, they are now at least willing to believe that I do have a job. They are the best reminders of how important it is to think about the future.

Finally, it is hard to express how much I owe Pamela Swett, whom I am fortunate to call my wife. She never complained about reading chapter drafts three times over — and her comments on democratic governance are far more astute than my thoughts on German history. Her indomitable character, her commitment to her scholarship, and her faith in me contribute immeasurably to my life and work. This book is a tribute to our partnership.

Foreword

by U. S. Senator Bill Bradley

In 1995, I learned firsthand about an idea that was stirring among public officials and community organizers across America. Shortly after O. J. Simpson's acquittal, Los Angeles city officials convened "Days of Dialogue" to give people throughout the city an opportunity to share their views on the complex and intensely personal topic of race relations. I was invited to sit in on a session at a drug rehabilitation center, where a member of the Nation of Islam served as an evenhanded facilitator, making sure everyone had a chance to speak.

Seeing the willingness of people to come together amid highly charged circumstances to talk about their lives, their fears, and their hopes made a deep impression on me. I was moved by the participants' civility and honesty, and I believe these discussions may have helped avert a wave of violence like the one that accompanied the 1992 Rodney King verdicts. Just as important, the dialogues gave participants a much-needed chance to talk plainly about racism and racial division with people from backgrounds different from their own. The Days of Dialogue—which expanded to take place nationally in the late 1990s—were an early example of the sort of civic engagement Matt Leighninger describes throughout *The Next Form of Democracy.*

In this book, Leighninger chronicles a movement that is still too new to have a name (although groups like the National League of Cities refer to it as "democratic governance"). The phenomenon—which is taking shape across the country in many different ways—is fueled by the notion that public life is too important to be left solely to the professionals. When we create real, ongoing opportunities for all sorts of people to work together and to become active citizens in meaningful ways, we strengthen our communities and improve relationships between public servants and those they serve.

Leighninger brings outstanding credentials to his task of document-ing the rise of democratic governance. Through his work with the Study Circles Resource Center, the National League of Cities, and many other civic organizations, Leighninger has helped hundreds of communities in forty states launch local efforts to bring citizens to the table on many issues, including education, racism and race relations, criminal justice, and growth and development. The stories he tells are rooted in his own experience—he really knows these people and has worked side-by-side with many of them. He has learned why civic engagement initiatives work—and how they sometimes fail. Drawing on this experience, he describes ways that local organizers have made room for the talents and passions of all citizens, not just the traditional power brokers. Leighninger's stories illuminate the highest principles of collective life in the context of real communities and challenging circumstances. That is why this book conveys so much hope.

Too often, public officials and other organizers try to sort citizens into categories—"seven different narrow definitions of what citizens ought to be and do," as Leighninger puts it. People may be viewed solely as voters, or as "consumers" of public services, or as volunteers, social beings, advisors, dispossessed people, or public intellectuals who can help deliberate and explain issues of the day. Leighninger explains how these narrow definitions lead to the failure of many citizen involvement efforts, and argues that successful projects embrace a more holistic view of citizenship. In the best examples, Americans become true partners in our democracy, filling a range of civic roles in "a heterogeneous, candid, cooperative culture" of ongoing dialogue and opportunities to work for change.

I have described American society as a three-legged stool, where government and the private sector provide two legs, and the third is anchored by civil society—our shared institutions, including schools, churches, and community organizations. The best way for local communities to tackle our toughest problems is through innovative collaboration among all three sectors. Leighninger describes how democratic governance points the way to a more sustained, creative interplay among the three, fueled by the voices and commitment of citizens.

How do we get there? Leighninger doesn't ignore the challenges posed by these new, more open and participatory forms of democracy, and he raises many intriguing questions about whether hands-on democratic governance is compatible with bureaucratic realities, partisan politics, technology, and ever-growing constraints on people's time. But he shows how, by continually tapping into citizens' energy and common sense, officials and the public are reaching new levels of cooperation, efficiency, and mutual respect.

The Next Form of Democracy shows common challenges faced by people working in a wide range of fields, including education, public finance, urban planning, and race relations. Leighninger details their struggles, shows how the most enterprising public employees are trying to do things differently, and offers words of hope and caution to light the way. In these pages, candidates for public office also will find wisdom on how they might lead efforts to increase citizen engagement before and after Election Day.

This book is sure to prompt deep thought and lively discussion among public figures, community organizers, and everyone who cares about our country. Leighninger gives example after example of democratic governance projects that include the broadest possible array of participants—people who are fulfilling their promise not only as individual citizens but also as part of more democratic communities. Readers will discover countless ways to build a nation where the next form of democracy—one where all people will have better opportunities to be heard and make a difference—can take root and flourish.

Introduction
Things Your Mayor Never Told You:
The Recent Transformation
of Local Democracy

Lakewood, Colorado
September 9, 2004

It was an offhand comment, blurted out by someone in a crowd of people, and I was never able to figure out exactly who said it. The room was full of citizens and public officials; they were talking about why there was a lack of trust between the residents and local government of Lakewood, a small city just west of Denver. The mayor and city manager just didn't understand how taxpayers could be dissatisfied with a city administration that had won awards for efficiency and innovation. Finally, someone said it: "Look, we know you're working hard for us, but what we've got here is a parent-child relationship between the government and the people. What we need is an adult-adult relationship." It was the perfect summary of what I'd been watching in communities all over North America for the last ten years: a dramatic, generational shift in what people want from their democracy.[1]

For researchers, journalists, and other observers, this change in citizen expectations has been hard to recognize and harder to explain. But it is a daily reality in the kind of work I do: helping local leaders figure out how to involve residents in addressing key public issues.[2] To recruit effectively for those kinds of meetings, you have to understand your audience, what their interests are, and what motivations they might have for participating.

When you strategize with public officials about how they can engage citizens, they sometimes give you an unusually revealing assessment of their constituents. To them, ordinary people seem more capable, confident, and skeptical than ever before. Citizens may have less time for public life, but they bring more knowledge and skills to the table. They feel more entitled to the services and protection of government, and yet have less faith that government will be able to deliver on those promises. They have more to contribute to the solving of public problems, and less patience for those

1

situations where they feel shut out by public officials. They are less connected to community affairs, and yet they seem better able to find the information, allies, and resources they need to affect an issue or decision they care about. At the beginning of the twenty-first century, citizens seem better at governing, and worse at being governed, than ever before.

On the other side of this divide, local leaders are becoming tired of confrontation and desperate for resources. If they try to make important policy decisions the way they used to, they are faced with angry, informed, articulate citizens. If they try to make budget choices the way they used to, they are faced with voters who don't trust their expertise or their integrity. Elected officials aren't the only ones affected: all kinds of leaders, from school superintendents and police chiefs to nonprofit directors and neighborhood activists, are feeling the same kinds of pressures. These challenges cut across the major fields in the public sector, including education, planning, law enforcement, human relations, environmental protection, housing, economic development, public finance, and public health. In all of these areas, the psychological toll of local politics and the high cost of unresolved public problems are forcing communities to find new ways for people and public servants to work together. For reasons that are political, economic, intellectual, and emotional, leaders and citizens are attempting many different civic experiments—some successful, some not—to help their communities function more democratically and more effectively.

The proliferation of these efforts, and the conditions that have produced them, herald the next stage in the development of our political system. We are leaving the era of expert rule, in which elected representatives and designated experts make decisions and attack problems with limited interference, and entering a period in which the responsibilities of governance are more widely shared. "When you get down to it, what we're really talking about is whether the current form of representative government is obsolete," says Steve Burkholder, the mayor of Lakewood and the first chair of the Democratic Governance Panel of the National League of Cities. "We seem to be moving toward a different kind of system, in which working directly with citizens may be just as important as representing their interests."[3]

From Big Government to Big Governance

As they try to adapt to these changes, Burkholder and other local leaders have pioneered a concept called "democratic governance." This term is being used to describe a whole new array of projects and structures, a series of successful principles that have emerged from those efforts, and, above all, a new relationship between citizens and government. It is no longer simply a local phenomenon, either—most of these civic experiments have been based in cities and towns, but they are now being used to address state and federal policies as well. Perhaps the most useful way to define democratic governance is to call it the art of governing communities in participatory, deliberative, and collaborative ways.

So far, democratic governance has taken two main forms: temporary organizing efforts and permanent neighborhood structures. The best examples of both types employ four successful principles: First, they recruit people by reaching out through the various groups and organizations to which they belong, in order to assemble a large and diverse "critical mass" of citizens. Second, they involve those citizens in a combination of small- and large-group meetings: structured, facilitated small groups for informed, deliberative dialogue, and large forums for amplifying shared conclusions and moving from talk to action. Third, they give the participants in these meetings the opportunity to compare values and experiences, and to consider a range of views and policy options. Finally, they effect change in a number of ways: by applying citizen input to policy and planning decisions, by encouraging change within organizations and institutions, by creating teams to work on particular action ideas, by inspiring and connecting individual volunteers, or all of the above.

Temporary organizing efforts are often labeled as "citizen involvement" or "public engagement" projects, but these terms are broad, vague, and increasingly outdated; they don't necessarily reflect these four strategies. It seems more useful to refer to the projects built on these ideas as examples of "democratic organizing." Since 1990, democratic organizing efforts have taken place in hundreds of cities and towns, allowing hundreds and sometimes thousands of citizens to address issues such as race, crime, education, corrections, immigration, growth and sprawl, youth development, public finance, community-police relations, and economic development.[4]

During the same time period, dozens of cities have created new systems for decision-making at the neighborhood or ward level. They have established official committees—with names like "neighborhood councils," "priority boards," or "neighborhood action committees"—that give citizens a say in decisions that affect their neighborhood or ward, and sometimes on citywide policies as well. The first neighborhood council systems emerged thirty years ago in cities like Dayton and St. Paul; the current wave is much larger and more diverse, including places like Basalt, Colorado; Roanoke, Virginia; and Santa Rosa, California, as well as large cities like Los Angeles and Houston.[5]

Some of these neighborhood council systems seem to be permanent structures for democratic governance. They have been driven by the same changes in citizen expectations and local politics as the democratic organizing efforts, and they have adopted some, but not all, of the same tactics. Most neighborhood councils seem to be impartial arenas, allowing their members to consider a range of views and options, and they are clearly oriented toward action and change. A small number of councils recruit large numbers of citizens and involve them in participatory meetings; others rely on neighborhood associations and block clubs to do this kind of work. However, some councils feel that their job is to represent, rather than involve, their fellow residents; the council members are trying to make public decisions on behalf of others. The shortcomings of these groups mirror the typical weaknesses—low turnout, high burnout—of traditional neighborhood associations. In a way, these councils are smaller imitations of the city councils and state legislatures they are designed to support: they are examples of republicanism with a small "r," rather than the "small 'd' democracy" that is so evident in other democratic governance efforts.

The potential, and the difficulty, of combining democracy and republicanism is a major plotline in the recent history of local politics. As leaders react to changing citizen expectations, they are trying to create spaces within our political system where ordinary people will feel like they are legitimate, powerful public actors. This challenge is complicated by the fact that it is being addressed simultaneously by leaders in different fields who are not working together. Educators, planners, city managers, community organizers, police chiefs, human relations commissioners, and elected officials are all trying to involve citizens in more active ways. It is unclear whether communities are creating a more holistic, citizen-centered public life, or simply trying to pull people in too many different directions.

Another plotline in this drama is the reframing of our long-running debate about the role and size of government. Twenty years ago, the Reaganites argued that "big government is the problem"; ten years later, the Clintonites claimed that "big government no longer exists." Today, it is increasingly apparent that the size of government doesn't matter as much as how it connects with its constituents. We seem to be moving from a dispute about big government to a difficult conversation about how to achieve big governance.

Currently, these trends are flying under the national radar, beneath the sound and fury of pundits and partisanship. That is partly because democratic governance efforts are divided between different fields of practice and scattered all over the country. Most civic experiments have been initiated by people with very specific analyses and needs who have neither the time nor the inclination to think about the implications of their work for democracy and governance. But, whether they realize it or not, these organizers are challenging our traditional notions of politics. From their efforts, we can learn more about why people are dissatisfied with the traditional ways of addressing public issues. From the words and deeds of project participants, we can discover what citizens believe is missing from public life. From the successes and failures of these civic experiments, we might also get glimpses of the next form of democracy, and all the benefits and challenges it may bring.

Race, Violence, and the Appeal of Dialogue

Of all the issues and conditions that have propelled and shaped democratic governance, a single event stands out: the violent aftermath of the 1992 Rodney King verdict in Los Angeles. Suddenly, the question of racism and race relations made public dialogue seem more critical than ever before. Elected officials across the country became convinced they had to approach community relations in a different way. They realized that, while they might address race-related issues through their work in areas like economic development or housing discrimination, they also had to deal directly with the race-related perceptions, biases, and beliefs of their constituents. This kind of public outreach had rarely been done before; most communities lacked venues for people of diverse backgrounds to talk to each other about race.[6]

Local leaders began researching public engagement approaches and contacting national organizations that promote dialogue and deliberation on race and other issues. They hoped that involving people in discussions of race could help to overcome community divisions and prevent public debates from being dominated by extreme voices. A wave of local public engagement efforts swept the nation, involving hundreds and sometimes thousands of citizens in forums, trainings, workshops, and small-group dialogues.[7] Big cities weren't the only venues: some of the most influential programs were initiated in smaller cities like Lima, Ohio; Aurora, Illinois; and Springfield, Illinois. As these organizers experimented with different kinds of meeting formats and recruitment methods, they discovered tactics that were also being pioneered in fields like education, planning, and crime prevention.

Like most of these public issues, race affects people at a personal, emotional level. To allow participants to share their experiences in a productive way, local organizers gravitated toward strategies that emphasized small-group discussions, either on their own or as breakout groups within larger forums or workshops. Organizers either realized from the beginning, or learned by trial and error, that these small-group sessions would function more effectively if they included four main components:

1. Having an impartial facilitator seemed critical for the success of the discussion. Many organizers felt that if the facilitators tried to "educate" the participants or direct the group toward a particular conclusion, the dialogue would backfire. They found that facilitators could be successful if they remained impartial: giving everyone a chance to speak, helping the group manage the allotted time, helping the group use discussion materials, and trying to manage conflicts within the group.

2. Allowing groups to set their own ground rules was important. When the participants in a small group set their own norms for the discussion, they were more likely to abide by the rules, and the sessions tended to be more civil and productive. Participants typically proposed rules about not interrupting others, maintaining confidentiality, and keeping an open mind.

3. People valued the opportunity to compare personal experiences. Encouraging participants to talk about their cultural backgrounds and experiences with racism turned out to be a critical way to begin the discussions. It defused some of the tension, allowed participants to get to know each other better, and helped people see how our policy opinions are often based on our personal experiences.[8] This initial conversation also established a level of trust within the group, and at that point the participants usually found they had a lot to talk about. It wasn't just a difficult political discussion: it could actually be fun. In fact, the dialogue groups—which had been intended to meet for only a few sessions—sometimes went on long after the organizers had expected them to conclude.

4. Using a written guide to help structure the sessions proved to be critical. Groups tended to be more effective when they followed a guide that provided discussion questions, background information on the issue, and suggestions for managing the sessions. Some of the guides also presented viewpoints that mirrored the main arguments being made about race; these views were intended to present a sampling of the ideological spectrum, so that participants could analyze different ideas and options and relate them to their own experiences. These guides were sometimes written by local organizers but more frequently supplied by national organizations specializing in race dialogues or public deliberation.

None of these techniques for successful small-group discussions were entirely new.[9] They had been used, in one combination or another, by dialogue efforts and organizations well before the 1990s; in fact, they can be traced back to the civil rights movement fifty years ago, the Chautauqua adult education methodology of a century ago, and other precedents in other eras.[10] And, just as some organizers were employing these techniques to address race, other leaders were using them on other issues. School superintendents and principals in places like Kuna, Idaho, and Inglewood, California, wanted to engage parents and other citizens so that they would tutor students, help with extracurricular activities, and find ways to raise school funding. In cities like Buffalo, New York, and Fayetteville, North Carolina, police chiefs and other law enforcement professionals wanted citizens to revitalize neighborhood watch groups and form more productive relationships with police officers. Directors of youth programs in places like Racine, Wisconsin, and Portland, Maine, wanted young people and adults to work together on youth activities and find ways to combat substance abuse. Across the board, these leaders were frustrated by their inability to solve the public problems they faced every day in their jobs. Their traditional problem-solving tools had been blunted by budget cuts and lawsuits. To these organizers, the idea that citizens would devote their time and energy to local solutions seemed promising.

In all of these areas, small deliberative groups were appealing because they helped citizens gain information, forge connections with public employees, and take ownership of action ideas. On a host of issues, in countless communities, organizers used some combination of impartial facilitators, ground rules set by the group, a focus on personal experience, and a guide to structure the sessions.[11] The acceptance of these techniques, along with the acknowledgment that small groups could be effective for addressing a public issue, was an essential step in the development of democratic governance.

The Critical Need for a Critical Mass

There was another key realization that emerged, across fields and across communities: holding a few small-group dialogues would not be enough. In order to make sufficient progress on any of these issues, it was clear that large numbers of people, and many different kinds of people, had to be participating in the discussions. The best way to fight racism, boost volunteerism, or develop trust between citizens and government was to involve a critical mass of citizens in the effort. On this score, the national dialogue and deliberation organizations weren't nearly as helpful; they tended to focus on how to run the meetings rather than how to recruit participants.

To attract hundreds or even thousands of citizens, organizers realized they had to name their issue broadly. They worried that if they invited people to discuss the pros and cons of "zoning practices," "community policing," or "affirmative action," only a handful of confident, opinionated, well-educated residents would participate. Successful local organizers avoided jargon and narrow policy questions in their recruitment messages, and pitched their projects as opportunities to address issues—"crime," "race," or "our schools"—that people experienced in their daily lives. They assured citizens that the conversation would delve into policy questions, but that it would start with personal experiences and allow participants to address many ideas and concerns within the broader topic.

Another reason to frame the issue broadly was that local leaders knew they wanted participants with varied opinions and beliefs. To address conflicts and divisions in the community, they needed people who lived on different sides of those barriers. Organizers didn't want their projects to be confused with advocacy efforts; people had to know that all kinds of opinions would be respected, and that the facilitators would not be trying to push the groups toward any particular conclusion. When public officials were heavily involved, this position of neutrality became even more necessary; local governments wanted to avoid the perception that they were biased toward any one segment of the community.

Local organizers also learned that no single group or organization would be able to recruit the large numbers and different kinds of people that would make the project credible. Outreach through the media or by public officials would help to legitimize the effort, but citizens would be much more likely to participate if they were approached by someone they already knew. The only way to accomplish this kind of large-scale, one-on-one recruitment was to reach out to all kinds of community organizations—businesses, churches, neighborhood associations, clubs, and other kinds of groups—and ask the leaders of those organizations to recruit their own members.

Together with the small-group discussion techniques, these recruitment tactics became key ingredients of democratic organizing. Organizations with missions that focused explicitly on race, such as the National Conference for Community and Justice, the YWCA of the USA, and state and national associations of human rights workers, began to popularize and promote these strategies, as did civic groups like the Study Circles Resource Center, the National League of Cities, the League of Women Voters, America*Speaks,* the Kettering Foundation, and the National Civic League. As some of the same lessons were learned by organizers working on school issues, groups like the National School Public Relations Association, the Annenberg Institute for School Reform, the Southwest Education Development Lab, and the National School Boards Association began to tout them as well. City staffers who interacted with neighborhood councils and neighborhood associations began to use these strategies in their work. The NeighborWorks America Training Institute offered democratic governance courses to planners, housing builders, and employees of community development corporations. The National Crime Prevention Council and the National Organization of Black Law Enforcement Executives taught these techniques to their constituencies.[12]

Democratic governance was a new approach, but it seemed to demonstrate an old and recurring phenomenon: if you want to mobilize citizens, you have to make them feel that they are part of something larger than themselves. Asking people to join a fascinating small-group dialogue usually isn't enough to tempt them. To persuade them to spend some of their free time this way, organizers had to show citizens that high-profile leaders had "bought in" to the idea, that many different organizations were involved, and that taking part would give them a real opportunity to effect change. Citizens needed to know that their small-group discussion would be one of many—one small part of a community capable of solving its problems.

More Talk, More Action

Just as they learned how to recruit large numbers of people and involve them in productive meetings, local leaders have also learned how to help those citizens achieve tangible changes in their communities. For some organizers, especially those working on issues of race, action planning didn't seem important at first; some of them saw racism as mainly an interpersonal challenge, and they felt that creating civil, educational discussions would be enough. Many neighborhood council members were in the same boat: they considered themselves advisors to government, and felt that it was up to the public officials and city employees to implement their recommendations. But in the small-group sessions, it became clear that talk was not enough.[13] Participants wanted to see changes happen, and they didn't always expect—or trust—government to put their ideas into practice.

In democratic governance efforts focused on school improvement, crime prevention, or other priorities, achieving tangible changes was always a primary goal. But the fact that none of those changes had been decided before the project began made this a complicated and confusing message to give potential participants: "This project will make a real difference, but it is up to you what that will be." People aren't used to having that kind of opportunity: they are usually asked to sign a petition, send a check, or devote some volunteer labor to a cause that has already been chosen. They are also used to situations where their input is solicited, but nothing seems to happen as a result. Democratic organizers were trying to promote projects where action was assured but not predetermined. To get the point across, some organizers highlighted the broad coalition of groups supporting the effort, implying that the project welcomed different views and that the organizations would help support the action ideas that emerged. They also pointed to the tangible outcomes of civic experiments in other communities, and talked about how the concluding forums would help influence policy and launch action efforts.

The leaders of these projects also wanted to be clear that participants would be expected to lend some of their own time and energy to action efforts: the projects would do more than just generate recommendations for others to implement. It didn't matter to the organizers what kinds of actions participants decided to take. The important thing was that they did something: volunteering to help organizations already working on the issue, continuing the small-group meetings to implement an idea a group had developed, working within the community organizations they already belonged to, or finding ways to affect the policymaking process. This message also led organizers to talk more hopefully about their communities' assets, rather than focusing on problems and deficits. They wanted to create a more positive atmosphere in the groups and give citizens greater confidence that their communities could meet major challenges by building on their strengths.

To live up to this rhetoric, organizers in places like Syracuse, New York; Orford, New Hampshire; and Fort Myers, Florida, began holding large-group events for all the participants after the small-group sessions had ended. They used names like "action forum" to describe these meetings, which were designed to categorize and prioritize the enormous variety of ideas that emerged in the small-group meetings, match promising ideas with sets of people willing to work on them, and highlight action efforts that were already underway. The forums followed different formats in different places: in some communities they looked like volunteer fairs, while in others they resembled old-fashioned political conventions, but most of them succeeded in attracting public officials and other decision-makers and giving participants a chance to connect with other problem-solving allies.

Some action forums have given momentum to policy ideas that emerged in the small-group discussions. The democratic organizing effort held in Orford in 1996 attracted 100 citizens in a town with only 1,000 residents. The project focused on education, and many participants talked about the problem of falling enrollment at their high school. The small-group meetings helped establish some common ground among the school board members, the leaders of a taxpayers' association, and the town officials who had been at odds over the situation. At the action forum, program participants voted unanimously in support of a resolution that the "economic problems of the town not be solved by sacrificing educational quality or accessibility." At the annual town meeting a few weeks later, citizens voted to appropriate $5,000 for a planning process for a regional high school. Three years later, the Rivendell School District became the first two-state K-12 district in the country, spanning four small towns in New Hampshire and Vermont.[14]

At some of these concluding forums, local leaders launched new task forces or committees to take on action ideas that were popular in the small-group discussions. Many of these new citizen groups foundered once the enthusiasm of the forum had worn off and the group members had begun to feel isolated and powerless again, but organizers realized that they could overcome some of these challenges. In some cases, they recruited people with professional expertise and authority to assist the groups (for example, police officers for a task force devoted to crime prevention). In others, they worked to get media coverage of the task forces. Other, more basic techniques were also successful, such as simply checking in with task force leaders periodically, or holding a subsequent forum several months later at which task forces reported on their progress.

One particularly successful task force emerged from a civic experiment on issues of race in Fort Myers in 1997. Over 600 people were involved in the project. In the small-group dialogues, participants had talked about the fact that one low-income neighborhood had no grocery store, forcing residents to shop for food at convenience stores. A task force set up at the action forum began working with the city, the county, a local supermarket chain, and a minority business development organization to explore the idea of a new grocery store. The task force members, several of whom had business expertise, conducted a market survey and drafted a financing plan.

They found that the city and the minority business development group were arguing about how to spend their Community Development Block Grant funds. The task force helped to settle the dispute and promote the shopping center idea as a way to provide job opportunities and basic services for low-income citizens. Two years later, the Dunbar Shopping Center was built.[15]

As these programs proliferated, local leaders realized the importance of involving rank-and-file public employees in the small-group discussions. When teachers, police officers, social workers, or city planners were in the room, the solution ideas developed by the group were usually more informed and more influential. Action efforts were more likely to succeed because they were backed by stronger citizen-government relationships. Neighborhood councils have been particularly effective in this regard, because they provide regular occasions for residents and practitioners to interact.

In Buffalo, New York, one example of this kind of partnership emerged in a project on police-community relations in 2001. In one neighborhood with several halfway houses for the mentally ill, police officers and small-business owners had complained about ongoing disturbances. In the small-group meetings, people discussed how business owners often called the police about incidents involving halfway house residents. They also pointed out that officers are not trained to handle such situations. A state legislator, the director of mental health services for the county, and several peer leaders who had successfully battled mental illness attended the meetings. The participants came up with the idea of a trained emergency response team—one which would include business owners, former halfway house residents, and county mental health professionals—that would be on call for every neighborhood in the city.

Another unexpected development was the tendency of these projects to produce new leaders. This was particularly evident in some of the neighborhood council systems and in programs organized by neighborhood associations or other grassroots groups. As they participated in the small-group discussions, people who hadn't thought of themselves as leaders gained confidence in their speaking abilities and made connections with other participants. Having "found their voices" in this way, new leaders began to take more visible roles in the program and in the community. In many places, leaders who emerged through neighborhood councils or democratic organizing projects have been elected or appointed to the city council, the school board, the human relations commission, or another public office.

In Northeast Kansas City, Kansas, democratic organizers recognized this trend and found ways to encourage it. The United Way initiated a project in 1999 to help residents make an impact on school decision-making and school improvement. The effort has involved over 1,300 citizens and educators in small-group discussions, and has resulted in a number of after-school enrichment programs that were conceived and staffed by project participants. To help some of these participants take the next step as community leaders, organizers formed a formal partnership with a citywide leadership program, one which provides a year-long curriculum that teaches formal leadership skills and connects graduates with other leaders.[16]

As local organizers devised these kinds of strategies to ensure that public dialogue led to tangible outcomes, they used and validated a number of theoretical principles. Some of these were very old ideas, while others were contemporary concepts that developed alongside the growth of democratic governance. For example, using a combination of small-group and large-group meetings to empower citizens is a time-honored practice; this phenomenon has been described by historians and political theorists in many countries in many eras.[17] An example of a newer concept is the theory of asset-based community development popularized by John McKnight and John Kretzmann in the mid-1990s. Kretzmann and McKnight argued that past neighborhood revitalization efforts had failed because they emphasized needs and deficits—crime, poverty, inadequate housing—rather than assets such as historic buildings, cultural heritage, and the skills and talents of residents.[18]

Some democratic organizers have been guided by these kinds of theoretical principles, while others were totally unaware of them. In either case, the true test of an idea or strategy was not whether it conformed to the thinking of theorists, national civic organizations, or other experts: it simply had to work. So while the growth of democratic governance has rich implications for any observer of politics and democracy, it is a field that has been driven by practice more than theory.[19]

Shadow Government

Driven by the need to find more workable forms of politics, local leaders are adding controversial new twists to time-honored questions about rights, representation, and power. Officials often initiate democratic governance efforts with the seemingly straightforward goal of finding out what citizens are thinking. Along the way, these leaders begin to recognize that there are new implications and opportunities inherent in this work: they realize they have to allow policy options they don't agree with to be put on the table; they enlist citizens to help them find the necessary resources; they give people ways to take action that range from simple volunteer acts to much larger initiatives. Though these projects are intended to inform and supplement the traditional political process, they often seem to supersede it. All the same actors are there—citizens, interest groups, public officials, public employees—with all the same goals, but the language, procedures, and formats are different. What they end up with is, in effect, a "shadow" political process—one that is participatory and democratic but not official or legitimate.

In that sense, democratic governance is very different from past attempts by public officials to gather input on important decisions. Input gathering was quite prevalent in the 1960s and 1970s, when a number of federal laws were passed which required "maximum feasible participation" by citizens.[20] At the local level, the neighborhood council systems that emerged in the mid-1970s were also designed to connect citizen voices with city policymaking processes. The tradition of input gathering still runs strong in Europe and Canada, where public officials and employees sometimes organize "consultations" with the public.[21]

From the beginning, the desire to gather input was frustrated by a lack of infrastructure for citizens. Most public meetings—from city council sessions and zoning board meetings to public hearings held by federal agencies—were structured in ways that ruled out small-group deliberation, discouraged people from describing their experiences, and failed to give citizens a meaningful chance to be heard. Ironically, many of the laws passed to encourage citizen participation actually hindered it because they mandated unworkable processes and meeting formats, or made it impossible to hold confidential discussions of sensitive issues.[22] Another problem was that input-gathering opportunities seemed discouraging to citizens: the meetings were often held in situations where public officials were deadlocked over a decision, or when the community was in the midst of a crisis. Finally, in most cases very little attention was given to recruitment— officials would simply announce meetings and hope for the best. Depending on the level of controversy, these hearings either attracted a handful of attendees or a large, angry mob of people who would rail at public officials and leave more frustrated than they had been before.[23]

Some of the original neighborhood councils were successful at gathering input from a broad range of residents, but many faltered because they failed to recruit broadly or give people meaningful chances to participate.

Over time, some councils devolved into small, exclusive clubs, made up of expert residents who lacked either the skills or the inclination to involve their neighbors in important decisions. In places like Los Angeles, this led government officials to wonder whether the recommendations made by neighborhood councils were adequately representative of the neighborhood as a whole.[24]

Faced with these challenges, many public officials eventually gave up on the idea of gathering citizen input. Others had never understood the need for it in the first place: they had been elected by citizens to make decisions, so why should they spoil the soup by inviting more chefs into the kitchen?

But by the 1990s, a growing number of elected leaders and other policy professionals were coming around, once again, to the need for greater interaction with citizens.[25] Perhaps the most important reason for this current shift is that activists and citizens have become more sophisticated and skeptical than ever before. When officials try a "decide and defend" approach to major decisions, it is more likely to backfire. The policymaking process is under greater scrutiny, and whenever a decision goes against a particular interest group, activists use the media to throw a spotlight on the situation. People often react angrily to the decision, and officials find themselves in the midst of a political fiasco. Many leaders have been scarred enough by these experiences to conclude that, while working directly with citizens may be difficult, not working with citizens can be dangerous.

Deliberative processes seemed to present a way out of this predicament.[26] Officials noticed that when citizens on different sides of an issue were brought into facilitated discussions where they set ground rules, shared personal experiences, and considered a range of views and options in depth, the meetings rarely degenerated into shouting matches. In fact, these kinds of small-group dialogues were completely different from public hearings and other traditional input-gathering sessions: citizens didn't just complain, they actually learned about the issue and the various policy options. Activists were part of the discussions, but they weren't able to dominate them. Participants were able to think through their recommendations carefully, and they seemed to emerge with a much greater appreciation for the time and commitment that officials gave to their jobs.

One of the first democratic governance approaches to become popular in the 1990s was the idea of "visioning": involving citizens in creating a broad plan for the future of their community. The early icon of visioning was the city of Chattanooga, Tennessee, which involved 1,700 people in discussions and goal-setting sessions dealing with the economic future of the city. It is now estimated that Chattanooga Vision 2000, which began in 1984, produced 223 separate development projects, created 1,381 new full-time jobs, and led to investments of $800 million in the community.[27] Many other communities followed Chattanooga's example, but many of them stumbled because they failed to keep citizens and community organizations involved in implementing the visions. If a vision did not include measurable benchmarks, and specific commitments by people and organizations, it stood little chance of becoming reality.[28]

Meanwhile, public officials and civic groups began using deliberative approaches on more specific policy decisions. Some of these experiments used an approach more akin to opinion polling than to large-scale organizing. Instead of recruiting large numbers of people, the organizers tried to select a set of participants—usually 100 people for a Deliberative Poll®, or a much smaller panel for a "citizen's jury"—who mirrored the demographic characteristics of the community as a whole. If this perfectly mixed group discussed a policy decision in a deliberative way, the organizers reasoned, the resulting recommendations would be more valid and influential. In situations where public officials gave their active support to the forum, the input gathered seems to have affected the policymaking process. In others, the impact on policy has been harder to determine.[29]

Other leaders used the full range of democratic organizing strategies, recruiting a diverse critical mass of citizens. In Oklahoma, state legislators, policy analysts, and members of the League of Women Voters became convinced that this kind of approach could help resolve one of the worst legislative deadlocks in the state's history, over the issue of corrections reform. With the support of state legislators, corrections officials, and other organizations, they embarked on the first statewide democratic organizing effort in 1996. Perhaps because of its historic role as a guardian of the political process, the League used language to describe the program that conveyed a sense of "political legitimacy" and convinced citizens that they had a place on the public stage. "Balancing Justice in Oklahoma" involved almost 1,000 people in thirteen communities. After the meetings had concluded, the legislature enacted a landmark corrections reform bill that upheld the main recommendations made by the participants.[30]

In addition to describing the major policy options in an impartial way, it became clear that organizers had to leave room for options that hadn't been part of the public debate before. When the county commission of Sedgwick County, Kansas, launched a program on solid waste disposal in 1996, they expected that the main focus would be the question of whether to build a new landfill. While the 1,300 project participants did give their opinions on that matter, they were even more interested in ways to increase recycling: citizens concluded that they had to do a better job of reducing the amount of trash in the first place. Maintaining and improving the recycling system became one of the major priorities of the county commission.[31]

Some of these civic experiments have made greater use of technology than other kinds of democratic governance efforts. Though the Internet has not completely revolutionized democracy, as some observers had predicted in the mid-1990s, a number of agencies and organizations have used on-line dialogues and other electronic arenas to involve citizens in decision-making.[32] Some of the most promising experiments are the ones using technology in the service of face-to-face meetings: the local government of Washington, DC, has used keypad polling and laptop computers to summarize the conclusions of small-group breakout sessions at its annual "citizen summits."[33] The most successful of these high-tech programs have relied on the same methods for recruitment, facilitation, and meeting structure as the more low-tech civic experiments.

Though gathering input was a major goal of all of these efforts, organizers learned not to focus too narrowly on the most visible policy decisions. In Cleveland, hundreds of people took part in a mid-1990s project that focused on racial segregation in the school system. A lawsuit had been brought against the district, and a federal judge was considering ways to reconfigure the schools. The citizens who took part in the project spent a great deal of time and effort drafting a comprehensive desegregation plan; ultimately, the judge disregarded it in his ruling.[34] Since the entire project had focused on the decision, rather than including other ways to strengthen education or address race relations, participants had nothing to show for their labors. From examples like this, some organizers concluded that a broader focus was better. They gave participants time to consider the controversial question, but they also asked them to address other aspects of the issue. This widened the pool of potential participants beyond the people who were already focused on the policy decisions, and it also gave citizens a wider range of action opportunities.

The participants often surprised themselves: some of the citizens who took part in Balancing Justice in Oklahoma in order to comment on state policy ended up taking action at the local level, helping to establish local drug courts and youth courts. Many New Yorkers who participated in a similar statewide effort began their discussions with a great deal of frustration about the corrections system; some of them joined that system by creating citizen advisory panels that were embraced and sanctioned by the New York Department of Corrections.[35]

Though they may not intend to, public officials are blurring the line between the governors and the governed. This seems to have a number of good consequences—better communication, higher levels of trust, stronger support for public policies—but it also creates new complications. Communities have to decide, collectively, how much authority citizens should be allowed to wield, how volunteers and public employees can work together effectively, and how the lines of accountability should be drawn.

Is Democracy Evolving or Revolving?
Reading the Signs

Whether you are caught up in this struggle or observing it from afar, it is difficult to decide how the new developments fit in the larger history of democracy. Some people describe these civic experiments as the elements of a movement—a return to the social consciousness of the 1960s. Others assume that democratic governance is an attempt to turn back the clock even farther, to a time when the average citizen felt a much higher degree of public responsibility and civic virtue. To these observers, the proliferation of new projects and structures is not a sign of any dramatic transition into the future, but simply a continuation of the important work that has been done, repeatedly, in the past.

It is true that democratic governance employs some of the same tactics as past social movements; it is true that many different kinds of people in many different eras have worked together in small groups to share concerns, analyze problems, and decide what they should do. However, some aspects of the recent history of democracy suggest that a larger, more transformative shift is underway.

First, the people initiating these civic experiments cannot be easily categorized. They do not uniformly belong to any one political party, ideological agenda, occupation, or generation. They include nonprofit directors, clergy members, human relations commissioners, leaders of interfaith groups, public officials, policy practitioners, community organizers, school superintendents and school board members, police chiefs, youth program directors, recent retirees, members of the League of Women Voters, neighborhood association presidents, and activists. Some of these people bring the perspective of grassroots organizations and citizen groups that try to affect government "from the bottom up," while others approach it from the standpoint of government officials and other decision-makers who want to reach citizens "from the top down." All of these different kinds of people are experiencing the shortcomings of expert rule, and trying solutions that employ democratic principles.

Second, these local leaders do not rely on a predetermined cause or a shared sense of identity—of race, class, religion, gender, unions vs. corporations, or neighborhoods vs. downtown—when they are recruiting participants. Rather than establishing new rights or roles for particular sets of people, these civic experiments are changing how governments interact with all kinds of citizens.

Finally, this shift toward shared governance is wrapped up in other changes—pushing them, pulled by them, part of them—that we face as we enter the twenty-first century:

- Our desire to have some control over our physical surroundings is driving both urban sprawl and participatory planning.
- As the vision of a colorblind society becomes less realistic and less appealing, we are beginning to accept the need to deal with and build upon racial and cultural differences.
- As the responsibility for reducing poverty shifts increasingly from public agencies to nonprofit and faith-based organizations, we face new questions about how low-income residents can affect the decisions that affect their lives.
- The struggle over school accountability and the need for parent involvement is forcing citizens and educators to decide how they can work together on a regular basis.
- The capacity of activists to pressure public officials on increasingly technical issues, at higher levels of government, is provoking attempts to "scale up" democratic governance to the state and federal levels.

All of these challenges demonstrate the weaknesses and increasing unpopularity of a political system that relies too heavily on experts and elected representatives to make public decisions.

This may not be a movement, but it is certainly moving. Democracy shudders forward as leaders and citizens adapt to changing conditions and the changing expectations they have of one another. They are not simply trying to recapture the attitudes of some earlier era; they are building new institutions and modifying old ones so that they fit what communities need today.

Democracy in the Real World

The rest of this book describes the challenges and opportunities that are emerging as we shift from expert rule to shared governance. Unlike many of the books written recently about democracy, it is neither a dismal critique nor a Utopian vision of the future. Citizens and local leaders are striving toward a next form of democracy that may well be an improvement, but will not be a nirvana. This work solves old problems, and it may create new ones.

The people driving these changes are acting on a whole range of motivations. Sometimes it seems like the citizens are the "good guys" and public officials are the enemy; sometimes it seems like the other way round. It seems to me that people are starting from different vantage points with generally good intentions; the essence of the struggle is whether they can relate to one another, work together, and develop structures and procedures that maintain shared governance over the long term. The real world—the *realpolitik*—of deliberative democracy is an emotional, chaotic, powerful, invigorating struggle for common understanding and community change.

The book is not intended to be a catalogue of all the civic experiments undertaken in the last fifteen years; instead, I will use particular case studies to illustrate the motivations behind them, the principles they embody, and their implications for the future of politics. In my role providing technical assistance to communities, I was able to experience some of these scenarios firsthand. Therefore, my perspective on the case studies is more direct and up-close than if I were writing as an academic or a journalist. I will offer critiques, but they will come from a different vantage point than if I had been a complete outsider to each example. The vast majority of these examples are from the United States, but I have done enough work in Canada, where I now live, to suspect that Canadian school boards and local governments are facing many of the same pressures and challenges as their American counterparts.[36]

Some of the foremost challenges are covered in the first section. Chapter 1 represents the view "from the bottom up," describing the difficulties faced by ordinary citizens when they try to improve their neighborhoods and communities. It explores how our entrenched attitudes about "getting involved" limit our political imaginations, and how the lack of active citizenship affects our ability to address public problems. Chapter 2 turns to the "top-down" perspectives of the people who are trying to work with citizens: not only local leaders, but the national "civic field" of practitioners and researchers who are trying to resuscitate public life. It explains why traditional citizen involvement efforts often fail, and describes how the civic stereotypes we fall into—thinking of people only as voters, or consumers, or deliberators, or volunteers—are unappealing to real, well-rounded citizens.

The next six chapters trace the development of democratic governance in different policy areas, among different sets of leaders and practitioners. The chapters in Section 2 cover some of the ways in which leaders are appealing to citizens. Chapter 3 handicaps the race between choice and control in metropolitan development, providing the broader context for planning efforts at the neighborhood, community, and regional levels. Chapter 4 describes how the evolution of race dialogue programs may be changing our vision of the post-racist future. Chapter 5 delves deeper into the psychology of input gathering and argues that the mutual need for validation is bringing officials and citizens together, not only at the local level but increasingly in state and national policy decisions as well.

The third section delves more deeply into the attempts to realize shared governance in local institutions. Chapter 6 charts the progress of community organizers, who have diversified their tactics and assumptions over the last twenty years, and shows how the efforts to empower low-income people have led to a new model of "government by nonprofits." Chapter 7 describes how parents and educators have reached a critical crossroads: having found ways to work together over the short term, they are now grappling with long-term questions about how parent groups should be structured, how young people should be involved in school governance, and how school decisions should be made. Chapter 8 shows how communities are moving beyond the traditional assumptions first formed in the Progressive Era, which held that the role of government is to provide services and the role of citizens is to pay taxes for those services. The chapter describes how participatory budgeting, neighborhood council systems, and new forms of policing are reshaping how communities handle public finance, crime prevention, and economic development.

The conclusion summarizes the lessons we might learn—immediate and practical or long-term and theoretical—from the recent history of democracy. It surveys the frontiers of our political evolution and anticipates how these developments will affect elections, polling, lobbying, the media, the Internet, and our attitudes toward democracy in other parts of the world. These changes may surprise us, because we tend to assume that our political systems are entrenched and unchanging. We laugh ruefully at Winston Churchill's famous joke, that "democracy is the worst form of government, except for all the other forms," and ignore the fact that democracy is constantly evolving, right under our feet.

In twenty years, the political landscape will certainly be different than it is today. As the residents of Lakewood and other places cast off the constraints of expert rule, they are forcing governments to become more inclusive and interactive. Instead of concentrating on how people should be represented, the next wave of political reforms may be built around the day-to-day interests, concerns, and talents of the people themselves. In an increasingly busy and sophisticated world, we seem to be headed toward a new form of democracy, in which public officials bring politics to the people, politics takes place in small groups, and people take active roles in problem-solving.

Section 1

The State of Democracy

1

Good Citizens and
Persistent Public Problems

Most of what we hear about the state of citizenship today seems dismal and abstract. There is the persistently bad news about voter turnout and public mistrust of government. There are the constant reminders that young people in particular feel disconnected from public life. There are the concerns of experts who believe that volunteerism and membership in neighborhood associations, political parties, community organizations, and other groups is lower than ever before; this is a subject of great debate among political scientists and sociologists, who pore over opinion polls and historical data, and though the tone of the discussion is ominous, the answers are never clear.[1] It is a cloudy and depressing vista, and there doesn't seem to be much we can do about it. We have become apathetic about our supposed apathy.

The picture becomes a little less blurry when we take a closer look at how citizens and public employees typically interact, how neighborhood associations and other grassroots groups operate, and what happens when residents try to "get involved." At that level, the capacity of ordinary people is clear; this book is filled with examples of what citizens have accomplished. But one of the other realities is that people only participate when they feel like they have to: when a problem has gone from bad to terrible, or when an important decision is being made (or has already been made) that will affect them directly. Usually, the crisis is something that could have been averted if citizens had been part of the process earlier on, but for a number of reasons, the regular opportunities for this kind of participation—neighborhood associations, parent-teacher associations, public meetings, and so on—fail to attract people until the crisis hits.

At the local and neighborhood level, most communities don't provide the kind of meaningful political opportunities that will compel and sustain long-term involvement. Local leaders talk about the need for persistent, widespread participation, but what they get are occasional bursts of active citizenship, often occurring in situations where the energy can't be channeled in any productive way. In most places, local democracy is like a boring college lecture course with a tedious professor: most of the students skip every class until the final exam, when they troop into the room, chewing their pencils with fear, anger, and determination.

On one hand, looking through the eyes of the average resident gives us a view of citizenship that is dismal and specific rather than dismal and abstract. On the other hand, it affirms that most people are not in fact apathetic, or incompetent, or permanently alienated from government, or so busy they are incapable of participating in public life. It helps us understand why expert rule is increasingly unattractive to citizens and leaders alike. It shows us how the sad state of our democratic infrastructure reinforces our guilt-ridden avoidance of active citizenship. It helps us see why neighborhood council systems and democratic organizing efforts are proliferating, and how these experiments in shared governance are different from the usual kind of local politics. It gives us a picture of citizenship that is both more hopeful and more complicated.

Looking carefully at the state of democracy in communities also reminds us why active citizenship matters so much. When we take stock of our progress on key public priorities like education, race relations, land use, and crime prevention, the consequences of the disconnection between citizens and government become more apparent. On almost every public issue, there is a lack of cooperation and coordination between residents and public employees. Citizens are often unaware of the nature of a public problem, the steps they might take to address it, and how they might get assistance. Citizens are unconvinced of the need to support and fund public services and capacities, while public employees are unconvinced of the need to legitimize the roles of active citizens and consult with the public on questions of policy. Some of the greatest difficulties are caused by the erosion of shared community values and by deepening divisions between different groups of people. The state of citizenship seems like an abstract idea when boiled down to a statistic like voter turnout; it becomes more real when we see how it affects the issues that affect our lives.

Overwhelmed by these limitations, expert rule is slowly being overtaken by forms of governance that foster and reward active citizens. So while most of what is written about citizenship focuses on the apathy or alienation of people *en masse,* we can learn the most from the experiences of individuals who, despite all the obstacles, are doing their best.

A Good Citizen

Providence, Rhode Island, 1997

I am standing with Lisa Giordano on the sidewalk in front of her house on Willow Street in Providence, Rhode Island. We are talking about all the things she has done for her block.

During the last ten years, Giordano has spent much of her time making life better for her neighbors. Despite the fact that she has a full-time job as a housecleaner, she has spent countless hours with the young people on the block—taking them on field trips, organizing activities, talking with them about their problems. She has worked with the police to make the neighborhood safer. She has put pressure on absentee landlords to clean up their properties. She has led efforts to clean up graffiti and litter. She has brought neighbors together for block parties where people got to know each other.

But for Giordano, active citizenship comes with a price. When she tells me about her greatest achievement of the past year, she lowers her voice. ". . . And so far the drug dealers have been doing a lot less dealing out of the blue house across the street," she says. "Since the landlord, after repeated requests from us and the police, threatened to evict the tenants who lived there, things have been quiet."[2]

I make the mistake of looking over at the blue house. "Don't!" she says quickly. "They might see you—they're pretty sure we're the ones who've been making waves, but I don't want that confirmed. We've received threats already."

Being a good citizen is more difficult than it ought to be. People like Lisa Giordano are sometimes praised for their acts of kindness and generosity (usually with an aside: "I don't know where they find the time!"), but the way they are singled out reinforces the notion that their actions are unusual, uncalled-for, and done out of saintly virtue rather than any direct individual or community interest. Giordano is a "good" citizen in the sense that she is active and effective for her neighborhood, but for most people, this quality is overshadowed by a different kind of goodness: her altruism and self-sacrifice. Giordano is an admirable person, but not a realistic role model for other citizens. Though it is dismaying, it doesn't surprise us that her efforts have earned her threats from drug dealers. This appears to come with the territory—the consequence of being a "good" citizen in a "bad" neighborhood.

Even in neighborhoods without drug dealers, few people question the assumption that improving your community is—and must be—lonely, arduous, thankless work. Knowing that a clean conscience may be the only reward, the average person is likely to forego good citizenship in favor of some safer, more pleasant activity, less connected to public problem-solving and community decision-making. It is easier for most of us to demonstrate our virtue by giving blood, helping with a food drive, or donating to charities.[3] If we are active in our communities, it is a direct reflection of our own intrinsic virtue and devotion; if we do not, it is because we just aren't virtuous enough, or because we choose to demonstrate our goodwill in more convenient ways. "Getting involved" seems like an old-fashioned cough syrup: it is "good for you," so it has to be unpleasant.

Lisa Giordano moved into her house on Willow Street in 1990. She was single and in her twenties. She had been looking for an older house for a reasonable price, expecting to do some renovation work. She hadn't thought much about the diversity or quality of life of her new neighborhood.

The West Broadway neighborhood in Providence is dominated by a colossal, 1903 armory building just around the corner from Willow Street. It has a mix of Latinos, Asians, African Americans, and whites, of all different income levels, living in Victorian houses in various states of repair. It is a beautiful neighborhood.

As soon as Giordano moved in, she started recognizing Willow Street's challenges. Litter and graffiti kept appearing on the street, and it was clear that drug dealers were operating in some of the houses. What pushed her over the edge was a very simple problem: every day, kids chasing one another would hop over her back fence, trampling parts of her garden in the process, and run off. When she talked to a few of them, she found out they were just playing a game.

"I stopped them from jumping the fence, and I was surprised when they didn't understand why I was mad," she says. "That was the first hint I got—when they didn't understand that what they were doing was wrong—that they should respect other people's property, not to mention all living things (my poor plants!). I started to notice differences between their lives and experiences and mine. I started telling them about the principles I learned—not to change them, but so that they could understand me. The farther I got, the more I realized some of my own prejudices—before I got to know them, I hadn't understood or respected them as much as I should have."

As Giordano got to know the young people who lived on her block, they began spending more and more time with her. "We started playing basketball, playing video games. I remember helping a couple of them make birthday cards for their mother." Giordano's interest in protecting her property led her into relationships she hadn't expected; in order to maintain her good fence, she became a good neighbor.

The Plainclothes Problem-Solver

The more involved Giordano got in the lives of the young people, the bolder she became about some of the other problems on Willow Street. As well as the drug dealing, there was some prostitution activity, and there were reports of domestic violence in some of the houses. One Halloween, someone set fire to all the trash cans on the block and scattered burning refuse in the street. "But that wasn't the worst part," Giordano recalled. "When the police and firemen came to put out the trash fires, some of them started making jokes about the situation. They seemed to think that the people in our neighborhood ought to expect things like this."

When Giordano tried to get help from the police department and other offices of local government, the results were mixed. Some departments would respond to her calls, and some wouldn't. Luckily, a neighbor named Gerry Roy, who lived a few blocks away, encouraged Giordano and gave her tips on who to talk to in City Hall. "Gerry was a key person for me," she says. "I would tell him about the problems on the block, and he's the one who always said, 'Yes, that *is* a problem. You should talk to so-and-so.'"

Dealing with graffiti was one way of demonstrating to outsiders that the residents of Willow Street were determined to get things done. "We got so efficient that we had cans of paint to match the color of every house on the block, all tagged and lined up in my basement. We would clean things up right away, since the longer you wait the more likely it is that the property will be vandalized again."

The Department of Code Enforcement, which monitors the maintenance of buildings, was usually the quickest to respond to Giordano's calls. "Usually, they did something within twenty-four hours," she remembers. The state's Department of Environmental Management, which deals with lead paint, asbestos, and other hazards, was also responsive. Big, wisecracking John Lombardi, the local city councilman, often helped her out when she couldn't get calls returned.

Responses from the police, who were so critical for dealing with many of the problems, were more varied. "Some of the community police officers we've had have been great—really involved with the kids, really friendly and easy to work with. Others were awful. There's this image of power that a lot of people buy into when they become cops—they want to make the big drug bust, catch the bad guys. Being a good role model to the kids just isn't as popular with them."

The worst were the officers on the narcotics unit. "You had to call and call and call to ever get a response. I started to document every call, so that I could complain to John [Lombardi] or someone in the police department when they never responded. At one point, I even gave them keys to my house, so they could do stakeouts."

Several times, Giordano actually confronted people living in the blue house or one of the other houses that were sites for drug dealing and prostitution. "Sometimes we'd actually have good conversations," she said. "Other times, especially after they knew I'd called the police, I'd get yelled at, or have my house vandalized. Sometimes people would call me a racist—not all the dealers were people of color but many were. It made me question myself—question why I was doing this."

Finally, the narcotics police recognized what a problem the notorious blue house had become and were able to make some arrests. Afterwards, some of the detectives apologized to Giordano. "They actually told me, 'We thought you were just some snooty neighbor.' I couldn't believe that! Here I was trying to help the police and help my neighborhood, and their first inclination was not to believe me." Giordano may have been a good citizen, but to the police her complaints were illegitimate until proven otherwise.

Legitimacy seems like a strange word to use when talking about citizenship. After all, we know that one essential feature of our citizenship is that we have rights—as long as we obey the law, we are entitled to "life, liberty, and the pursuit of happiness." People are used to the limited kind of legitimacy that comes with these individual rights, and in the abstract, it may be hard to imagine what else we might ask for.

The rights guaranteed to us in the Constitution allow us to vote, give us freedom of speech, protect us from various forms of persecution, and provide us with many other liberties. But nowhere does it say that narcotics detectives have to return our calls. As she struggled to improve life on Willow Street, Lisa Giordano started asking her government for more than just the protection of her rights: she wanted to be considered a legitimate partner, an unpaid problem-solver, a citizen with powers and responsibilities that went beyond voting.

Certainly, some of the public employees of Providence responded to Giordano right away, and eventually even the narcotics unit became more cooperative. Invariably, however, she had to make the first call, she had to introduce them to the neighborhood, and she had to justify her concerns. Even the Office of Code Enforcement, always there within twenty-four hours, had no presence on Willow Street until Giordano came along.

Our limited citizenship is an immediate, practical problem at the neighborhood and community level. At one of the meetings in the West Broadway neighborhood, one of the policemen Giordano worked with said, "Maybe once in your career as a cop you will turn a corner and find the burglar coming out a window with a VCR. All the rest of the time, you need citizens to tell you what they saw, to help you identify problem spots, and to take good precautions against crime." Police officers can't enforce the laws by themselves—they rely on citizens.

Despite the reception she got from local government, Giordano was determined to be a good citizen. The fact that Giordano was willing to do all of those things—even to confront the drug dealers and let the police set up shop in her home—should have earned her legitimacy in the eyes of the police. In our romantic visions of the Old West, the sheriff would be handing her a shiny deputy's badge. Instead, most of what Giordano said went unrecorded, her offers to help unanswered, and her role unrecognized.

Willow Street Values

Though the drug dealing, prostitution, and vandalism on Willow Street began to decline, what pleased Giordano most was the time she spent with the kids. During most of those years, there were ten or fifteen young people living on Willow Street; Giordano estimates that she got to know about fifty kids. "We really started to get creative about all the activities," she says. "I took them fishing, we had cookouts and pizza parties, we always went to a haunted house on Halloween. We went on a tour of Brown University, and went to the art museum at the Rhode Island School of Design. We delivered Christmas presents to needy families. I just wanted to get them out of the neighborhood once in a while—spark their ability to dream."

In the beginning, she got more suspicion than encouragement from adults on the block. "Some of the parents questioned my motives—they wondered if my interest in the kids was partly sexual. That fazed me for a while, but then I figured, 'If it isn't true, why should I let it bother me?' "

Setting limits with the kids was always important. "From that first conversation about jumping my fence, we had to agree on what the ground rules were. Eventually we even created a written contract—what their responsibilities were, and what mine were. They were all simple little rules of conduct, like 'Don't litter,' 'Don't disrespect people and their property,' 'Respect all living things.' From there we got into other lists, like lists of goals for each kid. I really felt like I was being a mentor to them.

"We had a shared pool of money we got from doing odd jobs, which we used to pay for the pizza parties and things like that. If the kids broke one of their rules, though, they had to donate the money to St. Michael's Church. One time, when this happened, I made them deliver the money in person—they were mad. But when we went into the church, we found some of the parishioners cooking for a soup kitchen. We started chopping vegetables, and helped them with the whole meal. Afterwards, the kids felt really good about themselves."

Giordano could tell that the young people valued her friendship. Some of them would come to her with problems or give her information on a crime that had been committed. One young woman, in her twenties now, still calls Giordano regularly. "When she was a teenager, she would try my loyalty constantly. We got through that, and now we talk all the time. 'I'm not pregnant yet,' she tells me—that's what has happened to so many of her teenage friends."

There was little in Giordano's background to suggest that she would emerge as a neighborhood leader. "I really had no formal preparation for any of this," she says. "I was never in any kind of organization, not even Girl Scouts. I guess the biggest influence was my family. From my grand-father, I inherited a huge respect for nature and for all life. My parents were always at odds with each other, so I grew up in the middle, always trying to repair things."

Aside from the encouragement she got from Gerry Roy and a few other adult neighbors, her main source of motivation was the young people. She wanted to make things better for them, and she felt she had to prove that commitment to them. As a group, they looked up to her, they believed in her, and after a time they expected that she would solve Willow Street's problems.

Giordano also had little preparation for dealing with the diversity of Willow Street. "I grew up in a middle-class Italian neighborhood," she says. "There were only a few students of color in my school. When I first moved here and saw people doing things I didn't agree with, I would dismiss it as a trait because of their race," she admits. "I had to recognize my racism and deal with it. Now, it is nice to see some of the similarities we share, to feel like I'm like everyone else in some important ways. It's humbling."

Strengthening community values, dealing with racism, helping young people learn about ethics and standards and goals—these are priorities that have almost universal appeal. From the right wing to the left, public officials and political candidates talk about them all the time. And yet it is very difficult to strengthen values through legislation. More commonly, leaders try to exhibit "moral leadership" by taking a highly visible stand on an issue like racism or abortion or drunk driving, hoping that this will influence the behavior of large numbers of people. While that kind of moral leadership is admirable, the person who had the greatest influence on the kids of Willow Street was Lisa Giordano. She communicated with others, she forged relationships, she changed her own thinking and behavior, she helped young people understand rules and set goals for themselves—these are things that sound bites rarely do.

The growth in Giordano's awareness of others and her development as a dynamic neighborhood leader sprang from the same source: she needed her community and the community needed her. Understanding the young people she spent time with and gaining the confidence to solve public problems were not things she had learned in school. Her status as a good citizen was not dependent on her intrinsic "goodness." It was her relationship with her neighborhood that made her both a more virtuous citizen and a more active one. Willow Street brought out the best in her.

The Power of Public Happiness

In addition to improving her neighborhood, Lisa Giordano has found her Willow Street experiences to be personally rewarding. "This has brought to life parts of my personality I didn't know about because I hadn't been exposed to certain things," she says. "It made me realize what I want to do for the rest of my life: I have a strong interest in working with middle school kids. I have a knack with them, and now I'm studying to be a science and math teacher."

But even when the benefits are apparent, most people find good citizenship a difficult ideal to achieve. Among the adult volunteers who have helped her on Willow Street, Giordano has witnessed plenty of turnover. "People come in waves, then burn out. The needs of our neighborhood are always so obvious and always so great; eventually, people put them aside in favor of their own needs. You have to surround yourself with things that make you happy, and volunteering to fight problems makes that hard. It is easier to stay in your house, surrounded by your family and the things you own."

Sustaining active citizens may require surrounding them with a unique kind of happiness. Giordano had a sort of epiphany several years after she moved to Willow Street, when the drug traffic and many of the other problems on the block had begun to subside. "Through all the frustrations, I reached a point where I had great relationships with the kids, with my neighbors, with the police. It was a real community—the true definition—not just preaching it but being in it. We were all communicating. We got past the racism, we got past the stigmas about the police and by the police, we got past it all. That kind of communication is powerful.

"Unfortunately, that feeling didn't last very long," Giordano remembers. "Some of the kids moved; there was turnover in the community police officers assigned to us; things just changed."

Some time later, Giordano set out to revive that spirit by forming the Willow Street Association. "We started just by inviting all the neighbors over for a cookout. I suggested that we meet every month or so." It took some work to keep it going—Giordano had to coordinate the meal and make sure everyone got invited—but eventually the street association meetings became part of the regular routine of Willow Street.

Part of each meeting was a discussion of some of the challenges facing the block. As they talked about their concerns and came up with solutions, people got excited about solving problems together. Though some of the neighbors had been very helpful to Giordano before she created the street association, the group brought out more people than ever, and they worked together in a more concerted way. Organizing the youth activities became more of a shared endeavor, rather than something that depended entirely on Giordano. More neighbors started talking to and working with the community police officers. Others began tutoring the young people and helping them with homework. The Everett Dance Troupe, which operates out of an old carriage house nearby, began giving free dance lessons to the Willow Street kids. The street association members acquired and planted eight trees on the block, conducted several street cleanups, bought new trash containers for every house, and created a telephone tree for meetings and emergencies.

But, beyond these accomplishments, people went to the street association meetings because they enjoyed them. "We had surrounded ourselves with connections to others," Giordano says. The spirit that was evident in the meetings of the Willow Street Association is significant, and yet difficult to define. Most people today, looking at the way the residents talked, worked, and made decisions together, wouldn't even know what to call it. One set of historians and theorists, influenced by the political philosopher Hannah Arendt, would characterize it by using a term from the eighteenth century: "public happiness."[4]

Some of these historians argue that, two hundred years ago, ordinary citizens had more frequent opportunities to conduct public business together. Officially, these privileges were only open to male, property-owning citizens, but when John Adams, our second president, described public happiness, he was much more inclusive: "Wherever men, women, or children are to be found, whether they be old or young, rich or poor, high or low, wise or foolish, ignorant or learned, every individual is strongly actuated by a desire to be seen, heard, talked of, approved and respected by the people about him."[5] Experiences of public happiness may have had a great influence on Adams, Thomas Jefferson, Thomas Paine, and the others who helped draft the Declaration of Independence, the Constitution, and the Bill of Rights. In fact, the famous phrase "life, liberty, and the pursuit of happiness" may refer specifically to the kind of public happiness enjoyed by the residents of Willow Street.

Other historians disagree with these claims. There is considerable debate about how democratic America really was in the eighteenth century, both in terms of how meetings were run and what kinds of people were allowed to attend them.[6] Regardless of the historical debate, "public happiness" seems like an apt term for what the residents of Willow Street experienced at their meetings. It is also a good description for the kinds of feelings people talk about when they have been involved in democratic governance. The idea of public happiness is important because it explains why this kind of active citizenship is more than just a means to an end. When people get together in small groups and large groups to share concerns, make decisions, and solve problems, they don't just appreciate the tangible outcomes—they place a high value on the experience itself.[7]

Most Americans are familiar with one descendant of those eighteenth century town assemblies: the neighborhood association. Willow Street and the surrounding area are served by the West Broadway Neighborhood Association (WBNA). Throughout its history, the WBNA has been successful at winning grants and other kinds of funding. The WBNA has encouraged the restoration of historic buildings, hosted neighborhood events, and lobbied local politicians on behalf of the neighborhood. It is a very accomplished group.

But the WBNA has not been a source of public happiness for Lisa Giordano. "I started going to the meetings soon after I moved to the neighborhood, but I got disenchanted because many of the people there were outspoken, abrasive, idealistic, and not all that interested in kids."

Part of the problem is the way the WBNA runs its monthly meetings. The president and executive director set the agenda, which usually consists of 1–4 speakers who give presentations to the audience, and then answer questions. In the question-and-answer periods, the people who are angry or outspoken tend to dominate, and there is little actual discussion.

The monthly meetings of the WBNA never attract more than 30–40 people out of a neighborhood of over 8,000 people. By contrast, some of the Willow Street meetings had roughly the same number of attendees, even though their members were from only one block in the neighborhood. Though West Broadway is extremely diverse in terms of race, ethnicity, age, level of income, and level of education, the people involved in the WBNA are almost all white, well-educated, and middle-class. The Willow Street meetings attracted a broader range of people.

Almost all of the work of the WBNA is carried out by a handful of highly motivated citizens. What gets done reflects what they think is worth doing. "The main priorities of the WBNA were always things like traffic, old houses, and tree planting—generally making the neighborhood a better-looking place," says Giordano. Some of the other West Broadway residents were more interested in issues like whether the public schools were succeeding, how the police were treating neighborhood residents, and whether rising rents and property taxes would force more people out of the neighborhood. "The WBNA members always wanted to have people of different cultures involved, but they didn't know how to make Hispanics, Asians, or African Americans feel welcome. They wouldn't turn them away, but people of color would turn themselves away—they would come to the meeting, see that the issues being discussed weren't the ones they cared most about, and never come back. Then the WBNA members would shake their heads and talk about how hard it was to get people of color to participate. I thought to myself, 'You pride yourselves on the diversity of the neighborhood, but you still don't know anybody who is unlike you.' "

Several years later, when Giordano started organizing the Willow Street Association, the president of the WBNA urged her to come back to the monthly meetings. She did for a while, but then a debate arose over what to do with a small abandoned school in the neighborhood. Giordano wanted it to be a community center for young people. Some of the WBNA board members literally laughed at her idea. "That didn't make me feel very good," she says. "Now I bake cookies for the meetings, because I think the people there are making a great effort for the neighborhood, but I don't go."

So Lisa Giordano, the best citizen in the neighborhood, bakes cookies for the WBNA but does not feel comfortable attending their meetings. This would be an embarrassment for the WBNA—except for the fact that so many other neighborhood associations have the same limitations. In fact, most parent-teacher associations, neighborhood watch groups, small business networks, and other community groups, in addition to most neighborhood associations, share the same flaws as the WBNA. Few of them are able to involve large numbers of people, represent the full diversity of their constituencies, or foster public happiness. One reason is that so many of their meetings are run in the same kind of non-participatory format.

These groups face other difficulties as well. As organizations, they tend to be awkward hybrids, somewhere in between formal institutions and informal clubs. They have many of the same burdens of formal institutions—the need to establish and maintain bylaws, the need to raise money—and yet most of them don't have any of the benefits, such as paid staff or an official role in local decision-making. Members spend large amounts of time on organizational upkeep rather than working toward the main priorities of the group.

Having worked so hard to establish themselves, group members are often ambivalent about sharing their limited power with "newcomers" who don't have the same priorities as the founders or core members of the organization. Many of these organizations were created in order to meet pressing public needs; the founders and core members sometimes have a frenetic, "take-action-now" mindset that makes it difficult for the group to pause long enough for other people to join up, form relationships, weigh in on the options, and begin to feel at home in the organization. Knowing that the organization's members are determined to implement an idea or combat a problem, most people are content to cheer from the sidelines, admiring the group's efforts but not pitching in to help.[8]

Even when they want to recruit more widely or function in a more welcoming, participatory way, most of these groups don't have the time, staffing, or skills to be successful.[9] Even when they want to deal with the challenge of cultural difference, as in the case of the WBNA, these groups usually don't know how to address those issues in a productive way.

Finally, most of these community groups limit their recruitment appeal because they are not as holistic as the term "community" implies. In addition to the political side of community life, there are social, cultural, and economic aspects. In other words, the residents of any place have a wide range of interests: socializing with their neighbors, eating good food, going to concerts, building things, finding new jobs and other kinds of entrepreneurial opportunities, going to sporting events, winning prizes. Children are a particularly powerful motivator for community participation: all kinds of people will take part in something if it involves watching kids (and not just their own kids) dance, sing, act, receive awards, display their artwork, or play sports. They will also take part in something if child care is provided, if it will allow other adults to get to know (and look out for) their kids, or if it will benefit their children in some other way. Some residents are motivated primarily by the need to solve public problems—these are the people you find in neighborhood associations, PTAs, and neighborhood watch groups—but most of us are not so single-minded. We care about improving the community, but we are more likely to attend if, as in the case of the Willow Street group, some of these other incentives are offered as well.

Though many community groups at least provide food at their meetings, most of them aren't aware of this larger need to provide a range of reasons for people to participate. As a result, these neighborhood associations—which should more accurately be called "neighborhood problem-solving groups"—limit their recruitment pool to only the most motivated and confident political actors. Most of the time, this is not sufficient for sustaining public happiness or addressing the root causes of public problems.

Lisa Giordano has done so much for her neighborhood, and yet her place in the political landscape doesn't seem to have changed. In order to return to school and get her teaching certificate, she sold her house and moved to another street in the West Broadway neighborhood. There is no street association on Harrison Street, and now that she is back in school, Giordano can't face the prospect of starting another one. Neither the city nor the WBNA has the staff time to help mobilize the Harrison Street residents.

In fact, neither the city nor the WBNA ever officially recognized the Willow Street association—never asked the group for input on any decisions, never gave it any funding, never listed it as a legitimate organization. Without Giordano's leadership, the Willow Street association eventually stopped meeting.

Giordano was recently given an award by a local foundation for her volunteer work. But, despite her status as an honored citizen, she doesn't seem very powerful. When you ask her about the affairs of the city, she talks about the taxes, scandals, and city council decisions as if talking about the weather—circumstances to contemplate and complain about, but not anything you can change. Even within her neighborhood, she doesn't try to play a role in decision-making: "I guess I have a voice within the WBNA, but I know that if they're set on something, it is as good as done. I know the way things work, so I'm usually not inclined to speak out." Her energy, experience, and ideas are great assets for her neighborhood and her community, but Giordano still feels like she's standing on the sidelines.

On her new block, Giordano knows that, if she could find time away from her schoolwork, she could start all over again as a good citizen. But when you ask her what citizenship means to her, she only uses words like duty, and responsibility, and work. "Citizenship means, in a broad sense, responsibility; a sense of responsibility not just to a community but to the larger community. That is really the fuel for everything I do." Her take on citizenship doesn't come across as a complaint; indeed, Giordano feels obligated to soldier on. But, in the future, she'll be fulfilling her sense of civic responsibility as a schoolteacher, not a neighborhood organizer. There she'll be able to help others in a setting that is more supportive of her efforts—surrounded by other educators, in the midst of an institution dedicated to her cause, with a paycheck arriving every two weeks.

For all the personal rewards Giordano has gained through being a good citizen, when she speaks, what stands out are the negatives: loneliness, powerlessness, and responsibility. These emotions are enough to keep most of us from trying to be good citizens in the first place. We believe it is our duty to "get involved"—but the opportunities we have to get involved are mainly on the edges of public life. By and large, these tasks are thankless, disempowering, and devoid of the benefits of democracy.

"We've Got to Stop Meeting Like This!"

Neighborhood associations, PTAs, and neighborhood watch groups are clearly not the only political opportunities for good citizens like Lisa Giordano. In almost every community, people have the chance to attend a wide variety of officially sanctioned, government-initiated public meetings: public hearings, school board meetings, city council proceedings, zoning and land use meetings, town assemblies, and other kinds of formal citizen-government encounters. Unfortunately, it is extremely difficult to attract people to these meetings, because they usually don't satisfy the goals citizens might have for attending them.

Perhaps the most basic reason for citizens to attend public meetings is that they want to make an impact on an issue they care about. People seem more motivated to participate when they can view challenges with some degree of optimism: they want to know that we can make some kind of progress on the issues facing our neighborhood or community, and they want public meetings to reinforce this confidence. But public officials want to keep people from having expectations that can't be fulfilled (at least by government alone), so they often stress that public resources are limited. This emphasis on difficult problems and half-hearted solutions helps create an air of pessimism and dissatisfaction.[10] In the absence of a crisis, the prospects of addressing an issue usually seem brighter, but the turnout is usually lower—and the low numbers sap the determination and confidence of the few citizens who do attend.

A related but more common motivation that brings citizens to public meetings is the ability to affect policy: people participate because they are concerned about a government decision that will affect their lives. Sometimes, public hearings are held *after* a controversial decision has been made, making this goal unreachable from the start. But even when a public meeting occurs before a major decision, the policy options have usually been whittled down to a few narrow choices, dramatically limiting citizens' ability to affect how the community addresses the broader issue. For the public officials, it is difficult to judge whether the citizens who attend the meeting are truly representative of the neighborhood or community as a whole, so they may be unsure how much weight to give the input they are receiving. As a result, most public meetings do not have a discernible effect on policy decisions, and in those rare instances when they do change the minds of decision-makers, most citizens never know it.[11]

Public meetings are more compelling if citizens have a chance to build relationships with one another, and with public officials, in the process of addressing community problems. Yet very few traditional public meetings allow the attendees to get to know one another; in fact, citizens often don't have much chance to say anything at all. This is partly because most hearings and council meetings are large-group affairs, but even in small-group settings the agenda usually plunges the discussion directly into the most controversial questions. Participants rarely get the chance to find out why public officials made a certain decision, or why other citizens feel the way they do.[12]

Finally, many citizens who are troubled by divisive issues in the community want to be able to deal with those conflicts and differences in a civil, candid, nonconfrontational way. Once again, the format of speakers followed by an open microphone makes that difficult. There are other difficulties, including the fact that these meetings leave little space for sharing personal experiences and the fact that issues and policy options are often described in very technical terms.[13]

Traditional public meetings usually allow the most extreme voices to dominate the discussion, and they often put both citizens and officials on the defensive. "There is no 'hearing' at public hearings," says Ruth Ann Bramson, a public administration professor and former county administrator.[14] These obstacles have a particularly discouraging effect on young people, people for whom English is a second language, people without college degrees, and people who simply haven't been involved much in community life before.[15]

When most of these citizen goals go unfulfilled, what's left is the final reason people attend traditional public meetings: to complain. Privately, many public officials will tell you that they dread these meetings and much prefer talking with citizens one-on-one or in small groups. The Healthy

City Office for the City of Toronto summed up this frustration in a typically humorous, typically Canadian way: their official citizen participation handbook is entitled *We've Got to Stop Meeting Like This!*

It's the Democracy, Stupid

As cities like Toronto try to find better ways for residents and public officials to work together, and as people like Lisa Giordano struggle to improve their neighborhoods, they help us get beyond the statistics on voter turnout and public mistrust of government. Examining democracy at the local level reveals the *real* citizenship dilemma: the absence of regular, meaningful political opportunities for ordinary citizens is a key factor in so many of the public problems facing communities today. Democratic governance efforts are a direct response to these shortcomings of local politics.

At the neighborhood level, the pioneers of shared governance are motivated by the kinds of challenges so evident in West Broadway. Democratic organizers and neighborhood council leaders will tell you that most citizens don't know their neighbors and don't feel a sense of attachment or belonging to the place where they live. People feel hard-pressed to affect even the most basic quality-of-life issues on their street—problems like excessive noise, dogs without leashes, graffiti, littering, and inadequate trash pickup. They feel powerless about most land use decisions, fearful that the empty lot down the block will soon be occupied by a housing development or a landfill or a drug treatment center. They compare the places they live now to the neighborhoods they grew up in, where everyone knew everyone else, and they worry about their own kids growing up without any of those support networks.[16]

The leaders who are experimenting with democratic governance in suburbs or across metropolitan regions are witnessing a different aspect of this dynamic. When people don't feel attached to their current neighborhoods and don't think they have the power to make improvements, they are more likely to move somewhere else. Usually they move somewhere that is less populated—they have had to put up with all the drawbacks of living near other people, and have reaped few of the advantages, so suburban or rural areas seem more appealing. In the suburban or rural communities they are moving to, the current residents don't have enough control of land use, public works, and economic development to plan adequately for population growth. The subdivisions become larger and the strip malls more extensive, but the residents' sense of community and political capacity diminishes, and so people begin to move out once again.[17]

Some of the mayors and city managers who have adopted democratic governance strategies are reacting to new realities in public finance. In many cities, residents give high marks to the public services they receive and yet consistently vote down bond issues and sales tax increases to maintain those services. Without the same level of financial resources, and without a strong working partnership between government and citizens, public services begin to erode—which in turn provokes a backlash from citizens who want to know why the streets aren't being plowed or the roads repaved.[18]

Other civic experiments are designed to address the effects of limited citizenship on our public schools. Without networks of adult relatives, role models, and mentors for young people, the burden of raising children shifts to parents and schools. With less buy-in from parents and other community members, schools receive less funding and other kinds of support. Parents and teachers fail to cooperate effectively to encourage student learning. The way in which schools and teachers operate does not change, since reform ideas aren't adequately analyzed, understood, adopted, or adapted. Schools do not adequately address the achievement gap or other race-related education issues. The school climate is tense, and deep rifts exist between students of different races and classes.[19]

Most democratic organizers and neighborhood council leaders working on crime-related issues are responding to the lack of connections between citizens and police officers. When that relationship is weak, it becomes more difficult to prevent crime and enforce the law: officers don't respond to citizen requests, citizens don't give officers the information they need, and there is less support for youth programs and other shared endeavors.[20] When the police-community relationship is marked by mistrust, the forces of crime prevention end up fighting each other in the courts. Residents start to feel that the justice system no longer reflects and upholds community values. Without that sense of fairness, criminals aren't held accountable (judged, sentenced, punished, rehabilitated) by the community, but by the abstraction of "the law."[21]

Finally, many local leaders are responding to the breakdown of communities along lines of cultural difference. Racism and other kinds of cultural conflict reflect the lack of good citizenship in a variety of ways. People don't understand, are unsure how to interact with, and are more likely to stereotype people who are unlike themselves. Simmering, longstanding resentments and injustices aren't brought into the open until they explode in a crisis. People haven't had chances to think about how racism affects policy, society, and institutions—and they don't know how to take action against racism, bias, and prejudice.[22]

With most of these public issues, the conventional public policy tools seem to treat the symptoms rather than dealing with the root causes. The dearth of active citizenship is not the only cause—there is no single source for any of these problems—but it interacts with other trends and challenges in subtle and pervasive ways. The lack of cooperation and mutual support among potential problem-solvers, the lack of consensus behind community values and plans, the lack of awareness and knowledge, and the lack of social cohesion between different groups corrode our ability to address all kinds of public challenges. This analysis could be summarized by paraphrasing the old Clinton campaign line: "It's the democracy, stupid."

These are daunting, persistent public problems, and the illusion that they can be solved single-handedly by government is finally fading away. All kinds of local leaders, from elected officials to neighborhood activists, are turning to new governance approaches because they realize how badly they need active, productive citizens. They come to this realization in different ways: because they are confronted by angry people who are upset about a particular problem or decision; because they are convinced of the need for parent involvement in education, or for "eyes on the street" to prevent crime; or because they are terrified of the grim forecasts for their city's financial future. In order to deal with any of these challenges, leaders find they need to work differently with the public.

Spurred by their fears and frustrations, local leaders are creating environments where citizens, governments, and community organizations can pool their ideas and resources. These projects and structures for shared governance can boost the problem-solving power of communities by involving many more people in defining, analyzing, and working to address the problems. In the process, they seem to be changing people's conceptions of good citizenship. By offering participatory, empowering, and holistic opportunities for ordinary people, they are proving that "getting involved" can be both politically effective and personally rewarding. They are showing that Lisa Giordano does not have to be an isolated, unusual, altruistic figure: she can be a realistic role model for all of us.

2
Is Everything Up to Date in Kansas City?
Why "Citizen Involvement" May Soon Be Obsolete

Dr. Ray Daniels knew all about the key role that parents play in student achievement. Daniels was the superintendent of schools in Kansas City, Kansas (KCK), an ethnically diverse, blue-collar city of 150,000 people that sits right across the river from Kansas City, Missouri. From his experience as an educator, he had no trouble believing what the researchers claim: that the involvement of parents and other family members is one of the most critical factors in helping students succeed.[1]

Involving KCK parents was not going to be easy, however. Many longtime residents distrusted the schools, partly because of past controversies over busing and school segregation. Teachers felt that some parents weren't adequately preparing their children for school. People who had moved to KCK more recently, including a growing number of immigrant families, needed help adjusting to a new language, a new education system, and a new set of cultural norms. All of these difficulties were apparent in the low test scores of KCK students, which were well below the national averages.[2]

Daniels knew that raising those scores would require internal changes as well; the KCK schools were in the midst of "First Things First," a systemwide reform initiative that would get teachers and administrators talking about how to improve teaching practices, the curriculum, and other aspects of how schools function. But those changes wouldn't make a difference if the role of parents stayed the same. "I was looking for a way to get more community involvement," he says. "Not in the same way as parents traditionally get involved, with cookies and cupcakes. I was looking for ways to get the business and faith communities involved as well."[3]

But Daniels was facing a problem that so many other officials, organizers, and activists have to deal with today: citizen involvement efforts often fail to attract many participants. This is partly because the whole notion of "citizen involvement" centers on the needs and goals of the person doing the involving, not the citizen. It is based on the assumption that elected representatives and public employees can handle the business of governing without much help; ordinary people are only needed to play limited roles on certain occasions. Even the term itself implies that there is an existing institution, process, or meeting that citizens must be brought into—people must be brought to politics, rather than the other way round.

This makes for a recruitment message that is not compelling enough to attract many citizens. Most people are too focused on their families, their careers, or just making ends meet to understand the needs and goals of all the different kinds of local leaders who want some of their time and attention. So while leaders like Daniels may start out with a narrow view of citizen involvement, they often realize the need to broaden their horizons in order to succeed. They begin to recognize the great variety of skills and motivations people bring to public life, and begin to help citizens address a range of issues, in a range of ways, on their own terms and their own turf. "Citizen involvement," which once seemed like the wave of the future—the great leap beyond traditional public meetings—is now being treated like a well-worn stepping-stone on the path to more democratic forms of governance.

It Isn't Rocket Science: It's Harder

If you, like Ray Daniels, are trying to involve citizens in some kind of civic endeavor, you may not realize exactly what you are up against. You may be starting out with very limited, specialized citizen involvement needs that are dictated by the demands of your job:

- you are a public official who needs input on a particular policy decision;
- you are a community organizer trying to recruit low-income people for a march on city hall;
- you are a principal and you want parents to raise money for the school;
- you belong to the League of Women Voters, and you want to register large numbers of voters in a neighborhood where most people have never voted before.

You begin to realize that these specific goals tend to attract very specific—and small—sets of people.

So instead of trying to do all the recruiting yourself, you decide to use institutions and organizations that are already set up to host and facilitate citizen participation. You begin looking for places where diverse sets of people are discussing, deciding, and acting on public issues in a public way. Roger Bernier, an administrator for the Centers for Disease Control (CDC), went on this kind of search when he needed citizen input on vaccine policy decisions. "Vaccines are critically important to public health, but not many people are aware of the policy decisions that the CDC has to make. I knew we couldn't get a huge national turnout for meetings about vaccines; the ideal thing for us would be to introduce some of these questions and policy options in environments where people are already deliberating on public issues. After gathering their input, we could then come back a few months later to those same sets of people to ask them more specific questions, and tell them how their input has affected federal policy. So I looked for those kinds of regular, popular, deliberative meetings—unfortunately, I didn't find many."[4]

Like Bernier, you realize that most public meetings and hearings aren't all that deliberative or well-attended, and that other kinds of citizen involvement efforts are too narrowly focused to accommodate your needs. There simply aren't that many meaningful opportunities for people to participate in public life. You have run up against the same barrier that ordinary citizens face—you have just approached it from the top down rather than the bottom up.

Finally, you arrive at a surprising conclusion. You thought you were just trying to get input or find volunteers, and it turns out that what you really need to do is full-scale organizing. Your to-do list may include developing a recruitment message, finding sites for whatever meetings you plan to hold, finding and training facilitators or moderators, writing a guide that provides background information and describes key options, and arranging for an evaluation of your efforts. You may need to find translators or multilingual facilitators, and have your discussion materials translated into different languages. You may need to provide food, transportation, and child care. If you plan on holding large-group events, you may need to find good speakers and moderators, or even arrange for high-tech aids like simultaneous translation equipment or instant polling devices. If you can't get all of these services donated in-kind, and if your employer can't afford to let you spend large amounts of time on this project, you will need to raise money. Most important—and time-consuming—of all, if you want to attract a broad range of people, you will have to recruit groups and organizations that can recruit participants for you from within their networks and memberships. "Being a democratic organizer is hard work," says Shakoor Aljuwani, former director of the United Neighborhoods Center in Buffalo,

New York. "I felt like a combination of a movie director and a referee at a hockey game—putting on the show, getting groups to the table, occasionally keeping them from each other's throats, reminding people of the big picture."[5] You may not have the time or the skills required to complete all these tasks. You may not have the budget to hire someone—and even if you do, where do you look for someone with all these capacities?

Your plight is shared by local leaders all over the country: most would-be democracy-builders have narrow citizen involvement needs, they have few democratic structures to lean on, and they have trouble finding people with the skills to mobilize citizens effectively. As these barriers become clear, "citizen involvement" begins to seem like a quaint abstraction, a trite phrase mocking you with its apparent simplicity. You have discovered the complicated truth: if you want to succeed, you can't just involve citizens in ways that supplement the political process—you have to construct new arenas where citizens are at the center of the system. It is easier said than done.

Beyond "Cookies and Cupcakes" in KCK

In 1999, at the very beginning of his efforts in KCK, Ray Daniels made a couple of breakthroughs that helped his project overcome some of these challenges. First, he realized that, because of the mistrust and the cultural barriers between citizens and educators, the schools couldn't engage parents effectively on their own. So he reached out to Terry Woodbury, the director of the local United Way, and the two men began talking about how to increase parent involvement. They won a grant from the Ewing Marion Kauffman Foundation, the leading philanthropic organization in the region, to help fund the project.

Daniels and Woodbury wanted to focus their initial efforts on the northeast side of the city—the set of neighborhoods where they felt the need was greatest. The Old Northeast, as it is known locally, has a population of 11,000 and much higher percentages of low-income residents, people of color, and recent immigrants than the rest of the region. It has an unemployment rate that is five times higher than the regional average.

The second breakthrough was the hiring of Brandi Fisher to run the project. Fisher was uniquely qualified: she had graduated from the public administration school at the University of Kansas, one of the first such schools to include democratic governance as a core part of the curriculum. She had also worked on "Americans Discuss Social Security," an effort to connect citizen voices with national policy makers that was coordinated by a national civic organization called AmericaSpeaks. Both of those experiences had given her a sense of the national "civic field," the loosely connected network of people—professors, consultants, program officers at foundations, and employees of national nonprofit organizations—who think and talk about democracy, citizenship, and public life.

Referring to this set of professionals as members of a field is somewhat misleading, however. For while they all refer to their work as being "civic" in some important way, there is tremendous variation in how they use that term. These practitioners, researchers, and observers—who include conflict resolution practitioners, deliberation experts, campaign finance reform advocates, democratic theorists, dialogue specialists, and representatives of many other related fields—tend to have very different ideas about democracy and citizenship. Some of them think of citizens in very narrow ways; they are using stereotypes that prevent them from understanding what ordinary people want out of public life. Some of them have built their reputations around specific citizen involvement "tools" or models that they have developed, trademarked, and promoted. Because they are so divided and disconnected, the members of the "civic field" are not providing a clear, consistent message to local leaders about how they might change their relationship with the public.

As a result, some of the most innovative democratic governance efforts are being pioneered by local leaders who have very little contact with the national "civic field"—and who may not even think of their work as civic. Ironically, most of the people who are trying to change how democracy works are disconnected from the people who write about how democracy ought to work.

Fisher has been one of the few to make this jump from the national civic scene to the local realities of democratic governance—from the debates about citizenship to the challenge of how to recruit citizens on a rainy Tuesday night to talk about difficult issues with people they've never met before. Her intellectual background gave her a set of principles she could use to guide her work; her interactions with the residents of the Old Northeast helped her figure out how to apply those principles in the real world.

The Seven Deadly Citizens

Fisher began her work in the Old Northeast with the main goals of the school system in mind: to help parents feel more comfortable with the schools, and to help them understand how to help their children succeed. But the more she connected with parents and other community members, the more she understood the many different motivations—and misgivings—they had about getting involved. By reacting to the needs and goals of well-rounded, flesh-and-blood people, Fisher was moving beyond the civic stereotypes that dominate the national debate about what citizens ought to be and do. These seven narrow definitions of citizenship handicap many citizen involvement efforts before they even get started.[6]

1. Perhaps the most common of these stereotypes is that of the citizen as voter. Enormous amounts of money and effort are spent every year registering Americans to vote. Incredible quantities of political capital are marshaled in support of campaign finance reform, greater use of initiatives and referenda, and other changes to our electoral system. Advocates of election reform assume that raising the number of voters and reducing the role of money in the political process will produce better candidates, more satisfied citizens, and—once the election is over—improved political leadership.

Voting is clearly an essential public duty—our ultimate safeguard against tyranny. If electoral reform will improve the quality of our leadership, even to a small extent, then it is worth pursuing. But despite all these efforts, voter turnout continues its inexorable one-step-forward, two-steps-back decline. Turnout is particularly low among young people, who are the primary targets of most campaigns to promote voting.[7] It may be that all the pro-voting messages ("Your Vote Counts!") have backfired; implying that voting can cure all of our dissatisfactions with politics may leave citizens more cynical than before.

While the way candidates raise money may disillusion citizens, perhaps the most important reason for declining turnout is that voting can be such a solitary, routine activity. Voting advocates haven't fully realized that citizens want more than just to pull a lever: they need that critical sense of being part of something larger than themselves, part of a community that is capable of solving its problems. Instead, they are confronted by daunting issues and sound-bite candidates. "It is possible to vote and still be disenfranchised," says the sociologist Michael Schudson.[8] By itself, voting seldom provides the feeling of unity and capacity that makes our electoral choices meaningful.

2. Public officials have reinforced the second civic stereotype, the citizen as consumer, by trying to make government more efficient and entrepreneurial. To advertise this approach, many of them have borrowed terms from the private sector, referring to their constituents as "customers" or "patrons" rather than citizens.[9] The implication is that residents are busi-

ness clients, rather than allies who can help make public decisions and solve public problems. This mindset has been characterized as the "vending machine" theory of government: when residents insert their tax contributions, they receive trash pickup, police protection, education for their children, and other products in return.[10]

To the extent that this philosophy encourages public employees to be efficient, and encourages citizens to demand government efficiency, it can be a positive influence. But as a remedy for citizen mistrust of government, it may not be very effective.[11] Perhaps this is because it discourages direct communication between citizens and officials; Americans don't expect their banks or phone companies to ask for their input or their help, so when government acts like a business, we tend to think of citizenship in purely financial terms. The consumer stereotype also reinforces the assumption that government alone bears the responsibility for solving public problems. This burden is much more difficult and complicated than selling products, and it may create expectations that government cannot fulfill.

3. Robert Putnam's article and subsequent book, *Bowling Alone,* helped define the third civic stereotype: the citizen as socializer. Putnam observed that Americans no longer join social clubs, neighborhood associations, or even bowling leagues in nearly the numbers that they used to, and he claimed that this solitary behavior has undermined our culture and democracy itself.[12] Putnam and his allies want to rebuild the "social capital" of our communities by strengthening connections between diverse residents and finding more organizations that can unify citizens around common goals. They argue that cities, regions, and countries with high social capital tend to be more democratic and prosperous than places with low social capital.

Some observers have loudly rejected Putnam's thesis, pointing to increased enrollment in youth soccer leagues and yoga classes. Others have joined him in urging Americans to join things and trying to predict what the popular new organizations will turn out to be—as Putnam puts it, "What will be the Kiwanis Club of the 21st Century?" If these efforts fail, there are sure to be dire consequences: Putnam claims that if Americans keep watching so much television, democracy may never recover.[13]

This is a discouraging vision: that, with one more click of the remote control, civil society might vanish altogether. Putnam doesn't mean to blame citizens, but his message can come across that way. While the social capital approach is much more holistic than some of the other stereotypes, it is such a high-level, macro analysis that it is difficult to know how to apply it to citizen involvement efforts. It may be true that social and cultural connections make communities stronger, but most people don't see the link between joining the Kiwanis Club and reshaping local politics.[14]

4. Many of those who reject Putnam's grim view of public life tout the fourth civic stereotype as a kind of antidote: the citizen as volunteer. Like his father, George W. Bush has made volunteerism a cornerstone of his domestic agenda. In advocating his USA Freedom Corps and Citizen Corps, Bush has used dramatic language about citizenship. The president and his advisors feel that increasing volunteerism, especially through faith-based initiatives, will cause Americans to rethink their public roles. "America needs more than taxpayers, spectators and occasional voters," Bush says. "America needs full-time citizens."[15]

Like the statistics about membership in clubs and organizations, the question of whether Americans are volunteering more often is a subject of some debate.[16] Even if they are, it isn't clear whether increased volunteerism will repair the citizen-government relationship or revitalize public life. In fact, most of the rhetoric used to promote this stereotype describes volunteering as altruistic and apolitical, rather than a way of solving public problems. This may be the wrong language to use, since it downplays the capacity of citizens to make an impact on big issues through their own effort and ideas. It also casts volunteerism as a solitary activity with purely personal benefits—we should do it because it will make us feel good. For most people, good feelings are probably not enough; organizers must show convincingly that the volunteering opportunity is part of a larger effort that can make a real difference.

5. Some public officials promote the fifth stereotype, the citizen as advisor, when they ask for their constituents' input on major public decisions. The assumption is that bringing citizens into the process will lead to better, fairer, more informed policies that have broader public support. The practice of input-gathering evokes a democracy where everyone is well-informed, and everyone has a say.

But, once again, the role being offered to citizens may not be meaningful enough to sustain their involvement in the long run. Of course public officials should ask their constituents what they think, but if people don't see the broader context—if they don't understand how these policy questions affect their daily lives, or they don't feel their input is being used to solve public problems, or they don't see how they can take action themselves on the issue—then either they won't participate in the first place, or their enthusiasm will wane over time. Sooner or later, the only residents to attend the meetings will be the ones who believe that their participation could have a direct effect on the decision—and this small group is already informed, educated, and passionately involved.[17]

6. The sixth stereotype, the citizen as a dispossessed or disempowered person, is reinforced by the kind of traditional community organizing first pioneered in Chicago in the 1940s. This approach, which is often associated with Saul Alinsky, focuses on particular sets of citizens: low-income residents, people of color, and others who have been on the short end of the political process. By building a critical mass of people, these organizers hope to make the "disempowered" a force in the political process.[18] One key assumption in this approach is that there are basic conflicts of interest between decision-makers and citizens, between the rulers and the ruled. Traditional organizers worry that if citizens and government work together too closely, public officials will dominate, manipulate, or co-opt the residents. Instead, organizers try to build a separate base of power, so that they can then deal with powerbrokers by confronting or negotiating with them.

Many traditional community organizing strategies are still used today, in all kinds of projects. Appealing to people on the basis of their attitudes toward the system can be effective for recruiting certain sets of people, but like the other civic stereotypes, this is not usually the best way of reaching a broad base of citizens. Starting out with a predetermined cause or an explicit focus on people who feel disempowered tends to exclude people who disagree with the cause or do not feel part of that group.

7. Finally, a number of civic foundations and academics uphold the seventh stereotype: the historic vision of citizens as deliberators—public intellectuals who read and talk about public issues. They cite Thomas Jefferson's famous edict to "educate and inform the whole mass of the people." They encourage citizens to read the newspaper religiously, study the issues diligently, and discuss politics with each other in a logical and respectful fashion. This vision of citizenship has had a strong influence on the way civic education is conducted in high schools and colleges.[19] The courses, forums, salons, Deliberative Polls®, and other kinds of meetings organized under this philosophy put an emphasis on learning and dialogue; participants are expected to listen rather than just talk. Sometimes public officials are invited to these events to hear what citizens have to say, and there is usually some kind of report that is circulated to decision-makers, but the organizers of deliberative meetings want to do more than just gather input: they want to impress everyone with the insight and integrity of the discussions, rather than simply assembling a summary of the most common opinions.

Deliberation advocates think highly of ordinary citizens. They affirm that people are capable of discussing complex problems and finding common ground, even when a divisive issue is on the table. Supporters of this approach have also made a valuable contribution by emphasizing the importance of process: citizen meetings are more likely to be successful when organizers provide facilitators, guides, and other kinds of structure. As recruiters, however, advocates of deliberation often come up short. Most deliberative processes attract a fairly exclusive crowd, perhaps because the possibility of action and change seems even more distant. Because it emphasizes dialogue and analysis at the expense of other activities, the deliberator stereotype may have limited appeal.

Each of the seven civic stereotypes is based on good intentions: we would all presumably like to see a future where every citizen votes and volunteers, where every government is highly efficient, and where we all have chances to socialize, deliberate, give input, and advocate for our interests. However, local organizers have learned that these are complementary, interconnected aspects of a civic whole: none of these parts of the body politic works as well on its own. When you ask citizens to deliberate on an important issue, they also want their input to affect public policy. When you ask them to provide policy input, they also want to volunteer for action efforts. When you ask them to vote, they also want to know whether candidates will back up their promises. When you ask them to fight for causes, they also want to form productive relationships with public officials and other citizens. If you don't allow participants to explore all the ways they can be citizens, you cut short the larger potential of well-rounded, active citizenship, and you may just leave people frustrated.

These stereotypes are also tempting because it seems easier to focus on a narrow slice of citizenship than to give people a range of political opportunities. But, in the big picture, piecemeal citizen involvement leads to redundancies and failures. As the United Way beats the bushes for volunteers, the League of Women Voters resolutely registers voters, government agencies ask for input, bowling leagues languish, neighborhood associations beg for donations, and hundreds of well-meaning public and nonprofit organizations try to involve citizens in one issue or forum or another. If these efforts don't hang together, they may all hang separately.

The Evolution of Citizenship in Greater Kansas City

To make democratic governance work, you have to move past the civic stereotypes and create environments that will appeal to real citizens. As

Brandi Fisher tried to do this in KCK, some of her peers across the river were facing the same challenge. In fact, the recent history of Greater Kansas City shows how numerous attempts at citizen involvement can produce a few successful adaptations. In a metro area that spans two states, eleven counties, and 1.9 million people, many different civic initiatives have been launched over the last fifteen years, reflecting many different roles that citizens might play in public life. Some of these efforts faltered from the beginning; others have survived by appealing to one set of residents and carving out their own niche in the political process. A few seem to be growing and diversifying, attracting larger numbers of people, giving them a variety of ways to practice active citizenship, and establishing new arenas for policymaking. In the process, these projects seem to have evolved beyond traditional "citizen involvement."

One of the largest civic initiatives in the region is FOCUS Kansas City, which began in 1992 as a large-scale visioning effort. The project was initiated by the city government of Kansas City, Missouri, as a vehicle for developing "a comprehensive and integrated plan to guide the future of Kansas City for the next 25 years." FOCUS is funded by the city and has a staff of four. In two planning phases, one in 1992 and another in 1994, several hundred citizens served on seven work teams to flesh out the plan. The teams held a number of forums and hearings in order to involve even more citizens; Denise Phillips, the current manager of the project, estimates that those events reached 5,000 people. The FOCUS plan was adopted by the city council in 1997 as a guide for city government operations over the next twenty-five years.[20]

After 1997, FOCUS shifted to the implementation of the plan. The organizers had researched the fate of visioning efforts in other cities and concluded that they had to involve citizens in this stage as well. "We realized that, five years out, few of those visions were still alive and kicking," says Phillips. "When you ask thousands of people to help create a plan, you better make sure it doesn't just sit on a shelf." The FOCUS plan included 600 proposed initiatives, grouped into twelve categories. Phillips estimates that "about 90% of them are being done by the community," and that another 5,000 people have been involved in this process, though these numbers are difficult to track.[21] In each neighborhood, FOCUS staff helped residents conduct a Neighborhood Assessment that identified action ideas for both citizens and public employees to work on.[22]

In 1998, the city won a federal grant for improving and streamlining public services, which was one of the central ideas in the FOCUS plan. The money came from the federal "Hassle-Free Community Initiative," which takes the language of the citizen-as-consumer stereotype to an extreme.[23] The goal is to create "hassle-free" communities where people can access "seamless," "customer-driven" public services from local, state, and federal agencies. Each of the communities receiving this funding was urged to reach a "90% customer satisfaction rate" among the citizens who use the services.[24]

While FOCUS Kansas City was initiated by local government, another major civic initiative, the Kansas City Church/Community Organization (KCCO), is rooted in the faith community. As an heir to the faith-based community organizing tradition, KCCO's mission is to help people "participate in and influence our political system and democratic institutions. Those who were previously ignored, excluded, or apathetic become involved."[25] The group is affiliated with the Pacific Institute for Community Organizing (PICO), a national network of faith-based community organizations. The strength of KCCO is its member congregations. Each congregation has an organizing committee that selects issues and priorities based on dozens of one-on-one conversations with congregants and other community members. Congregations sometimes mobilize around an issue facing that particular neighborhood; one recent example is an effort to reduce housing blight in the Ruskin neighborhood, which has led to massive neighborhood cleanups and the formation of the Ruskin Neighborhood Community Development Corporation. Sometimes all the KCCO congregations work together on an issue of citywide concern. They will often hold an "action" on that issue—usually a rally or an event where residents will ask questions and make demands of public officials.

In the last ten years, KCCO has changed its tactics. Instead of expecting public officials to solve problems single-handedly and using the "actions" to sway them, the KCCO congregations are more likely to see themselves as part of the problem-solving process. "Our actions are less likely to be stand-alone meetings, focused on a single subject," says KCCO director Warren Adams-Leavitt, "and more likely to be one point in a series of meetings and actions taken to resolve a problem. In that sense, we are no longer simply coming to public officials, presenting them with a problem, and asking them to solve it. We are more likely to be presenting them with some possible strategies or solutions, and bringing other necessary partners as well."[26]

One of the newest civic experiments, the Kansas City Forums, recruits participants from across the metro region. Begun in 2003, this effort was inspired by the publication of a major report on the state of the Kansas City region by Curtis Johnson and Neil Peirce, two national observers of regional issues. The process is modeled after the National Issues Forums (NIF) promoted by the Kettering Foundation of Dayton, Ohio. A "deliberative forum" is held each month on an issue of national and local concern; the issues have included healthy neighborhoods, regionalism, economic development, race relations, transportation, and children and youth.

Jennifer Wilding, who coordinates the Forums, says she does most of the recruiting via e-mail. "People participate because they're interested either in the process, or in the issue we're deliberating about," she says. "We tend to get people who want to create change—for example, people who want to reduce growth and sprawl—but we don't usually get radicals from either political extreme."[27] Over 500 people participated, roughly fifty per forum, in the first year of the project.

At the beginning of each forum, participants are handed a guide that provides some background on the issue and lays out three overarching choices. For example, on the topic of transportation, the choices presented were: 1) develop new modes of travel; 2) improve the current system; and 3) expand the roadway system. The crowd breaks into small groups to discuss these choices, one at a time, before coming back together to share their summary conclusions at the end of the evening.

Participants are then invited to join a task force that will work on the main action ideas that emerged at the forum. The organizers of the KC Forums are particularly proud of the way they are helping citizens move from deliberation to a more active role in the community. According to Wilding, "Most NIF programs use discussion guides published by the Kettering Foundation, which conclude with a ballot where people can vote for their favorite choice; these ballots are designed to be mailed to Members of Congress. We are the only NIF program in the country that creates task forces where citizens can help implement their ideas, and the groups have already made great strides." One task force is producing an economic development guide, another has created a tourism pamphlet highlighting the city's downtown, and another is producing a play on the school district's desegregation case.[28]

The KC Forums also helped provide facilitators for another civic initiative, a forum on foreign affairs hosted by the local public television station in January 2004. Kansas City was one of several cities to participate in this national PBS initiative, called *By the People*, which used the Deliberative Polling® approach pioneered by political scientist James Fishkin.[29] In each city, organizers selected a set of 100 people who perfectly mirrored the demographic characteristics of their city and had them discuss three different potential priorities for American foreign policy. The selected citizens were paid a stipend of $75 to take part, though in Kansas City at least, this inducement wasn't enough: only fifty-two of the selected hundred actually turned out for the forum.[30] The goal of most Deliberative Polls® is to provide citizen input that is so demographically representative, and so thoroughly discussed and refined, that it carries weight with public officials.

Meanwhile, at the neighborhood level, Kansas City's Community Development Corporations (CDCs) have been involving residents in decisions about housing and economic development. In fact, citizen engagement is a major component of the "CD2000" plan that guides all of the community development in the region. The plan requires each CDC to meet specific goals for resident involvement in order to ensure their continued funding. Citizens are invited to serve on the CDC advisory boards and to take part in periodic "listening sessions" where they talk about their concerns and priorities for their neighborhood. As the connections between the CDCs and the neighborhoods have become stronger, citizens have begun taking on more active roles: they now monitor the performance of the CDCs in their efforts to meet the financial, construction, and citizen engagement goals in CD2000, and they sometimes work closely with developers and architects on specific construction projects. CDC staffers have also realized the need to go beyond the decisions concerning the "built environment" and help citizens address social issues like crime. "We try to assess the needs of the neighborhood," says Leslie MacLendon, an organizer for a CDC called Swope Community Builders. "We're here not only to build houses, but to assist residents and make sure that they know we are not taking over the neighborhood they've lived in for twenty years."[31] The CDCs may have started out with a simple desire to gather resident input, but they now seem to be helping citizens take on a variety of civic roles on a whole range of issues.

Many other Kansas City civic initiatives have come and gone in the last ten years. Some have survived as small-scale efforts, like the "Dialogue Dinners" organized by a nonprofit called Kansas City Harmony. The Dinners are informal gatherings of 7–9 people and are meant to build "social capital" by fostering new relationships among different groups. Others couldn't be sustained, such as the "Community Conversations" on race and neighborhood issues that were initiated by Kansas City Harmony and several other organizations in 2001. Inspired by President Clinton's "One America" initiative, two city council members organized a set of "One Kansas City" forums on race relations in 2000, but these events too were discontinued.

During the same period, organizations like the League of Women Voters and the United Way have been trying to cast Kansas City residents in the traditional civic roles of voter and volunteer. These kinds of efforts aren't usually considered "citizen involvement," but they do reflect a desire to pull people further into public life.

At least one thing is clear in Greater Kansas City: this endless array of projects, programs, campaigns, and other attempts to involve citizens shows how badly our political process needs the time and attention of ordinary people. Some of these civic experiments were modeled after approaches promoted by national organizations, and sometimes the Kansas City organizers received advice and technical assistance from these groups. But in most cases, the local leaders did a great deal of adapting and innovating on their own, and the success of each project seemed to depend primarily on local variables, such as the capacity of the coordinator or the level of shared commitment from the local groups supporting the effort.[32]

So is everything up-to-date in Kansas City? Perhaps not, but a fundamental shift in the state of democracy in the region does seem to be taking place. One challenge almost every initiative has struggled with, especially at first, is recruiting an economically and ethnically diverse array of participants. This may be because most of the projects started out by projecting a specific civic stereotype: they reached out to citizens as deliberators (KC Forums and *By the People*), as socializers (Kansas City Harmony's Dialogue Dinners), as policy advisors (the CDCs for neighborhood-level decisions and FOCUS Kansas City on citywide and regional decisions), or as members of the disempowered and dispossessed (KCCO). The League of Women Voters and United Way asked citizens to serve as voters and volunteers, respectively. These recruitment messages attracted the citizens who already gravitated toward those roles.

Some local organizers recognized the danger in this lack of diversity. They knew that their projects would be more powerful, and produce outcomes more reflective of the public as a whole, if they could successfully incorporate a broader array of people. Some of the Kansas City initiatives broadened their recruitment appeals by giving participants a wider range of political roles to play: FOCUS involved citizens in implementing the vision, the CDCs began enlisting citizens in crime prevention efforts, KCCO worked more collaboratively with public officials, and the Kansas City Forums began creating task forces. These civic experiments have gone beyond the initial citizen involvement stereotypes and are helping participants exercise other aspects of their political personalities.

A related adaptation that seems to be emerging in Kansas City is the creation of new arenas for making public decisions. Instead of gathering citizen input and treating people like outsiders to the political process, some of these projects are establishing alternative venues for decision-making. This shift is apparent within the history of one organization, KCCO: instead of trying to influence public officials, they are trying to solve public problems (successfully, in many cases) by assembling all the necessary actors and asking them to work together. In their shift toward more well-rounded citizenship, FOCUS Kansas City, the KC Forums, and the CDCs all seem to embrace this approach. Their actions imply that, within the context of their meetings, power and authority is shared between citizens, government, and community organizations.

Learning and Teaching in KCK

The same shift toward well-rounded citizenship was also evident in the efforts of Brandi Fisher and her KCK colleagues. As they struggled to achieve Ray Daniels's vision for parent education and involvement, they demonstrated how local leaders can learn from the national "civic field," from local organizers in other communities, and—most importantly—from the citizens themselves.

As Fisher began working with KCK residents, she began to understand the depth of the divide between schools and community. Many parents felt that educators had consistently either given them orders or ignored them completely. "The residents felt that the school had taken a top-down approach in the past," Fisher says. "Telling people what needs to be done doesn't build trust." [33] To create a more interactive relationship, Fisher and her allies decided to use small-group dialogues as the backbone of their effort. Each group of 8–12 people would meet several times, with an impartial facilitator present who could help manage the discussions. In the first session, the participants would talk about their own experiences in school. At the second meeting, they would weigh various options for improving the schools, and in the final session they would develop recommendations and action plans. At the end of the small-group meetings, the KCK organizers planned to hold an "action forum" where participants shared their conclusions and formed teams to work on particular solution ideas.

Fisher and her allies were inspired by the methodology for small-group dialogue and large-group action promoted by the Study Circles Resource Center (SCRC), one of the most prominent national organizations in the civic field. The KCK organizers had sifted through a sea of different models and techniques, discarding many of them because they seemed too limited, expensive, or proprietary. But instead of saying that Fisher and her colleagues adopted the model promoted by SCRC, it would be more ac-curate to say that they adapted it. Like most good examples of democratic governance, the "KCK Study Circles" took general ideas and guidelines and customized them to fit local conditions.

One of the most critical steps was developing a recruitment message that emphasized the schools' willingness to listen. KCK parents didn't just want to be educated: they wanted to have some influence over how the schools functioned. Fisher and her allies made this part of their general outreach efforts—printing flyers, putting announcements in school news-letters and church bulletins, even using billboards—but the more difficult and significant work was in reaching out to the leaders of neighborhood associations and church congregations. Pastor Stephen Robbs, who runs the "Jesus is the Answer" Street Outreach project, was one of those stake-holders. Robbs remembers having doubts at the beginning. "Would there be action at the end of our meetings? Would they lead to something? The United Way convinced us that this would be a partnership [between citizens and] the school board."[34]

This led the KCK Study Circles into unexpected territory. The project was not simply making parents comfortable with the schools and teach-ing them how to help their children succeed: the organizers were helping participants decide what they wanted out of the project and helping them articulate their concerns and ideas to the schools. "You can't go into this work with a narrow, preset agenda," says Fisher. "You have to be flexible about your goals, give citizens a chance to think things through, and be open to whatever they want to achieve."[35]

As they talked with the stakeholders, Fisher and her allies also realized they would have to adapt some aspects of their process to make it more appropriate for particular cultures. One example was the Hmong commu-nity of recent immigrants from the mountainous areas of Southeast Asia. Daniels says that for years, the school board had been trying—and fail-ing—to attract Hmong parents to meetings. The KCK organizers met with a Hmong pastor to talk about the divide. "He told us it would only work if it was a full-day event after a Sunday service," said former United Way direc-tor Terry Woodbury. "We adapted our efforts to meet their needs."[36] Unlike most meetings that deal with education issues, many of the KCK Study Circles were held at places other than schools. By convening the groups at churches, community centers, and other locations, they were able to attract parents and other citizens who were simply not comfortable coming to the schools.

Another adjustment made by the KCK organizers was in the way they involved local officials. Some participants were intimidated by the presence of a school administrator, police official, or city council member. The planners began keeping decision-makers out of the first session or two, then introducing them into the discussions after the participants had built some confidence and begun to clarify their ideas. Fisher recalls that "it was only after the participants had talked for a session or two that they began to trust each other and begin to feel like the educators respected them and took them seriously."[37]

Fisher and her allies tried to eliminate every possible barrier to participation. They provided food, child care, and transportation. They arranged for translators. They recruited churches, neighborhood associations, and other organizations to serve as "host sites" for the meetings. These efforts seem to have paid off: over the last five years, 1,676 KCK residents have taken part in over 100 multiple-session, small-group meetings.[38] In other words, over 10% of the people living in Northeast Kansas City have participated in the project so far. "I was disappointed that only seventy people turned out for our first big kickoff event," says Fisher. "But the educators and school board members had had so much difficulty connecting with citizens in the past that they were absolutely shocked."[39]

As it turned out, school issues were only one aspect of what the participants wanted to talk about. In the sessions, people brought up challenges like crime, prostitution, vandalism, and racism. In some of the groups, the facilitator abandoned the discussion guide after the first session because it was clear that the participants had their own, more compelling agenda. Many of the meetings held today focus mainly on neighborhood issues, including land use decisions, crime prevention priorities, and youth concerns. In the Belrose Manor public housing project, the participants have gone on to start a tenants' association, hold a youth sports camp, and rid their neighborhood of ten drug houses.[40]

The flexibility of the KCK Study Circles points out one of the main weaknesses of most citizen involvement efforts: they focus on the goals and agenda of the organizers, rather than the citizens. At the local, state, and national levels, most of practitioners and advocates of citizen involvement fail to see how their work intersects. For example, the education experts who promote parent engagement in schools and the criminologists who promote neighborhood involvement in crime prevention both embrace the idea that citizens can be helpful volunteers and useful policy advisors. The issues of education and crime are interconnected: they usually attract different sets of citizens who seldom work together but have many of the same interests, and these citizens could probably make more meaningful contributions on both fronts if they combined their energies. However, these two camps of civic professionals do not seem to be comparing notes or developing joint strategies.[41] They continue recommending processes and meetings that focus citizens' attention solely on school issues or solely on crime issues. Citizens must come to them: they will not consider a middle ground where citizens might address both issues and accomplish many other endeavors besides.

In the KCK discussions, the participants began to paint a more complete picture of the challenges facing their neighborhoods. "You had churches, schools, community agencies, government officials—each of us was working on one piece of a bigger problem," says Wendell Maddox, who succeeded Woodbury as United Way director. "This project connected us and helped us see our services and programs as part of a larger plan, one that is being created by the community."[42]

The picture of who is responsible for solving KCK's problems seems to have changed as well. "At our first action forum, people were pretty negative," says Fisher. "A lot of them pointed fingers at the superintendent and presented lists of changes for the schools to make. He wasn't defensive; he took the suggestions and implemented as many as he could. At the second action forum, several discussion groups had come up with their own action ideas that they wanted to work on. By the third action forum, everyone was really pumped: now they had all kinds of things to work on, and all kinds of people and groups are involved in making them happen."[43]

Stephen Robbs has experienced this change in attitudes at the school level. He and other neighborhood residents now volunteer at Hawthorne Elementary School on a regular basis. "When we come into the building, the teachers light up. They know us by name. They say 'we're glad you're here' and thank us for our support," he says.[44]

The citizens of KCK have found all kinds of ways to improve their community. As advisors to the school system, participants helped create school improvement plans, a school preparation program for new kindergarten students, and a concentrated system-wide effort to raise students' literacy levels; in many cases, they devoted their own time to implementing these changes.[45] They have also volunteered to create neighborhood associations, tutoring and mentoring programs, parent support groups, neighborhood watch groups, back-to-school fairs, neighborhood cleanups, school fundraising events, Cinco de Mayo celebrations, a youth talent show, an after-school homework help line, and a community garden. They also set up a breakfast meeting with Kansas legislators to discuss the state's budget and education issues. They developed and staffed "Black Roses," an extra-curricular Afro-centric drumming and dance program, and the "Missing Link" program for tutoring, mentoring, and mediation.

Statistically, the level of active citizenship in KCK seems to be having an effect on some of the major challenges facing the community. Student test scores have risen steadily over the last five years, and the graduation rate has risen from 50% to 70%.[46] The crime rate in KCK has dropped 24% since 1997. Police used to respond to twenty emergency calls per month from the Belrose Manor housing project; now they only get that many in a year. There are doubtless many other variables that have contributed to these statistical shifts in the Old Northeast, but few residents doubt that active citizens have played a huge role.

Part of Ray Daniels's original vision was correct: parents and other citizens had a lot to learn from educators in KCK. Likewise, the KCK organizers had a lot to learn from the national civic field and from their counterparts in other communities. But as it turned out, the organizers and participants involved with the KCK Study Circles had a lot to teach as well. Perhaps their most important discovery is the idea of the well-rounded citizen. Diverse sets of people are more likely to get involved, and stay involved, if you give them a supportive environment that allows them to experience a variety of fulfilling civic roles. They won't necessarily respond to vending machines, bowling leagues, and "hassle-free" government: they need to be able to socialize, advise, advocate, deliberate, *and* volunteer.

Staffing, Structure, and the Problem of "Public Goods"

Despite five years of dramatic success, you probably can't point to Kansas City, Kansas, as an ideal kind of democracy. No evidence has been gathered to test whether the KCK Study Circles affected voter registration or government efficiency, and traditional community organizers might argue that it has failed to shift entrenched local power structures. Furthermore, unless the project can meet the challenges of staffing capacity and long-term structure, it might not even survive another five years.

Finding and keeping a capable staff—which in most cases means one solitary coordinator—has proved impossible for many democratic governance projects. To run a project like this effectively, you need to hire staffers who have "people skills": the ability to make initial phone calls, forge partnerships, make requests without appearing greedy, nag without appearing rude, and operate comfortably in different cultural settings. It helps if this coordinator is already connected with different networks in the community. You need someone with the capacity to develop recruitment messages, write clearly, and work with the media. The coordinator needs to understand the issues that citizens will want to address and be sensitive to the fact that there are many different valid viewpoints on any topic. Good facilitation skills may be necessary, not only to manage citizen discussions but to run steering committee meetings and to train other facilitators. Finally, mobilizing large numbers of citizens can be such a circus that the staffer at the hub of the effort must be able to tend all the logistical details with great care.

"This can be a very discouraging job," says Fisher. "Especially at first, recruitment is very difficult. You can spend all this time and effort to find a site, provide food and child care, arrange for a facilitator and maybe a translator—and then two people show up. You made an incredible investment, and you got nothing."[47]

The United Way of Wyandotte County has been fortunate so far, not only with Fisher but also in hiring staffers such as Leona McIntyre, Shaun Hayes, Brenda Mortell, and Christal Watson, all of whom have kept the project moving and growing. But coordinators usually only last a few years before they "burn out" or simply move on to other jobs. Fisher, McIntyre, Hayes, and Mortell have all left the program for other organizations.

When you try to replace a coordinator, you roll the dice once again. It is different from hiring a police chief or a city planner: for those jobs, there are professional degrees applicants must have, and you can be reasonably sure that they have acquired certain skills in their past work experiences. You can also be reasonably sure that the applicant has at least some understanding of the kind of job you're hiring them to do. You may still end up with a bad police chief or city planner, but you've at least eliminated some of the uncertainties. With democratic governance, you don't have those kinds of assurances and understandings. You take a shot in the dark by hiring somebody, and they take a shot in the dark by accepting the job.

Perhaps the more daunting challenge is that of establishing a stable long-term structure for the project. In fact, this is a limiting factor in KCK today: the meetings only happen when a neighborhood association or neighborhood leader appeals to the coordinator of KCK Study Circles for help in convening, recruiting, and facilitating. Residents must either be confident and committed enough to set those wheels in motion, or they simply have to wait for their next opportunity to be active citizens. In the Old Northeast, democratic meetings have become popular and common but not routine.

The neighborhood associations that have formed because of the project could provide this kind of structure: regular opportunities for residents to bring up ideas or concerns that the coordinator or the neighborhood associations haven't considered. However, the new groups seem to be operating in the same haphazard, semi-participatory way as most neighborhood associations.

Why do citizen involvement efforts find it so difficult to avoid civic stereotypes, find capable coordinators, and build democratic structures? An economist or political scientist might answer by saying that these kinds of challenges illustrate the difficulty of providing "public goods."[48] What they mean is that things which everyone can enjoy equally, and which no one person or group can easily profit from—a public park, for example, or a reservoir, or a neighborhood council system—can be very difficult to establish. Creating and maintaining them requires funding, government support, a high degree of collaboration between community groups, or all of the above. Before a public good has been identified and valued, there is a natural tendency toward specialization and narrow definitions.

So organizations start out by trying to involve citizens in a specific, limited way, on a temporary basis, with staffers who aren't sure what they've gotten themselves into. They may realize—or grow to realize—that they can recruit a broader array of citizens and give them a wider range of political opportunities by working with other organizations in a larger effort. They may wish for public administration schools or other sources of professional training that would provide them with well-prepared job candidates. If they are successful, they may decide that these opportunities for active citizenship should be made available on a regular basis. But not everything that seems beneficial to a community will be supported, or funded, or achieved: these challenges still hover over Kansas City, Kansas, and almost every other community besides.

Keeping Up with Kansas City?
Evolution in the "Civic Field"

As communities like KCK race ahead, setting new standards and raising new challenges for democratic governance, the members of the national "civic field" are trying to catch up. The professors, program officers, and various kinds of civic practitioners are moving forward in three areas: collecting the lessons learned in local civic experiments, reconciling some of the divisions within the field, and sketching out the components and parameters of democratic governance as a profession.

The national membership organizations are driving many of these changes. Groups like the National League of Cities, the National School Boards Association, NeighborWorks America, the International City/ County Managers Association, the League of Women Voters, and the National School Public Relations Association occupy an intermediary position between local leaders and the foundations and nonprofit organizations of the civic field. In order to support their members, these groups are pushing the civic thinkers and practitioners to recognize that the experiences of real communities, rather than abstract questions about deliberation or power, are at the heart of this work. Academics have increasingly turned their attention to producing case studies, both in the United States and abroad, that show the benefits, challenges, and implications of democratic governance. Many of the membership organizations have developed training programs, commissioned research, and produced guides and handbooks on democratic governance. As these groups examine the theories and practices of the civic professionals and interpret the ideas for their constituencies, they are providing a major impetus for overcoming the challenges facing the field.

Civic practitioners and observers have also had more opportunities recently to connect with one another. Two major coalitions have formed in the last five years: the Deliberative Democracy Consortium (DDC) and the National Coalition for Dialogue and Deliberation (NCDD).[49] The DDC was initiated by Carolyn Lukensmeyer, the director of one of the most prominent national nonprofits in the field, America*Speaks*. The NCDD was assembled by a young civic entrepreneur named Sandy Heierbacher. Both coalitions are designed to help civic professionals compare notes and decide what they have in common.

Partly as a result of these discussions, the civic field seems to be coming to the conclusion that no single civic tool is sufficient by itself, and that all the various activities and approaches should be considered as part of a complete democratic practice.[50] Ten years ago, for example, it was common to hear "dialogue vs. action" debates, in which the dialogue proponents would claim that talk alone was sufficient to produce change, and action proponents would claim that dialogue was merely a vehicle for cooptation and delay. Now there is some agreement that both dialogue and action are necessary and that they complement one another.

Similarly, the debate about the role of the Internet in public life seems to be arriving at a more reasonable middle ground. When Internet use proliferated in the 1990s, some observers claimed it would revolutionize politics and make face-to-face meetings obsolete. Face-to-face organizers expressed solemn doubts about the value of online public dialogue. More recently, it has become clear that this is not an all-or-nothing proposition: both online and face-to-face formats have unique strengths, and using them in combination seems to hold the greatest potential.[51]

The advocates of collaboration, which has become a buzzword in public and nonprofit management circles, are also beginning to clarify how their ideas fit in the larger field. "For years, the literature on collaborative governance didn't even mention citizens," says William Potapchuk, who has written extensively on the subject. As local leaders realized that their resources were more limited than before, and that they faced problems that were more complex and more likely to cross jurisdictional boundaries, they began to see the need to include a broader array of people and viewpoints. Recently, collaboration advocates have moved farther away from their previous focus on cooperation between leaders of organizations—mayors and CEOs, for example—to a recognition that collaboration should occur at many levels of the organizations, and particularly between an organization and ordinary citizens. This idea, which could be called "complete collaboration," implies that partnerships between parents, teachers, and police officers are just as important as agreements between school superintendents and police chiefs.[52]

As tools and approaches coalesce into more comprehensive practices, a handful of public administration professors have begun to institutionalize democratic governance as a core component of the curriculum. Classes on these subjects are now offered in the public administration schools at Kansas, Harvard, Minnesota, Texas-Arlington, and other universities. Suffolk University in Boston has gone a step further by offering "Community Leadership and Public Engagement" as a concentration for master's students.

The ongoing professionalization of the civic field forces it to become more organized, coherent, and useful to local leaders. This is a much-needed development, but it is also ironic and somewhat dangerous: some historians observers argue that the professionalization of public management, education, planning, public finance, law enforcement, and other fields, beginning early in the twentieth century, is precisely what caused the alienation between citizens and government. Now, in their efforts to move beyond expert rule, local leaders are seeking more experts. This is one of the conundrums that public administration professors and other civic professionals will have to address as they try to support and advance democratic governance.

What's in It for Citizens?

As the next two sections of this book will demonstrate, citizens are being recruited from many different angles, by leaders in many different fields, in communities all over the country. In this mad, short-sighted, uncoordinated rush, organizers are learning the hard way that involving citizens is a more difficult, more transformative process than they expected. Reaching out to their constituents may seem like a just another organizational priority for a school district, a nonprofit, or a local government, but it often ends up changing the organization itself. Encouraging active citizenship may seem like a routine civic responsibility—an innocuous way to strengthen a community—but it often raises tough questions how the political process should function.

When community leaders like Ray Daniels and Brandi Fisher put themselves in the shoes of the people they are trying to recruit, they begin to realize the limitations of "citizen involvement" and all its synonyms (such as "public engagement" and "citizen participation"). Rather than a government of, by, and for the people, these expressions suggest a political drama in which government occupies center stage and citizens are bit players on the edges of the scene. The new civic experiments seem to be going a step further, illustrating the terms of a more meaningful, ongoing, multifaceted relationship between citizens and government.

Section 3 will describe some of the efforts to embed this relationship into the way that communities function. Creating durable democratic structures for citizens may make life much easier for leaders like Daniels: instead of having to assemble a new set of people for every new meeting or project, organizers will be able to bring their issues and questions to places where people are already assembled. However, establishing these new arenas will take much higher levels of collaboration, imagination, and foresight among local leaders.

No matter what the next form of democracy looks like, it will probably be shaped by our answers to one important question: What's in it for citizens? This line of inquiry leads away from two-dimensional stereotypes and toward the hopes and concerns of real people. It suggests that new arenas for democratic governance will be built around the day-to-day interests, concerns, and talents of ordinary citizens, rather than the immediate needs of political professionals or the far-off dreams of political observers.

Section 2

Appeals to Citizenship

3
Of Pigs and People
Sprawl, Gentrification,
and the Future of Regions

When Len Santini and his family moved into a nice new house in suburban Guilderland, New York, they knew what to expect. The street was next to one of the largest hog farms in the area. However, the Santinis loved the house and the location; the occasional whiff of manure from the pigpens only reminded them that they were fulfilling a longtime dream of living in the country.

Some of the Santinis' neighbors were not as content, however. Many of them grumbled about the smell, and several formal complaints were lodged with the hog farmer. Then, one day, two 300-pound pigs wriggled through a hole in a fence and went ambling through the neighborhood. At the school bus stop, parents grabbed their children and ran for cover. This was the last straw for some of the residents, who filed a formal complaint with the town board.

As a parent, Santini could see why his neighbors would worry about the safety of their children, but he didn't understand the general level of antagonism towards the hog farmer. "Didn't they realize that this was part of the package?" he asked. "They chose to live in the country—well, the country is where the farms are."[1]

Santini and his neighbors belong to what may be the most restless, itinerant new culture to emerge in hundreds of years. The North Americans of today are not quite as mobile as those prehistoric nomads who first crossed over from Asia, but our imprints are deeper because we leave strip malls and subdivisions in our wake. The combination of new suburbs, new highways, and rising incomes has given us a dizzying array of choices about where to live. But though Santini's neighbors are free to move somewhere else—and the hog farmer might be glad to see them go—most of them would rather try changing the place they live now. Despite all the options available to us on the real estate market, we still want to wield some influence over our current surroundings. This desire has become a palpable force, a threat to the expert rule of planners and public officials, and a major factor in the development of neighborhoods and regions. We value our power of choice, but we have never given up the need for control.

The Search for Control

The desire for control is a natural impulse, and it shows up all the time in all kinds of communities. Citizens turn out in droves to oppose developments that threaten to reduce their property values, or ruin the view from their living room windows, or make them fearful for their safety: new subdivisions, condominiums, affordable housing units, highways, halfway houses, drug treatment centers, shopping malls, and landfills. People who moved to the country for more "elbow room" are dismayed when they see their wide-open spaces closing in on them. Commuters complain about traffic congestion and argue that roads should be widened or subways extended—but then other groups of residents oppose the construction of new highways or subway stations near their homes. In city neighborhoods, residents worry either that new high-priced housing will lead to gentrification, or that new affordable housing will tip the neighborhood into blight. Rural residents fight against streetlights because they want to be able to see the stars; city-dwellers push for more lighting in order to prevent crime. "I spent the first twenty years of my career defending the planning department from developers," says Greg Hoch, a city planner in Durango, Colorado. "I've spent the last five years defending it from citizens."[2]

In some situations, there is a conflict between what is good for the neighborhood and what is good for the larger community. People may agree that a new school or highway would have great benefits, but they may also fight to keep it from being built across the street from where they live.[3] (Frustrated planners sometimes call this the "Not In My Backyard" syndrome—"NIMBY" for short.) In other cases, it isn't clear that the community has had a chance to decide whether the new development is worthwhile or not: does the community really need a new stadium, or landfill, or parking lot?

These situations become even more complicated when they involve issues that cross political jurisdictions. For example, decisions about highways, commuter rail, public utilities, and waste disposal are seldom made by only one local government: usually several cities and towns have something at stake. Elected officials sometimes feel they need to act aggressively; otherwise their constituents will think they are too "soft" to take on other cities. As a result, conflicts escalate and resentments form between local governments and between city and county governments.[4]

The desire for control is also having an effect on the size and structure of government. It is evident in places like the San Fernando Valley, a part of Los Angeles that almost seceded from the rest of the city in 2002. Many residents of the Valley, which has a total population of 1.2 million, felt that they would enjoy greater police protection, better schools, and more responsive local government if they were part of a smaller city. This kind of "localism"—the assumption that residents can get more of what they need from smaller governments than larger ones—is apparent whenever a suburb incorporates in order to avoid being annexed by a larger, neighboring metropolis, and whenever separate cities and school districts are carved out of larger jurisdictions.[5] But the localists aren't the only ones who want to manage their surroundings more effectively: David Rusk and other advocates of "regionalism" argue that larger, regional governments are necessary if residents want to address regional problems like urban sprawl and economic stagnation.[6] The regionalists want jurisdictions to be larger, the localists want them to be smaller, but both sides of the argument want citizens to have more control over the places where they live.

While the local-regional debate continues and the desire for control intensifies, some of the people most involved in land use decisions have come up with more democratic responses. They are planners, developers, architects, zoning board members, elected officials, and neighborhood activists, and they are influenced by their own bad experiences with controversial development decisions. In order to manage these situations more effectively, they are launching proactive, broad-based planning efforts that allow large numbers of residents to set the parameters for growth, understand some of the trade-offs involved in these decisions, and decide, to some extent, how plots of land can be used.[7]

The proliferation of these planning projects suggests that, while the size of the government may matter, how people connect with it matters more. At their best, these efforts strengthen citizen-government connections, creating environments where residents can decide what they want for their neighborhood or community, and then work together to realize those visions.[8] But like other democratic governance efforts, these projects face a number of challenges—and they may have negative implications as well as positive ones.

At their worst, planning efforts can do more harm than good. When a neighborhood planning process doesn't incorporate a wide range of people, it may produce gentrification: improvements lead to higher rents and property taxes, forcing low-income residents to relocate elsewhere.[9] In this case, some residents exert greater control over their surroundings—but at the expense of other residents. Because of these questions about equity, there is a higher bar for participant recruitment in this type of democratic governance.

A poor recruitment effort can make things worse in other ways as well. Without a wide base of support, planning efforts may be susceptible to ambush by residents who weren't involved in the project and realize, once the plan is almost complete, that they really don't like what they see.[10] Hannah McKinney, the mayor of Kalamazoo, Michigan, considered this the biggest challenge to the planning efforts in her region. "What you're up against is something an economist would call 'rational ignorance'—people won't participate at the beginning because it doesn't seem worth their time," she says. "But if you don't get them involved up front, they will often show up at the end of the process, when they can see how some of the specifics of the plan will affect them directly. That's how you get 'veto groups,' which can shoot down the entire plan and generate an immense amount of ill-will."[11]

Even when a planning effort displays all the best characteristics of democratic governance, including the involvement of large, diverse numbers of people, it may have some worrisome implications. As neighborhoods and communities try to gain or retain control, some of them move faster and more effectively than others. The places that generate far-sighted plans and a strong sense of community are often the ones that were already economically and politically successful, and the planning effort carries them even farther forward. Having worked so hard to improve their surroundings, residents of these places may actually become less willing to cooperate with other communities and more able to defend their own from outside influences. The result may be NIMBY on a whole new scale.

This possibility is particularly worrisome to those who believe that cooperation between cities and suburbs, and between local and county governments, is more critical to economic success than ever before. Many economists argue that metropolitan regions (rather than cities or nations) are now the basic units in the global economy.[12] For the metro area to succeed, it may be essential for citizens and public officials—whether they live in small jurisdictions or large ones—to consider their decisions about land use, development, transportation, and other issues with this broader regional context in mind. "The region is the new meaningful geography in people's lives," says Angela Glover Blackwell, who has written extensively on metropolitan development.[13] If residents are to exercise their control in effective ways, they need to weigh all the trade-offs and consequences that may affect them and their communities.

Whether we look on these situations with optimism or with fear, we will be better off if we acknowledge that residents have a basic desire to control their surroundings. As ordinary citizens become better educated and better connected, they will probably become even more likely to act on this desire. In fact, sprawl itself could be considered a continuing search for control, as people move farther away from unresponsive institutions and powerless neighborhoods toward tidier, more homogeneous places that look tamer and easier to handle. They may not find what they seek—like Len Santini's neighbors, they may just trade urban problems for rural ones—but that won't stop them from trying.

The Golden Egg and the Goose

Mark Linder brought two different kinds of experiences to his job as an assistant city manager in San José, California, a city of 900,000 that is the unofficial capital of Silicon Valley. He had worked in four different states as a community organizer in the network of the Industrial Areas Foundation. He also had a master's degree in public administration and had worked in several California city governments. He had witnessed conflicts between residents and planners from both sides of the divide: situations where a city government had tried to ram through a development over the protests of residents, and instances where residents had formulated vague, unrealistic neighborhood plans without gaining the support or expertise of the city.[14] In 2000, when San José decided to use $80–100 million in redevelopment funds to revitalize the city's nineteen most distressed neighborhoods, Linder was both excited and a little fearful: this golden egg could provoke a battle between residents, public officials, and other stakeholders, all arguing for their own visions of how the money should be spent. He also worried that neighborhood improvements would lead to gentrification, making it financially unfeasible for low-income residents to remain in their homes.[15]

Linder and his colleagues wanted the current residents to take charge of rebuilding their neighborhoods. The resulting Strong Neighborhoods Initiative (SNI) shows how participatory planning can combine expert advice and popular support. It also illustrates the limitations placed on it by the regionalization of our economy.

Linder knew that $100 million could buy a fair number of new streetlights, parks, housing units, and community centers. However, he was more interested in how it might leverage neighborhood leadership. The SNI plan called for the neighborhoods to establish Neighborhood Action Councils (NACs) of roughly twenty-five members each to compile lists of their top ten priorities for their areas. Linder and his allies tapped into strong existing neighborhood groups, but they also worked to bring in new leaders and new populations who hadn't been well-represented in local politics. "The additional money was the catalyst to get people to the table, but the goal was strong organizations with capable and confident leaders," Linder says.[16]

Each council elects its own chair and is supported by a Neighborhood Team of city staff with community organizing and redevelopment experience. Through this team, the groups have access to many other city employees who work with neighborhoods, such as community center staff, traffic engineers, project managers, police officers, implementation planners, and code inspectors.

To build their capacity to mobilize other residents, neighborhood leaders receive training at the Neighborhood Development Center, another facet of the Strong Neighborhoods plan. The Center helps people learn how to recruit, facilitate, and build stable organizations, not only in the nineteen original neighborhoods but all across the city. The Center also helps the councils find allies in community organizations and city departments.

Building the capacity of residents to revitalize their neighborhood seems to be a long-term process. Linder sees some differences between the most experienced councils and the ones that are "greener." Both seem able to develop good plans, but the more advanced neighborhood leaders are better at implementing them—not only holding the city accountable to its promises, but organizing residents to accomplish specific objectives of the plan. "The more seasoned neighborhoods also have the capacity to take on issues outside of the bricks-and-mortar focus of the planning process," says Linder. "As they gain credibility inside and outside the neighborhood, they attract more talented, enthusiastic people."

The priorities set by residents through the NAC process are probably different than the ones planners would have come up with alone. "In the Washington neighborhood, officials cite buildings too small to be developed, overcrowding, and garage conversions as big problems," reported the San José Mercury News. "But neighborhood leaders want to build a park and recreation center, fix alleyways and sidewalks, and alleviate bad drainage on one street."[17] Instead of focusing on private spaces, many residents were more interested in refurbishing public spaces like parks, streets, and community centers. In general, the kinds of changes ratified by the neighborhood councils may have been less disruptive to existing residents because they didn't involve as many changes to existing houses and apartment buildings. When the housing stock did change, it was resident-driven: people were able to get low-interest loans through SNI for home improvements.

Linder thinks that the councils' emphasis on public spaces has, in turn, encouraged residents to work on the private spaces. "Once you put up a community center, people start fixing up their houses. When people are working together on plans and other issues, they end up applying for rehab loans, making their yards nicer. They feel more attached to the neighborhood, and they feel like they will be there for the long haul."

The growth of neighborhood leadership has had corresponding effects on city government. Many public employees needed additional training to work effectively with the neighborhood councils and other citizens. City manager Del Borgsdorf also changed the way city finances are organized, moving from traditional departmental budgets to "city service area budgets" that cover offices in different departments. "We found we needed to break down some of the traditional hierarchies and boundaries between departments," says Linder. "Now we try to get teams of people, from different departments, working with residents on a particular issue." One of the Strong Neighborhoods progress reports proudly proclaimed that it is "not only an initiative, it is the way the City of San José does business."[18]

The SNI will have to adapt to new economic circumstances in the next few years. The initial funds have mostly been spent, and the city will be hard-pressed to find more redevelopment money, partly because the state has asked its cities to help close California's budget deficit. "Some of the councils already work on other neighborhood issues, like gang prevention or adult literacy," says Linder. "Those groups that focus solely on bricks and mortar may not do as well."

In the areas where it has been most effective, SNI seems to have promoted neighborhood revitalization in two ways. First, by improving the physical landscape and connecting people with their neighbors, it may have kept upwardly mobile residents from leaving for other neighborhoods or the suburbs. Jane Jacobs, the renowned observer of cities, once defined a slum as a place that could not retain the residents who had the choice to leave.[19] A neighborhood that people choose to live in, even when they have the option of going somewhere else, is demonstrating the first sign of success and the most basic ingredient—motivated residents—for continued revitalization. Second, by putting residents firmly in charge of their neighborhood plans, Strong Neighborhoods may have forestalled gentrification and increased the likelihood that low-income people will be able to remain in their homes. Kalima Rose, an expert on preventing gentrification, says that tools like land trusts and housing cooperatives can be effective, but that mobilizing citizens is an essential step in the process. "Achieving any of these things takes political will . . . and that means organizing."[20]

The Strong Neighborhoods Initiative has already made an indelible imprint on the landscape of San José. One neighborhood renovated its shopping center; another renovated a Boys and Girls Club; another designed a "school-community hub" building. There are new or rebuilt streets, parks, alleyways, houses, and apartments all over the city.[21] But while the residents of San José may continue to take control of their physical surroundings, their neighborhoods will continue to be affected by the fortunes of Greater San José. "For years, our 'golden goose' has been Silicon Valley," says Linder. "Having a world-class industrial center on our doorstep was a huge economic boost, and enabled us to do all kinds of things in the city. In the last few years, there haven't been too many golden eggs. We'll do our best to react to the ups and downs of the region, but we can't do too much to affect them."

Many other planners and public officials know the way to San José; participatory neighborhood planning has become far more common in the last fifteen years. By giving residents control of the process, these efforts are often able both to revitalize the neighborhood and avoid gentrification. But while their homes may be more secure, these residents also need jobs—and their career opportunities are more and more dependent on employers and industries far beyond the city boundaries.[22] Neighborhood control does not guarantee success in the new regional economies.

Community-Wide Planning

Over the last twenty years, the concept of planning has expanded in several different directions. First, the planners themselves have multiplied and diversified, with neighborhood residents and stakeholders in places like San José playing a much more meaningful role alongside the professionals. Second, the plans have become more multifaceted: instead of being limited to land use questions, they often set goals and benchmarks on issues like education, economic development, and crime prevention. Third, these collaborative, multi-issue planning processes have been used to mobilize citizens across an entire community, rather than a single neighborhood.

Some of these community-wide efforts began as single-neighborhood projects. In Hampton, Virginia, the city's new planning approach and

Neighborhood Commission emerged from the experiences of planners and residents in one neighborhood where a controversial new road had been proposed.[23] Others arose out of frustration with typical NIMBY struggles: residents of Pittsford, New York, just south of Rochester, had engaged in a bitter fight over the location of a new downtown library. In some places, community-wide planning projects were inspired by the accomplishments of democratic governance efforts on other issues. In Portsmouth, New Hampshire, "Portsmouth Listens" began as an effort to mobilize hundreds of parents and students around issues of bullying and violence prevention in the city's schools. The process was subsequently used to develop a plan for redistricting the school system. Having witnessed the success of those efforts, local leaders decided to use Portsmouth Listens to involve residents in creating a strategic plan for the city.

Finally, in some places, the character of the entire community seemed to be at stake. Decatur, Georgia, a city of 17,000 people just outside Atlanta, had experienced an influx of young white professionals, including a growing gay and lesbian population. People who had lived in the city for many years, including a large number of African Americans, had begun to feel the economic stress of gentrification, with rents and property taxes rising higher and higher. An African American minister in a neighboring community had incited controversy by attacking gays and lesbians in his sermons.[24] Longtime Decatur resident Jon Abercrombie decided that citizens should come together to decide what kind of community they wanted, and to plan out that future in areas like land use, race relations, and schools.

However they come about, citywide planning efforts usually receive strong support from chambers of commerce, real estate agencies, city governments, and other organizations that want to develop "social capital" and a stronger sense of community. Leaders of these groups see the identity and character of their city or town as something that directly affects their professional lives.[25] In some cases, they worry that the community's appeal is fading; they want to revive that feeling so that it continues to endure even in times when the population is changing dramatically. "A master plan is not just about bricks and mortar," says Jim Noucas, one of the leaders of Portsmouth Listens. "It is about accepting the social responsibilities we have, both as individuals and as a community."[26] This is a more ambitious quest than simply trying to determine how streets should look or how vacant lots can be used: these organizers are also trying to preserve the community's sense of itself.

Dining, Drinking, and Dancing

Decatur, Georgia, 1999

Jon Abercrombie is confident he knows the secret to the success of democratic governance. He leans back in his chair, smiles conspiratorially at the waiter uncorking the next bottle of wine, and announces that "dining, drinking, and dancing" are essential elements of a vibrant public sphere. Speaking in a leisurely Georgia drawl, he explains that if people can't have fun in their community, then they aren't going to like it, and if people don't like it, they aren't going to maintain it. To Abercrombie, "fun" doesn't have to be anything fancy—though he enjoys a nice restaurant, he's happy with a neighborhood barbecue—but it does have to be welcoming, affordable, and regularly available.

In organizing the "Decatur Round Tables" project, Abercrombie drew on the many relationships he had formed as a consultant, facilitator, and active resident in Decatur. He reached out to the downtown development authority, the local business association, the city commission, and many other official and unofficial community leaders. The people he talked to were anxious to find some way out of the conflict that had polarized their city. The shift in population was one aspect of their anxiety, but there were other, more specific incidents: an extremely contentious school board election, a conflict over a proposal to redevelop an historic hospital building, and an angry battle between Agnes Scott College and the surrounding neighborhood over the construction of a parking garage. The low point of the parking garage tumult was when a fistfight erupted between a neighborhood resident and the husband of the president of the college. Abercrombie figured, and his allies agreed, that Decaturites needed to take a deep, collective breath and begin a more civil, productive conversation about the menu of options in front of the community.

Because of the controversies, and because they didn't want participants to simply compile a laundry list of recommendations for city government, the leaders involved in organizing the project wanted the Round Tables to be highly structured. In one planning meeting, the city manager, Peggy Merriss, noted dryly that "I'm actually not a fan of unbridled democracy."[27] With the help of Merriss and others, Abercrombie wrote a guide for the discussions that would allow people to compare experiences, review policy options, and plan for action on issues of race, land use, and school-community relations.

To demonstrate the broad base of community support for the project, Abercrombie created a "leadership map" of formal and informal associations in Decatur (109 in all). Each group listed on the map, from gardening clubs to neighborhood associations, was asked to recruit participants from its membership. "We took the map to every meeting and presentation we did, as a way of showing people the scope of the project. It also reminded us of all the assets the community possessed, and helped us see where the gaps were in our recruitment process," Abercrombie says.[28] He also tapped into the web of community connections in a more proactive way, by providing "recruitment stipends" to two longtime residents who had extensive contacts in certain parts of the community. Above all, Abercrombie made sure that all the meetings, from planning discussions to the Round Tables themselves, included food and fun. The kickoff meeting for the project featured dishes from local restaurants and three different musical performances; when it was time to begin the proceedings, people were "drummed" to their seats by the Decatur High School Drum Corps.

In the fall of 1998, over 450 residents took part in thirty-five Round Tables. Each group met for three sessions, and all of the participants then attended a forum where they reviewed their conclusions and launched new task forces to take on specific action ideas. Staffers from the city manager's office and downtown development authority took the input gathered from the small groups and began to sketch the outlines of a ten-year strategic plan for the city. After the small groups had concluded, the planners enlisted over 200 of the initial participants to help flesh out the various categories listed under the plan. The resulting plan established goals and benchmarks for the city on economic development, race relations, traffic control, architectural design, environmental quality, and school services.[29] Other residents joined task forces to implement other ideas generated by the Round Tables.

The concerns about gentrification surfaced in many of the Round Tables and were well-represented in the strategic plan. As a result, Decaturites have found a number of ways to help people stay in their homes. One task force realized that the city's tax abatement program for senior citizens was underutilized and launched a new campaign to inform seniors about this public service. Former mayor Elizabeth Wilson, a strong supporter of the Round Tables, created an annual sale that raises money to help residents afford home repairs. More affordable housing is being built as part of "mixed use" residential and commercial developments, and the city enacted a "sunset tax" law that allows elderly residents to delay a portion of their property taxes to the settlement of the estate.

The task forces also found other avenues for action. The neighborhoods task force organized the Decatur Neighborhood Alliance, a coalition of all the city's neighborhood associations. In partnership with another task force, the city set up "Decatur 101," a free class on the workings of local government. Finally, the task force on land use experimented with changes to the zoning process. Working with the land use commission, they designed a new meeting format that brings the developer, the architect, and residents together in evenhanded, low-key dialogues. The new process was then used to address a potentially controversial proposal in which a developer wanted to site a low-rise condominium complex in a quiet neighborhood.[30]

Especially when compared to the heat that had accompanied public decisions before the Round Tables, Abercrombie's project created a more congenial atmosphere in Decatur. John Gastil, a communications professor at the University of Washington, called it an example of "collaborative deliberation" in which "the public and government were able to make choices together."[31] But for participants like Kecia Cunningham, those terms don't convey what was so gratifying about the sessions. "If you just asked people if they wanted to join a roundtable, and described it only as an informative political discussion, they'd say, 'Sure, right after I go to the dentist, sign me up,' " she says sarcastically. "To get people to come, you need to sweeten the pot."[32] Cunningham and her neighbors valued the discussions not just because they were informative and deliberative, but because they were social, enjoyable, and empowering.

Cunningham herself became a symbol of the project's success. After participating in the Round Tables, she ran for the city commission and won, becoming the city's first openly lesbian African American commissioner. To many, it was a sign that Decatur could resolve the kind of cultural conflict that was so apparent in nearby communities, where tensions still simmered between old-timers and newcomers, and between people of color and their gay and lesbian neighbors. To Abercrombie, it was a delicious irony.

Reaffirming the "Here Here"

Besides Decatur, many other communities have been able to mobilize large numbers of people to strengthen and reaffirm their attachment to the place where they live. Portsmouth Listens has involved 300 people, for example, and the Pittsford Community Forum turned out 200.[33] Many of these projects have had a deep impact on land use and other issues, but their intangible effects on the psychology of residents seem just as significant. They keep people from feeling the way that the writer Gertrude Stein felt about her hometown of Oakland, California, which she described by saying, "There is no there there."[34] The reaffirmation of the "here here" is a positive sign for these communities, but it raises interesting new questions about regional development and decision-making.

By emphasizing the good of the community as a whole, these projects seem to have created an environment where residents are willing to bargain with each other on controversial questions. The toughest test may be school redistricting decisions, as illustrated in Decatur and Portsmouth. Soon after the first set of Round Tables, a new state law on class sizes forced the Decatur school board to consider redistricting options for the schools. Knowing that parents would react intensely to any school closings, the board worked with Abercrombie to involve citizens in small-group deliberations. After considering seven different redistricting options laid out in their discussion guide, the 300 participants finally crafted their own preferred option that combined several aspects of the others. "It was an outcome that no one was overjoyed about—but no one hated it either," says Abercrombie. "In other words, it was a decent compromise."[35]

The possibility of school redistricting in Portsmouth had drawn fire for ten years, preventing the school board from correcting the imbalances within the district. Portsmouth Listens involved large numbers of people in small-group sessions that focused on a set of redistricting options. The resulting plan, which was adopted by the school board, provided increased funding for school renovations and resulted in only sixty-five students switching from one school to another.

Projects that reaffirm the "here here" may also be more likely to create changes in the way local decisions are made over the long term. The land use commission's new routine for dealing with controversial development decisions, the Decatur Neighborhood Alliance, and the "Decatur 101" class are all attempts to change the way people conduct public business. One outcome of the Pittsford project was a "Collaboration Compact" between the town government, the Village of Pittsford (a separate, smaller government inside the town), and the school system. These three entities had sometimes come into conflict before; as part of the compact, the town supervisor, village mayor, and school superintendent now meet regularly to address common concerns.[36]

Hampton has created a neighborhood commission that is even more far-reaching than the Decatur Neighborhood Alliance. Its members include representatives of nonprofit organizations, business, schools, local government, and youth, along with neighborhood leaders.[37] The city's planning efforts have also led to, and been aided by, a youth commission and a cadre of youth planners who help to mobilize hundreds of people for neighborhood planning efforts. This is not simply a civic education opportunity for young people: Cindy Carlson, who directs the Hampton Coalition for Youth, argues that "the true value of youth engagement lies in its impact on the overall quality of life of the community," not simply its effect on youth as future leaders.[38] Hampton is now working on a Community Plan that will meld goals and benchmarks on social issues with the land use provisions of the city's Comprehensive Plan.[39]

One key to the success of the recruitment efforts in Portsmouth, Pittsford, Hampton, and Decatur is that each of those communities already had a strong sense of itself. Architecturally, they have all the best characteristics of cities and towns developed before the Second World War: a well-defined downtown area, a large number of historic buildings, and strong cultural traditions. Though Decatur is sometimes considered a suburb of Atlanta, Decaturites proudly point out that their city is older—Atlanta is essentially a railroad terminus that outgrew its humble beginnings. Hampton and Portsmouth are port cities that were already thriving in the seventeenth century. Pittsford is much smaller, but it too has a distinct, picturesque downtown and a wealth of old historic homes. They are all communities with strong social networks and neighborhood connections; they seem to exhibit a high level of "social capital."

Most of the communities that have developed since the Second World War are not so fortunate. Cities like Lakewood, Colorado, grew in a more scattered way, with commercial strips and the occasional shopping mall taking the place of a more traditional downtown. Since it is adjacent to Denver, Lakewood is considered a "first-tier" suburb. As development pushes farther and farther away from downtown Denver, Lakewood is experiencing more of the problems that are typically associated with big cities. Crime has risen, the per capita income has fallen, and the population now includes a higher proportion of senior citizens and children in relation to the rest of the residents. Since older people and younger people require more public services but do not contribute as much to tax revenues, this has put greater strain on the city budget. Meanwhile, citizens have voted down local sales tax increases that would help address the shortfall. Lakewood mayor Steve Burkholder feels that the lack of a sense of community means that voters are less willing to contribute to their city, financially and in other ways. "Many of our residents don't form an attachment to Lakewood," he says. "They sleep here but they work elsewhere, and when they want to dine out or do something fun, they go into Denver or somewhere else. There was nowhere you could go in the city where you would look around you and say, 'I'm in Lakewood.' "[40]

To Burkholder, the lack of a cultural and architectural center is not simply a matter of esthetics: it affects the community's economic survival. Suburbs may not be as resilient as city neighborhoods because they don't have the same high density of people per square mile. Even when urban residents have very low incomes, the dense population base can still sustain local stores and create jobs. That is one reason why, as Jane Jacobs first observed, city neighborhoods are continually going through boom and bust periods.[41] It remains to be seen whether suburbs will have that same capacity to regenerate themselves: some of the most forlorn and crime-ridden areas can be found in first-tier suburbs outside cities like Los Angeles, where the combination of extreme poverty and low density has made it very difficult to turn neighborhoods around.

Burkholder and Lakewood city manager Mike Rock were so concerned about their city's economic future, and so convinced that it needed a "here here," that they decided to do something dramatic: build an entirely new downtown. Over five years, they marshaled community support for a plan that turned a bankrupt shopping mall into a new commercial and cultural center called Belmar. Scheduled for completion in 2007, the downtown is now partially built, with a town square, stores, restaurants, offices, a movie theater, small parks, a grocery store, and a hotel. Spanning nineteen city blocks, Belmar will have one million square feet of retail space and 1,400 new apartments and townhouses.[42]

Lakewood is not alone: similarly ambitious downtown construction projects are emerging in a number of other suburbs, and many older cities have worked to revive and renovate their downtowns. Local leaders are recognizing that the "built environment" of neighborhoods and downtowns, the connections people feel to the place where they live, and the ability of the community to control its destiny are all inextricably linked. Burkholder, Abercrombie, and Linder have all come to the same conclusion—they just approached it from different directions. In some cities, leaders mobilize citizens in order to change how the community looks; in others, they change how the community looks in order to mobilize citizens. No matter how they start, they are reinforcing the connections among people, place, and control.

Not in My Beautiful Utopia

As metropolitan areas spread out, our need to manage our surroundings leads to new complications. The more residential choices we have, the more homogeneous our communities become, with young families congregating in some suburbs, senior citizens in other locations, and wealthy households in yet another set of places.[43] At the same time, more and more of our prominent policy decisions have region-wide implications, requiring cooperation and bargaining among different parts of a metro area. So as residents become more vocal about what they want, and use democratic governance efforts—or plain old political pressure—to articulate their interests, we may see increasing gridlock among cities, suburbs, and county governments.

The Sedgwick County board of commissioners faced this challenge in 1996, when they had to make regional decisions about solid waste disposal.[44] More than 450,000 people live in Sedgwick County, which includes the city of Wichita as well as many suburbs and small towns. State officials brought the issue to a head when they decided to shut down the county's major garbage disposal site, Brooks Landfill, because it no longer complied with federal environmental regulations. Wichita and Sedgwick County officials began arguing about how the different governments would share the costs of a new waste disposal system.

The commission also worried that residents would be outraged about the possibility that a new landfill might be built near their neighborhood. They launched "Community Discussions on Solid Waste" to help people see the big picture and weigh in on the decisions. To reach a wide array of citizens, the commission enlisted the help of many different community organizations and neighborhood associations. A total of 2,445 people took part in the Community Discussions in early 1997.

The discussions were designed to help participants get past the most immediate Not In My BackYard arguments. "Unlike [other public] meetings, the small-group meetings were deliberative in nature," reported the *Wichita Eagle*. "They included a more representative balance of city and county folks as well. Discussion was between residents who—armed with 'fact sheets'—talked to each other. They shared values, considering both environmental and economic concerns. They jointly explored possible options and discussed what the consequences of their choices would be. In the end, each group determined what they felt was the best solution for the most people."[45]

Though the question of how to dispose of Sedgwick County's trash was the most controversial issue as the Community Discussions began, participants focused even more on how to reduce amounts of trash. "The options and availability of ways to reduce our trash volume" became the dominant theme in many of the groups. As this idea came to the forefront, many groups wondered about the possibility of a "pay as you throw" system, where residents would be charged for each bag rather than paying a flat rate for their trash.[46]

Ironically, the single greatest priority of the participants was not a new incinerator or a new payment system; it was recycling. "Almost every group brought up recycling as a method of reducing our waste stream," concluded the report. "There were a lot of comments about adding curbside recycling as a way to reduce trash bills."[47] By recycling more, citizens could lower their monthly trash bills, and by reducing the overall amount of waste, the county could lower its disposal costs.

Soon after the first round of Community Discussions had concluded in January 1997, the principal trash hauler for the drop-off recycling centers announced that it could no longer continue operating the drop-off program at a loss. Lack of demand for recyclable materials meant the hauler was losing $100,000 a year. Citing the findings of the discussions, the county commission took action. "This is, in my opinion, not the time to let this project go by the wayside," said Tom Winters, the chair of the county commission.[48] They recruited businesses to pick up the tab, and the Boeing Corporation was the first to respond. Corporate contributions kept the program going until the city of Wichita agreed to shoulder the cost of drop-off recycling over the long term.

As the Community Discussions continued that summer, participants learned things that would help them in their policy deliberations. "Participants frequently indicated a lack of knowledge about the disposal options and the status of planning efforts."[49] The county staffers and the more knowledgeable participants in the groups not only explained disposal methods like incineration, but gave information that would be helpful in participants' daily lives, such as how to use the recycling system and how to set up composting bins.

In October 1997, the county commission approved a solid waste disposal plan that upheld the participants' recommendations. The plan called for free curbside recycling, new "transfer stations" where trash would be gathered and then trucked to landfills outside the county, and the goal of a forty percent reduction in the overall trash flow.[50]

The fact that the participants had given such strong support to recycling may have been the key to the county commission's swift response to the sudden end of the drop-off recycling program. "The citizens spoke through this process," says Kristi Zukovich, the communications director for the commission. "The Community Discussions input helped resolve the crisis."[51] Wichita and Sedgwick County officials eventually agreed to share the costs of the recycling system.

The fact that the Sedgwick County participants embraced recycling as their major priority shows that they could develop their own analysis of the "big picture" and were willing to contribute some of their own time and energy to solving the basic problem: the general abundance of trash. However, the construction of the transfer stations means that Sedgwick County's trash will now be dumped in a landfill in some other community outside the metro area. Residents of that town may argue that Sedgwick County residents were mindful of each others' backyards, but less concerned with people outside the county.

Within the county, the Community Discussions seemed to change the landfill debate by ensuring that the elected officials were not the only ones at the bargaining table. Citizens had their chance to learn more about the issues, consider the interests of people in other parts of the county, and weigh in on the policy decisions. Presumably, the elected officials were a little less worried about looking "soft" in the eyes of their constituents, since a good number of those people were now focused on the decision itself. They were participants in the policymaking process, rather than spectators to a shoving match between the city and the county.

This regional initiative was a more difficult feat than mobilizing citizens within a neighborhood or a city, but when it comes to metro-wide issues, democratic governance efforts that are limited to one jurisdiction may be powerless to effect real change—and if they simply pressure local officials to fight harder for the interests of their jurisdiction, at the expense of other communities, they may actually make regional politics more difficult.

Regional Democracy?

The Community Discussions in Sedgwick County covered a broad geographic expanse, encompassing city-dwellers, suburbanites, and rural residents—but the project was limited to one issue, and it was initiated by the public officials who were about to make a major decision on that issue. Both these factors aided the recruitment process: people knew that, by taking part in the project, they could influence a policy decision that affected their lives.

When Hannah McKinney set out to help county residents plan for the future of the Kalamazoo region, her challenge seemed far more complicated. There was no single policy decision on the horizon, and the issue—land use—encompassed a wide range of social, economic, and environmental questions. Farmers, developers, neighborhood leaders, real estate agents, environmental activists, historic preservationists, public officials, planners, and residents all have something at stake in how land is used, but their concerns are usually focused on their own properties and neighborhoods. It is difficult for people to grasp the regional implications of all those local decisions or see the possibility of region-wide planning.

A number of problems were apparent in the region when McKinney, who was then the vice mayor, began designing the "Convening the Community" project in 1998. Kalamazoo has lost much of its industrial base in the last ten years, and the regional economy has worsened steadily. Meanwhile, sprawl has continued, swelling the small towns on the outskirts of the county and leaving farmers grumbling. The city of Portage, which used to be the destination of choice for people moving out of Kalamazoo, has begun to encounter the kind of "first-tier" challenges seen in Lakewood. Residents were frustrated with these problems, and there had been a few attempts at regional planning, but by and large the challenges had not been addressed on a region-wide basis. "We started with a fractured and jittery county with twenty-four individual land use plans, a county land use plan that was over thirty years old, and leaders that didn't even have land use issues on their radar screens," McKinney wrote.[52]

"The missing element in all of this was the public voice," McKinney says. "No one knew how to get citizens involved, and no one knew what they would say if they were involved." Slowly, McKinney and her allies built relationships with the major constituencies in the county, reaching out to all the organized stakeholders in addition to ordinary residents of cities, suburbs, and small towns. One key aspect of their approach was that they acknowledged their basic agenda (more coordination within the region) but did not hold out any one preconceived outcome—they didn't advocate for government consolidation or "smart growth" principles or any other single solution. They took no side in the regionalism vs. localism debate. They tried to help each constituency articulate its own specific interests in the context of the larger region.[53]

McKinney is also an economics professor at Kalamazoo College. In that context, she had encountered a social science methodology called "action research" that helped to guide the project. This approach differs from more traditional research methods, in which a researcher gathers data in order to write an article or report. In action research, the participants and researchers work together to study a public issue, so that the knowledge they both gain can be used to help solve the problem. Action research treats the experiences and capacities of the participants as assets, and assumes that everyone has something to contribute to problem-solving efforts. An action research project is not considered a success unless it has some kind of tangible effect on the issue and "increases the participants' control over their own situation."[54] Because it gives new powers and responsibilities to citizens, the development of action research may turn out to be yet another element of the shift from expert rule to shared governance.

Kiran Cunningham, an anthropologist at Kalamazoo College, helped

McKinney incorporate the action research principles in Convening the Community. Throughout the project, the two professors drew on the resources and credibility of Kalamazoo College and Western Michigan University.

McKinney, Cunningham, and their allies mobilized citizens in thirty small-group meetings that involved over 400 people in 1997 and 1998. Once they had sorted all the data and input into some basic categories, they involved roughly 100 people in small, intensive resource teams to convert the information into a set of principles for the region. They also gathered data through a random survey on regional issues that elicited 3,400 responses.[55] Using the input gathered from the small groups and the survey, they created an inventory of the county's natural and historical sites and its remaining open spaces. Finally, they held a Community Convention, attracting several hundred more people, to further refine their report and assign responsibilities for different steps and objectives.

Convening the Community has sparked a number of outcomes, including several municipal comprehensive plan revisions. At the county level, a coalition of citizens, public officials, and business leaders are developing a county-wide growth and development plan. Several townships created a Kalamazoo Community Enhancement Team to coordinate their planning efforts. The Chamber of Commerce established a committee to review developers' site plans. A number of homebuilders are working on farmland preservation initiatives.[56]

The participants in Convening the Community seemed to be thinking regionally, but this was not because citizens from different parts of the region came together in small groups: most of the meetings consisted of homogeneous sets of people. The organizers did not try to match up farmers with city residents, for example, or planners with real estate agents. The Community Convention allowed some of those different sets of people to interact, but the project did not focus directly on building those intergroup partnerships. Regardless, when people sat down to discuss their main concerns and priorities, in most cases they were able to see how their goals tied into the larger regional context, and they could anticipate how coordination across sectors and jurisdictions would be helpful. While the experience of many other democratic governance projects shows the power of face-to-face dialogue between people of different backgrounds and interests, Convening the Community seems to show another possibility: if the process helps participants consider a range of views, citizens can begin to understand those viewpoints even if the people holding them are not in the room. In the future, region-wide democratic governance projects will undoubtedly test this assumption, and provide more information on how to mobilize residents to address regional issues.

McKinney, who has since been elected mayor of Kalamazoo, feels that the greatest contribution made by Convening the Community is that it helped people see what they had in common, and recognize the importance of the region. "Everyone accepts the idea that growth affects fiscal health, that what happens in one city or township affects everyone else—that we really are one big community," she says.[57] Two other members of the Convening the Community steering committee were elected to the Portage City Council.[58] It is too early to say what the impact of the project will be over the long term, but at least in the short term, the willingness of Kalamazoo County residents to work together seems to back up McKinney's claim. Reaffirming the "here here" can be accomplished even on a regional basis.

Down the Stretch They Come

When you consider the pace of regional development, it is easy to feel like we are running out of time. Metropolitan regions continue to race farther and farther out into the fields, leaving hollow sections—deteriorating houses, rotting commercial strips—in both cities and suburbs. People continue to seek places that seem more peaceful and manageable, and they continue to create communities that are more homogeneous in terms of age, race, and class. Suburbanites end up living cheek-by-jowl with hog farmers.

Some local leaders are betting on democratic governance efforts, if not to stop sprawl, then at least to manage it effectively. But depending on how they are organized, these projects may or may not address the current shortcomings of regional politics. At the same time that Pittsford, New York, was engaging citizens in planning the future of their town, another democratic governance project was emerging in Rochester, the central city of that region (see Chapter 8). Rochester's mayor, William Johnson, made a strong plea for greater regional collaboration and took his message directly to the voters by running for the post of county executive. He was soundly defeated, and some political observers interpreted the election as a death knell for region-wide planning in Greater Rochester. This interpretation of Johnson's campaign and defeat is obviously open to debate, but it seems fair to say that successful democratic governance efforts can be going on within just a few miles of each other without citizens in either place knowing it—and that if each of those projects is focused on the improvement of that community alone, they may do nothing to help residents of different places understand what they have in common or how they might work together.

Can sprawl be overtaken? Some experts argue that, at some point, it will peter out simply because cities and counties will be unable to create the infrastructure—roads, highways, schools—that enable people to live farther and farther away from each other. Other observers argue that sprawl will continue because the Internet enables larger numbers of people to work from home. Frustrated by two-hour commutes, many people try to move closer to where they work; but, at the same time, many employers try to move closer to where their employees live, relocating their offices to the suburbs. This race is very difficult to handicap.

Mobilizing citizens around land use decisions is one way to satisfy their need for control in the places they live now, giving them less incentive to seek it somewhere else. But as automobiles, and now the Internet, change the way people work and shop, these communities may have a harder time sustaining cultural and architectural centers that people will rally around—increasingly, there is no "there" anywhere. As we search for control individually, we may lose our capacity to exercise it collectively.

It seems likely that different regions will handle these challenges in different ways. In some places, a stronger, metro-wide civic infrastructure will develop: residents and elected officials from different jurisdictions will be able to make planning and siting decisions together. In other places, democratic governance will emerge more unevenly, with citizens becoming more involved in their neighborhood or community than in planning the future of their region. In still other places, there will be very little civic experimentation, and other factors will dominate the development process.

Regardless of how all these dynamics play out, underneath them all will be the same basic motivation, the one need that will inspire participatory planning even as it drives urban sprawl: the need to manage our surroundings. Whether they look for it by working with their neighbors or by reading the real estate ads, citizens will be searching for control.

4

The Increasing Significance of Race in Public Life

I am often involved in meetings where people are introducing themselves, describing where they grew up, and talking about where they live now. It has always surprised me that in these settings, no matter what kind of issue or decision you have put on the agenda, one subject always seems to come up: race. Whenever you ask people to describe their backgrounds, or their hometowns, they usually include their racial, ethnic, or cultural heritage, and they often tell you what kinds of people lived in their neighborhood. In these conversations, they often describe incidents or experiences in which race played a key role. You might expect people of color to acknowledge race as a factor in their daily lives, but it seems to me that whites mention race just as frequently: sometimes they are defensive and uncomfortable, sometimes proud and passionate, sometimes matter-of-fact, but in any case, they keep bringing it up. Race is a remarkably persistent topic in American life.

This can be discouraging for people who remember W. E. B. DuBois's famous quote from 1903, that "the problem of the twentieth century is the problem of the color line."[1] Are we entering yet another century that will be dominated by the color line? Aren't we finally ready to follow the Reverend Dr. Martin Luther King's famous plea, and judge each other solely on the content of our character? The history of race in the United States, so different from the experience of Canada and other countries, seems so painful and problematic that we just want to leave it all behind.

But whether we like it or not, cultural difference and democratic governance are permanently intertwined. In many cases, you cannot mobilize large numbers of people unless you acknowledge and address race and other differences, and you cannot make progress on racism and bias unless you mobilize large numbers of people. Even when race is not considered the main issue—when the primary focus is education, crime, or growth—local leaders are creating spaces where people can discuss the racial aspects of the topic. Indeed, some of the tactics they employ—helping people connect their personal experiences to policy questions, using impartial facilitators, laying out a range of viewpoints—make it practically inevitable that race will be part of the discussion. These strategies also tend to reveal all the other kinds of cultural diversity in our increasingly complex communities: ethnicity, religion, sexual orientation, and so on. Sharing the responsibilities of governance means sharing our differences.

The increased attention to our differences does not mean, however, that racism and inequality are somehow inevitable. In fact, the people leading these efforts claim that acknowledging the benefits and challenges of diversity is essential for preventing prejudice, discrimination, and other forms of bias.[2] They are challenging three basic assumptions about race:

1. The participants in these local civic experiments question the notion that racism is just an easily identifiable, individual sin—that we are all either racists or non-racists. When people take a closer look, they usually begin to see racism as a blurry spectrum—a series of individual and institutional biases that get progressively more inaccurate and damaging.[3] Rodney King's question, "Can't we all just get along?" was a basic plea for tolerance, but once citizens begin to talk about race, they usually go much farther than that, addressing complex issues of institutional racism as well as simpler forms of prejudice.

2. People are examining the belief that we should learn to tolerate, compensate for, and eventually ignore the cultural differences between us.[4] Citizens cherish their cultures and traditions, and want to hold on to them. As they begin to recognize just how diverse their communities are, they often acknowledge that these differences will probably always affect how people interact with each other. Diversity is both a strength and a challenge: sometimes you celebrate diversity, sometimes you have to deal with it, but the challenge is how to do those things effectively, not how you can make differences disappear.

3. People are testing the assumption that a "level playing field," where every individual has a uniform opportunity at happiness and success, is the best outcome we can hope for. In its place, their actions seem to suggest a field where the players are equal but different, and the focus is on helping them work together.

So race has emerged, more explicitly than ever, as an enduring public priority like education or poverty. Local officials are one barometer for this change. "At the local level, we understand the critical role of race," says Charlie Lyons, a selectman from Arlington, Massachusetts, who served as president of the National League of Cities. "We deal with race every single day, in almost every aspect of our work."[5] Jim Hunt, a Clarksburg (West Virginia) city councilman, draws a connection between our ability to address race and our ability to address other kinds of divisions. "If we can get better at dealing with difference, we can tap into more of the strengths and assets of our communities."[6] Cultural difference is being recognized as both a positive and a negative, and as a core consideration in problem-solving and local governance.

Though specific issues like affirmative action or gay marriage tend to polarize liberals and conservatives, the desire to address issues of difference productively is not limited to the left. One example is George Voinovich, the Republican senator from Ohio, who claims that "the infrastructure of good race relations and human understanding is more important than any roads or bridges we might build."[7] In 1994, he presented awards to the Ohio Department of Health and Human Services, which has involved hundreds employees and citizens in small-group dialogues on race, and to the city of Lima, Ohio, where over 2,000 residents took part in one of the first large-scale democratic organizing efforts.[8] "People often have strong disagreements about how to address race," says Frances Frazier, who coordinated the HHS project, "but all kinds of people realize that cultural differences affect their lives. In my work, I've met plenty of conservatives who are curious about race, who want to know what the 'rules' are for interacting with people who are different from them, and who are genuinely committed to overcoming racism."[9]

This is a different kind of struggle, with new challenges and complications. One of the greatest obstacles is the structure and organization of local government. In most places, human rights councils and commissions devote most of their limited staff time to the enforcement of anti-discrimination laws; only a few have been able to mobilize citizens of different backgrounds and help them work together. There is often a disconnect between local governments and the organized groups and institutions that serve communities of color. Issues of race and difference among public employees themselves are not addressed successfully in most city departments. Race has become a core concern of public administration, but our local government administrations don't yet reflect that reality.

The fact that communities are pushing forward on these fronts, developing their capacities to deal with difference, has helped inspire new forms of shared governance. Racial progress has gone beyond lawsuits to large-scale projects for dialogue and action; it has expanded from a concern of the judicial branch to a priority for the executive. Instead of a homogeneous, colorless future, it promises a heterogeneous, candid, cooperative culture. Rather than a temporary "problem of the color line," race should perhaps be considered the great American project.

How Race Became a Mandate for Democratic Governance

This shift in our understanding of race was propelled by a number of key factors. The most dramatic was the series of race-related civil disturbances that exploded in major American cities in the mid-1990s. The turmoil surrounding Rodney King, and then O. J. Simpson, revealed a yawning chasm between the racial perceptions of whites and people of color. The sudden sense that we were divided as a nation, and the violent results of that division, spurred a wide array of local leaders to make race relations an immediate priority. Human relations commissioners, YWCA directors, heads of interfaith groups, elected officials, and other leaders began creating opportunities for people of diverse backgrounds to talk about race. These projects mushroomed virtually overnight, involving hundreds and sometimes thousands of citizens in forums, trainings, workshops, and small-group discussions. By the end of 2002, large-scale intergroup dialogue programs had been initiated in 266 communities in forty-six states.[10]

The civil disturbances, and the discussions that followed, threw a spotlight on the fact that stark economic, social, and educational inequities still exist between different racial and ethnic groups. Despite the laws against discrimination, many police officers practice racial profiling. Despite judicial efforts to end school segregation, many school districts are more segregated than they were thirty years before. Despite school policies embracing diversity, there is still an "achievement gap" between students of color and their white counterparts. Many other disparities surfaced: unequal sentencing of white and African American drug offenders, growing residential segregation, differences in trash pickup and street repair between wealthy neighborhoods and poorer ones, differences by race in high school graduation rates, and even the fact that African American students were more likely to be classified as needing special education.[11]

Some people saw these continuing disparities as a sign that we should redouble our legal and legislative efforts to guarantee racial equality. Many others concluded that laws alone would not be enough. As local leaders tried harder to involve citizens in solving public problems, our difficulties with difference became more obvious. Police officials who wanted to set up neighborhood watch groups didn't know how to reach out to residents of color. Local officials who wanted to hire more Latinos or African Americans for government jobs were unsuccessful in their recruitment efforts. Many educators were frustrated that they couldn't attract enough parents of color to parent-teacher conferences or parent-teacher associations. It also became clear that students themselves weren't dealing with cultural difference effectively: the title of Beverly Tatum's seminal book, *Why Are All the Black Kids Sitting Together in the Cafeteria?*, perfectly captured the alarm of parents and educators as they surveyed the racial climate in their schools.[12]

Local civic experiments also showed that when issues of race and difference were addressed openly and productively, communities could make some progress. For example, the "Clarksburg Unity Project" in Clarksburg, West Virginia, has involved hundreds of people and blunted an aggressive recruitment drive in that area by the Ku Klux Klan.[13] There are now twice as many people of color serving on city commissions in Corvallis, Oregon, as the result of a democratic governance effort involving over 400 people. In Burlington, Vermont, a community that has very few people of color, 250 citizens took part in discussions about race, leading to a school anti-discrimination bill that was adopted by the state legislature. When 100 residents of a neighborhood in Yonkers, New York, took part in a democratic governance project, they were able to change the city's trash pickup procedures for their area.[14] These projects have also revealed some new challenges, including the inadequacy of most human relations commissions, the ineffectiveness of many diversity training methods, and the increasing geographic separation between people of different backgrounds.

As communities delved deeper into issues of race and began to make some progress, their motivations for addressing cultural difference were transformed. Initially, race was a mandate for dialogue and personal growth: the first impulse behind these efforts may have been to inoculate people against racism, so they could be purged of bias once and for all. But as people began to realize the complexity of the issues and the increasing diversity of their communities, they began to see this as valuable, ongoing work. Instead of settling for a level playing field, where everyone would be treated uniformly by teachers, judges, principals, and police, communities began trying to build arenas where the players acknowledged differences openly, cooperated continually, and recognized each other as equals. In so doing, citizens and local leaders began to see race as a mandate for democratic governance. "There is a kind of natural progression here," says Roger Stancil, city manager of Fayetteville, North Carolina. "When you get different kinds of people talking to each other, they figure out they have interests in common and they start to act on them. They realize that they won't always agree, but they want to help each other anyway, and they begin to see how important it is that everyone is at the table."[15]

Uniting a "House Divided"

Springfield, Illinois, 1997

I am sitting in a coffee shop with Sandy Robinson II, the director of the Springfield Community Relations Department. We are at the table by the front window, and as people walk in to order their coffee, every single one stops to say hello. As people pass by on the sidewalk, every single person sees Robinson inside and waves. Robinson is always ready, flashing a big smile or leaping up with a handshake or a hug. A vote by Springfield pedestrians would make Robinson the governor of Illinois.

Looming across the street from our café is Springfield's most treasured building, the Old State Capitol. Almost 150 years ago, Lincoln gave his famous "A House Divided" speech under that rotunda. He decried the Dred Scott decision of the U. S. Supreme Court, which allowed Southern slave-owners to recapture their former slaves even in Northern states. "I believe this government cannot endure, permanently, half slave and half free," Lincoln said.[16]

The history of race in Springfield also has some truly horrifying aspects. In 1908, fifty years after Lincoln's speech, the city experienced one of the deadliest race riots in the country. Not far from where Robinson and I sat in the coffee shop, a crowd of people gathered to lynch two African American prisoners being held in the county jail. Turned away by the sheriff, the mob began destroying homes and businesses belonging to African American residents. They lynched two prominent African American businessmen, a barber named Scott Burton and a shoemaker named William Donnegan. After two days of violence, forty homes and fifteen businesses had been destroyed and seven people were dead. Nationally, the riot received a great deal of attention and was one of the main reasons for the formation of the National Association for the Advancement of Colored People (NAACP) the following year.

In the Capitol's shadow, Robinson tells me about the continuing influence of race and the efforts of his boss, Mayor Karen Hasara, to deal with issues of difference. Hasara is a Republican who served several terms in the state legislature before being elected mayor. Before she took office, the role of Robinson's department was limited to enforcing the laws on employment discrimination, fair housing, and landlord-tenant relations. The mayor and the city's community relations commissioners wanted to broaden the scope of the work, so that they could do education and outreach as well as law enforcement. "It seemed like we were dealing with the symptoms of racism, and not the cause," says Robinson.[17]

Why Experts Can't "Fix" Race

The racial climate in Springfield, as in many other communities, has several key elements: an appalling event from the half-remembered, half-acknowledged past; deep, silent patterns of racial segregation in neighborhoods and schools; and a never-ending stream of small daily racial incidents, as people of color are pulled over by the police or followed through stores by mall security officers. There are usually only a few people of color in high positions within city government, prominent businesses or churches, or other visible leadership posts. These people are often overcommitted, since as leaders of color they are asked to serve on many different boards and committees. Every so often, some kind of seemingly minor dispute—over hiring, or police conduct, or media coverage—becomes a "racial issue," and the consciousness of all those historical and everyday occurrences quickly crystallizes into anger and frustration. This turn of events often bewilders public officials, who wonder exactly where they went wrong.

Many white public officials are unaware that they are trying to govern a house divided. They may be lulled into an illusion of unity because they know community leaders who are people of color, but these working relationships don't usually allow room for a frank sharing of backgrounds and opinions. As a result, white public officials are surprised when ordinary citizens apply a racial interpretation to an incident—and absolutely stunned when their friends in the "minority" leadership agree. When you approach governance from the standpoint of an expert—a master technician who can solve public problems without much help from others—it becomes very difficult to deal with the human dynamics of an issue like race.

In Springfield, the latest straw was the case of Walter Meek, a police officer who had been fired after being accused of soliciting a prostitute. Meek, who is African American, was later acquitted of all charges, and in 1997 he tried to get his job back by filing suit against the city. The suit was eventually thrown out of court, but initially there was vocal support for his reinstatement, including a protest at City Hall by residents who felt he had been falsely accused.[18] As it had many times before, the city government found itself in the midst of a debate about race.

While Sandy Robinson is boisterous and demonstrative, former Springfield Mayor Karen Hasara talks slowly and quietly, enunciating each syllable with precision. Her common sense comes across in those carefully expressed words with her long Midwestern vowels as she speaks of the day-to-day victories and challenges that come with husbanding a small city in central Illinois.

Hasara could simply have waited for the Meek scandal to blow over, but her common sense told her she ought to do something more proactive, so she challenged Robinson and the Community Relations Commission to involve large numbers of people in addressing issues of race. She thought that the project should feature small, intensive dialogues, and she wanted to be sure that the discussions would lead to tangible changes in the community.[19]

The commissioners and staff were a little surprised that Hasara wanted to approach race head-on. Public officials tended to shy away from talking openly about racism and race relations in Springfield. "This was an issue that just wasn't discussed, although everyone knew it was there," Robinson says.[20]

Until recently, there were no plaques or markers to memorialize the 1908 Springfield race riot, and the city had done its best to forget it had even happened. In the early 1990s, the story began to be told more widely, and visitors can now take a short walking tour of the main sites relating to the riot. But even with the recent acknowledgement of this chapter in Springfield's history, race as a factor in everyday life still wasn't addressed. In the Land of Lincoln, it took some daring to say openly and publicly that racism was something Springfield still needed to resolve.

Recruitment as a Contact Sport

In October 1997, Mayor Hasara and the chairman of the Community Relations Commission sent out a letter to various community groups and organizations, asking them to work with Robinson and the commission to organize the project. Robinson also took advantage of cable access call-in shows and community events to promote the effort. Two thousand brochures were distributed in the community.

But Robinson and Hasara knew that they couldn't simply announce meetings and expect a wide variety of citizens to show up. Like democratic organizers in other communities, they realized that people would be much more likely to participate if they were approached by someone they already knew. Robinson and Hasara knew they had to reach out through all kinds of networks and enlist the help of different kinds of leaders. They saw recruitment as a contact sport.

"We went everywhere we could go, every part of the community, and we promoted, promoted, promoted," Robinson says. "We worked with people who had natural connections in those communities, and they promoted, and we had people going one-on-one, put the brochure in their hand, watch them fill it out, take it back, and bring it in."[21] Robinson mined Hasara's connections to leaders from different parts of the community and was able to convince many of those people to recruit from within their networks.

The combination of Hasara's visible support and Robinson's identity and personality proved to be very effective. An evaluation of the Springfield program found that "two important features stand out from the story of participant recruitment in Springfield. First, having Hasara herself, a white woman, championing the effort in a hands-on way, greatly increased the credibility and visibility of the program. Second, Sandy Robinson, an African American man, was able to do some recruiting and promotion that a European American/white person could not have done."[22]

African Americans and Hispanics were reluctant to discuss the painful, volatile issue of race unless they knew the project was legitimate. "We already spend our lives talking to white people about race," people of color will often say. Would this actually work, or would it be just another empty dialogue in which people learned a few things, felt better for it, and then failed to make any tangible changes?

Robinson agrees that his background and identity were critical for persuading people that this would be different. "Being African American, I kind of took it upon myself to make sure that I went into where there might be the hard sells, and make the hard sells . . . I wanted them in the pilots [sample dialogues held before the kickoff]. . . . And I frankly had people telling me, 'I'll be part of this for one session, I'll give you one session. If it's not what you say it is, I'm not coming back.' And they stayed for the whole process. And they were some of our biggest cheerleaders and some of our best salespeople."[23] The pilots helped convince community leaders that the project would provide safe spaces for candid dialogue, and enabled them to recruit others because they could talk about the process from personal experience.

Robinson realized that having well-trained facilitators would be critical for ensuring that the meetings were safe spaces for candid discussion. Citizens who signed up to be facilitators were required to invest ten hours in training and preparation. The Springfield organizers also opted to have them work in pairs rather than alone; that way, the facilitators could support one another, give each other feedback, and ensure that they were remaining impartial in the discussions.

Changing Closed Minds

When it came time to hold the kickoff event for the program, on March 29, 1998, there was one obvious location: the Representative Hall of the Old State Capitol, where Lincoln stood that day in 1857, warning the country that it was coming apart. "I have always felt the very presence of Abraham Lincoln in this room," Hasara told the crowd. "I think we can all know that he'd be happy for what we are doing here today."

There were still many skeptics in the audience that day. "They thought Hasara was just going through a political exercise so she could say she'd done something about the race issue, and then would sweep it under the rug," Robinson remembers.[24] But even the most cynical people in the crowd were impressed when Karen Hasara pledged to implement all of the recommendations made by the project participants. This promise would prove to be problematic, but it did show the residents of Springfield that their mayor meant business.

Another powerful component of the kickoff was the testimony of citizens who had taken part in the pilot discussions. They talked about what the sessions were like and why they thought the program would make a difference. "I would like to say, 'Go into this with an open mind,' " said Martin Michelson, one of the pilot participants. "But it doesn't matter—go into it with a closed mind. It will change."

Two weeks after the kickoff, eighteen small groups had begun meeting, with 215 people taking part. Each group was set up so that it had a mix of whites and people of color; overall, the demographic breakdown was 69% white, 31% people of color. Since the kickoff, over 1,500 Springfield residents have taken part in the project.[25]

The reports written by that first set of groups in Springfield are typical of the conclusions reached by citizens in other places, and they illuminate how race dialogue plays out in our communities. For most participants, the discussion seemed to be a cathartic experience—one that was both dismaying and transformative. "Everyone's ideas and opinions were changed by those meetings," one participant said later. "We had a woman in our group who grew up during the '60s, the civil rights days, in the Deep South, and she spoke of what segregation meant to her, yet I felt she did not hold any grudge against anyone for that treatment. That made a great impression on me."[26] The discussions helped dispel the notion of tranquil and progressive race relations in Springfield. "There are scars . . . moments when entrance was denied, or things were said," said one participant, a woman of color. "I'm excited about this. This is a beginning."[27]

In the safe, candid environment of the small-group discussions, it became clear how pervasive the color line has become, and how far we are from a world where difference no longer matters. The participants talked about the low number of employees of color in the police department, fire department, and school system. They explored the many kinds of segregation, including "white flight" to the suburbs, patterns of consumer spending that reinforce economic disparities, the effects of "tracking" in the schools on students of color, and segregation because of faith. "Church is the most segregated hour of the week," one group wrote in its report. They ranged into related issues such as economic development, public transportation, crime and violence, and youth programs. They discussed the effect of the local newspaper's "Police Beat" page on racial stereotypes. In their report, one group argued that "the most effective way to address the issue of race/racism is to address the root causes of economic inequality . . ."[28] By collecting the records of the discussions, Robinson compiled a rich and comprehensive analysis of Springfield's racial climate.

Robinson also compiled a long list of action ideas, ranging from volunteer efforts to policy changes, from the reports submitted by the groups. The participants recognized that people of different backgrounds are more geographically isolated than ever, and came up with a host of remedies; one of the more creative suggestions was to have "Boy Scout troops from both sides of town get together on a regular basis." Another circle recommended an "exchange program for children in distant schools."

Many of the ideas addressed some of the more systemic, long-term challenges. Multiple groups called on the city to hire more people of color. Some participants saw the entrance exams given to all candidates for the police and fire departments as a major obstacle, charging that the tests were racially biased. One group suggested that community organizations help candidates prepare for the exams, and another called on the city to "make changes in the Civil Service rules." Another devised a "police oversight board" to handle complaints about police conduct, and another voiced support for expanding the community policing program.

Many groups talked about increasing public investment on the east side of Springfield, where many people of color live. One group proposed an "east-side training and education center to offer courses on civil service exam techniques, computer and information technology, and various vocational courses." "We should develop a comprehensive citywide economic strategic plan with specific goals and objectives, supplemented with start-up funds," wrote another circle. "Ensure public transportation is available in all geographic areas," wrote another, with suggestions for smaller buses and establishing hubs in areas other than downtown.

There were many suggestions relating to the schools, particularly the lack of teachers of color. One group suggested that employers allow employees to volunteer for a certain number of hours as classroom aides; the idea was to have adults of different backgrounds working together in the classroom. "Both black and white students need to experience this type of teaming," the group wrote. Another idea was to "offer scholarships to racial minorities if they promise to return to Springfield to teach after graduation." Still another recommendation was for a new curriculum dealing with race and cultural difference. "We should teach history of race relations (both the negative and positive), appreciation of diversity and culture, communications skills, conflict management, ways of working together to change society." One group submitted a detailed proposal to "pool existing and potential community resources to develop before-school, after-school, and summer programming that is affordable, accessible, and enriching for elementary, middle, and high school students." The same group also advocated the restoration of an historic building downtown to serve as a "department store to be run by high school students," providing job training and job opportunities for young people.

Several groups called for the establishment of a new group or organization, made up at least partly of project participants, to oversee the implementation of these ideas and to serve as a locus for efforts to address racism. One group called it a "Coordinating Council on Racial Harmony." Some of the tasks suggested for this council were to:

- coordinate the efforts of volunteers and action committees emerging from the study circle program, and keep citizens informed of the progress being made by these groups;
- monitor the media and "challenge negative or inaccurate stories of race";
- help organizations attract people of color for their boards of directors;
- increase communication about race-related issues and "saturate the community with messages of racial reconciliation";
- and lend more assistance to future democratic organizing efforts.

But the participants were clear about not shunting the responsibility for implementing actions to the city or any new coordinating council. Almost every group explicitly recognized the need for participants to do their part, and some demanded it. "Participants Must Pay in Time, Money, or Personal Growth," declared one group. They expected to create progress with their own sweat equity.

The Giant To-Do List

Almost 200 people attended the action forum following that first round of dialogues, on June 13, 1998. Robinson structured the event like a political convention: participants from each circle sat together, and each group in turn solemnly presented their conclusions to Hasara and the community. The attendees were impressed by the breadth and variety of the action ideas. "It's kind of a nice mix," said Mayor Hasara's chief of staff, Brian McFadden, "because you have some that involve government, and some that don't." "A lot of the participants are interested in making changes not at the city level, but in their neighborhoods," added City Councilwoman Judy Yeager. "It was never just a 'you guys [the city] have to do this' kind of environment." [29]

Over the next several weeks and months, the excitement faded as Robinson and Hasara slowly realized they had made a critical error: by asking participants to report on their discussions without urging them to sign up for new task forces, action committees, or other volunteering opportunities, they had failed to capture the full potential of the project. They could have ended the action forum with a set of next steps for citizens, community organizations, and government. Instead, they were left with a giant to-do list.

Besides hiring more people of color for the police and fire departments, the top recommendation of all the groups was the establishment of a council that would oversee the implementation of action ideas. Robinson saw this as way to avoid the dilemma of too many ideas and too few implementers. He and Hasara set about creating a Race Relations Task Force. Most of the original members had been participants in the small-group discussions.

From its inception, there was some confusion about the role of the Task Force. "Some saw it as a vehicle whose sole purpose was to guide and grow the operations of the program," remembers Brian McFadden. "Some saw it as a means to implement the recommendations. Still others saw it as a formalized tool to be used to speak out on all race-related issues, regardless of any connection to the program." [30]

Meanwhile, Hasara was faced with the number one action idea—and the biggest challenge—on the list of recommendations: hiring more people of color for the police and fire departments. To those who work in the private sector, this might seem fairly straightforward. In government, however, a maze of public service regulations and union contract stipulations awaits anyone who wants to make fundamental changes in the public workforce. In Springfield, Hasara knew that the greatest challenge would be the police and fire unions. The unions didn't want the city to hire officers from other communities or rehire officers who had left the force because that might affect the seniority status of current officers. They were also attached to standardized tests as an important part of the hiring process; the tests had been used to select most of the union's current members. The police department used the Police Officer Standardized Test (POST) plus a physical fitness exam as virtually the only factors in determining whom to hire. Critics charged that the police and fire tests contained an internal cultural bias against people of color. For many young people of color, the tests were a deterrent to even thinking about a career in the Springfield police and fire departments.

Mayor Hasara was already committed to the goal of hiring more people of color, but the program put the issue on the front burner. "It was very powerful to hear group after group at the action forum say that an increased minority presence on the police and fire departments was their top priority," Brian McFadden said later. "The overwhelming response from citizens gave her a huge personal and emotional boost in what has been a bruising battle. The response also helped tremendously in the ensuing public relations efforts. In many ways, it gave the issue moral high ground, helping to elevate it above the ongoing political and labor relations wrangling that had plagued previous efforts and discussions."[31] The members of the new Race Relations Task Force were quite vocal on this front, reminding Hasara of her pledge and supporting her in her efforts. There were other kinds of pressure as well: the NAACP filed a lawsuit against the city over its hiring practices.

By 1999, Hasara was beginning to get results. After months of negotiations, the fire department agreed to Hasara's plan. The changes resulted in the first African American, the first Hispanic, and the first female to be hired in the last ten years, all in one firefighter class. The police negotiations moved more slowly, but in 2000, Hasara and the union agreed to institute personal interviews for the first time, and to drastically de-emphasize the POST test results as a factor in hiring.[32] They also agreed on several other measures, including a program to recruit and hire back former officers of color who had left the force, and a controversial "lateral entry" program that allowed the department to recruit and hire officers of color from other communities. That summer, the new class of officers included three people of color and four women. Meanwhile, spurred by the Race Relations Task Force, Hasara called a press conference to announce that she was committed to raising the number of police officers and firefighters of color to 15% in each department.

An Ongoing Struggle

Race continues to be a prominent public issue in Springfield. One reason is that the initial response to the city's democratic organizing efforts led to more organizing. "We believe a greater sense of community can be achieved through this kind of learning experience," wrote one of the initial small groups. "These should be ongoing community events," wrote another. The participants felt that the program presented an important avenue for community change. "As the program becomes more well-known and more people become involved, we as concerned citizens will have more power to effect change in our community," another group wrote. "Our recommendation regarding the program is to continue it with passion," yet another group concluded.[33] In addition to the 1,000 residents who have taken part, over 400 high school students and fifty police officers have participated in the small-group meetings and action forums.

The Race Relations Task Force rallied many of those participants in 2001, when Matt Hale, leader of the World Church of the Creator in Peoria, petitioned to give a speech at Springfield's Lincoln Library. Hale preaches white separatism and uses stridently racist rhetoric; his public appearances in other Illinois towns had often resulted in violence. In response to Hale's visit, the Task Force held a diversity celebration several blocks away that drew several hundred people. Only fifteen turned out to hear Hale, not counting the sixty police officers keeping watch over the proceedings.[34]

The democratic governance effort has also helped Springfield achieve a breakthrough in crime prevention. With the assistance of neighborhood leaders, officers now hold "Beat Circles" in every part of the city. The small-group discussions allow officers and residents to set crime prevention priorities, talk about how race affects police-community relations, and compare notes about what is happening in the neighborhood. Crime rates have dropped throughout the city, and Springfield's police chief feels that the increased focus on neighborhood partnerships has been one of the main reasons.[35] Another key recommendation made by project participants, for a citizen review board to monitor police conduct, was established in 2004, after several years of work by the Race Relations Task Force, the police department, and city council.[36]

But while the police department acknowledges race as a key factor in police-community relations, it has not adequately addressed the issue of race inside the force. The most damaging controversy involved an African American police officer named Renatta Frazier. In 2001, Frazier was dispatched to the home of a woman—the daughter of another police officer—who had been raped by two men. Other officers claimed that Frazier responded too slowly and could have prevented the crime. Though an internal investigation determined that Frazier did not receive the call until after the rape had occurred, police officials did not release this information to the public for almost a year. Frazier later resigned, filed a lawsuit against the department alleging that other officers had racially harassed her, and settled the suit for $851,000. Many other race-related incidents have plagued the police force, resulting in another lawsuit being filed by the Black Guardians, an association of African American officers. Some white officers say they are "too intimidated to speak their minds to higher-ups" about issues of race.[37] The department still doesn't seem to give officers sufficient opportunities to compare experiences, learn more about race, or work closely with people who are different from themselves.

These controversies have significantly weakened the police department's effort to shift its racial demographics. (The department has asked the Black Guardians to take a strong role in officer recruitment.) Though more and more people of color have joined the force, others have resigned or retired recently. The number of officers of color has reached 5%—higher than before, but still far short of Hasara's goal.[38]

Race in Republican Arenas

Through all these successes and frustrations, the struggle against racism in Springfield has taken its toll. Several members of the Race Relations Task Force have resigned in anger and frustration. Like Hasara, they tried to take the conclusions reached by citizens in the safe confines of the democratic organizing project and champion those causes in Springfield's republican political arena. This was no easy task. The police unions, the NAACP, and other key political actors had not taken part in the small-group discussions, and they saw the project participants as members of just another interest group. Policy opinions which have been developed through some kind of deliberative, democratic process may have a kind of moral weight, as Brian

McFadden argues, but that aura wears off quickly unless the critical mass of citizens supporting it continues to grow in size and power.

Hasara too has been frustrated by the constant struggle of trying to reconcile the democratic arena she helped create with the official, republican arena of local politics. After two terms in office, she decided not to run for re-election.

Robinson is still working away, helping to create more sustainable, routine ways to involve citizens in discussions of race. He feels that Springfield needs to develop a secondary tier of groups and institutions, "owned" by citizens and particularly people of color, that involve citizens in problem-solving and decision-making. Toward this end, Robinson has been working with a grassroots group called the Springfield Project, which helps neighborhood associations use small-group dialogues to involve larger numbers of residents in addressing issues like housing, race, and economic development. "Some of these neighborhood associations have become delivery vehicles for city services," says Robinson. The Springfield Project has also helped the police department set up its beat circles.[39]

The history of race in Springfield, sometimes glorious, sometimes ignominious, will continue unfolding for decades to come. The city may never again hear a speaker like Abraham Lincoln, and hopefully it will never again experience a tragedy on the scale of the 1908 riot, but race will still be part of the city's pulse. Springfield will be able to celebrate its diversity, but those differences between people will presumably continue to create problems as well. Even though Sandy Robinson, Karen Hasara, and their allies created a more level playing field for police hiring, their greater contribution to the history of their city was proving that Springfield residents could deal productively with the assets and challenges of diversity. "A lot more people have been able to see the world through other people's eyes," says Roderick Nunn, a participant who was subsequently elected to the Springfield city council. "It has been a tremendous learning for the whole community."[40]

Empathy and Self-Interest in Fort Myers

There is a new shopping center at the intersection of Martin Luther King Boulevard and Sabal Palm Boulevard in the Dunbar neighborhood of Fort Myers, Florida. At first glance, it looks like any other new shopping center on any other corner in any other city.

But this shopping center is different. It was backed by a developer, funded by a bank and an economic development corporation, and built by a construction company—but it took hundreds of citizens to generate the momentum necessary to build it, and it took many hours of effort by a smaller set of citizens to capitalize on that momentum and turn the proposal into a reality. The building stands in defiance of one of our most established political assumptions: that most of the time, ordinary people will only work for things that benefit them directly.

The Dunbar Shopping Center also represents one of the keys to progress on the issue of race and other cultural differences. For even if we could eliminate the idea of racism, and every racist idea and thought, we would still be faced with a legacy of inequity that plagues people of color in many tangible ways. Because of past and current racism, people of color are disproportionately affected by poverty, crime, and many other ills. Lawsuits and legislation may be able to undo some of these inequities, but not all of them. So our ability to defeat racism and other kinds of persecutions will rest not just on our ability to get along, but on our ability to work on one another's behalf.

That is what happened in Fort Myers, in a project called "Lee County Pulling Together" (LCPT). When a small band of people, most of who belonged to the same church, formed LCPT in 1997, none of them expected that a shopping center would be one of the end results. What had brought them together was a study showing that Fort Myers/Lee County was the most racially segregated community in the South. The group decided to mobilize large numbers of Lee County residents to address issues of race, racism, and segregation.

The people who formed LCPT included some influential local leaders, such as Fritz Jacobi, the publisher of the *Fort Myers News-Press,* and the Reverend Dr. Wayne Robinson, a prominent local pastor. But the key figure in LCPT turned out to be Annie Estlund, a recent retiree who decided to coordinate the project as a volunteer. Estlund had the conviction, the " 'people skills," and the tremendous organizational acumen necessary to make the project successful. LCPT recruited 600 citizens for small dialogues and large action forums in 1997 and 1998.[41]

Fort Myers participants generated all kinds of action ideas, ranging from simple volunteer activities to much more ambitious projects. Acting on those ideas, they have created a multiracial community choir, sorted canned goods at a food bank, painted and tiled a Habitat for Humanity house, and cleaned up a two-mile stretch of Martin Luther King Boulevard. They published a cookbook called *Lee County Cooking Together*, which includes recipes representing the various different cultural backgrounds of people living in the area.

In the end, the Dunbar Shopping Center proved to be the most visible outcome of the project. Participants in many of the circles were concerned about the lack of supermarkets in the low-income neighborhoods of Fort Myers. As in many other communities, people of color found themselves without easy access to basic services. At an action forum held at the conclusion of the first set of small-group meetings, a task force was formed to explore the possibility of a new shopping center.

To establish the economic viability of the shopping center, the task force members conducted a market survey. One of the members, a retired banker, drafted a proposed financing plan that was presented to a regional supermarket chain. The task force also reached out to other key stakeholders, convening a meeting of city and county officials and a minority business development corporation called LeeCo. LeeCo had received local and federal grants for economic development in Fort Myers, but hadn't spent the money due to conflict with local government. In fact, some of these funds were time-limited, and "millions would walk away" if the two groups couldn't agree fast. LCPT was able to get both sides to see the larger priorities at stake. "Once we had them in the room," Jacobi said, "it was easy to reach consensus."[42]

The groundbreaking for the Dunbar Shopping Center took place on November 23, 1999.[43] Estlund, Jacobi, and many of the people who had been mobilized by LCPT were there, ceremonial shovels in hand. They had devoted hours of volunteer time to the project and involved many of the groups and organizations they belonged to, even though most of them do not live in the Dunbar neighborhood and may never shop there.

The Fort Myers experience may be helpful for analyzing how other communities are dealing with cultural difference. The outcomes of Lee County Pulling Together can be grouped into several levels, which appear to be more or less sequential:

1. Citizens met, learned more about each other, and formed relationships across the lines of race and difference.
2. Having had a taste of the diversity in their community, they worked together on ways to celebrate it, such as the *Lee County Cooking Together* cookbook.
3. They worked together on action ideas that benefited everyone more or less equally, such as the cleanup of King Boulevard, a major thoroughfare used by most Fort Myers residents.
4. Finally, they took on action ideas that would only benefit those with the greatest need, like the Habitat for Humanity house and the Dunbar Shopping Center.

This sequence contradicts one of the most common concerns raised about democracy: that when you give citizens a greater say in decision making, they will vote according to their most direct interests, without regard for the well-being of others. Defenders of republican government sometimes argue that elected officials are better equipped to take various interests into account and decide what is best for the entire community.[44] In Fort Myers and many other communities, local civic experiments suggest that the way people form their political opinions is more complicated, and the process by which citizens make decisions is a critical factor. When people share experiences, become more knowledgable, and begin to empathize with each other, they often think and act in ways that political scientists would not have predicted. Certainly the Dunbar Shopping Center was an unexpected outcome in Fort Myers; left to public officials alone, it would probably never have been built.

Race as a Public Management Priority

Fort Myers is still one of the most segregated cities in the south, and it presumably still has a variety of other race-related issues to address. But Lee County Pulling Together, despite its successes, was disbanded in 2003. It had been an all-volunteer outfit from the beginning, and it wasn't able to attract enough funding to sustain itself. Eventually the core volunteers found they couldn't carry LCPT any longer. "We ran out of tenacious workers who just wouldn't let it die," says Estlund.[45] The city provided office space for LCPT, but local government doesn't seem to have taken on the role of mobilizing diverse citizens.

Like so many other public priorities, making progress against racism and discrimination requires, and warrants, a professional cadre of people in each community who can devote their time and skill to these issues. Though volunteers are critical for dealing with any public problem, we wouldn't consider placing the entire burden of education, law enforcement, or trash pickup entirely on the shoulders of unpaid citizens.

Many local officials have realized this, and made race a major focus of their administrations. In doing so, they have encountered several key strategic questions. The first has to do with how a community should deploy the staffers who will be working on race and difference. Some local governments have turned, quite logically, to their human rights or community relations departments, offices within city hall that are usually connected to human rights or community relations commissions. In most places, the commissioners are unpaid citizens who have been appointed by the mayor or city council. In addition to Springfield, the human rights departments and commissions in Champaign, Illinois; Springfield, Ohio; Columbus, Ohio; and Fayetteville, North Carolina, have mobilized large numbers of citizens to address issues of race. In most of these projects, the most basic obstacle is that the staffers who serve in the human relations departments spend most of their time enforcing civil rights statutes—responding to complaints of discrimination and investigating those cases. The narrow focus on enforcement, to the exclusion of other priorities, reflects the assumption that a "level playing field" among people of different backgrounds is our utmost goal.

Even when such a department has sufficient staff time to take on other tasks besides enforcement, there is a danger that the staffers will be isolated, both within government and in the community as a whole. City departments often have their own distinct cultures, and police officers or sanitation workers tend to see human relations workers as outsiders. "It was very difficult for me to get buy-in from some of the other city departments," said Sandy Robinson. "I had to work hard to gain their trust."[46] Outside city hall, community groups are often suspicious of any citizen involvement effort led by government. The usual combination of a professional human rights department with a volunteer commission is designed to overcome just this kind of credibility gap, and yet in most places the commissions seem to have difficulty establishing their own reputation as distinct from local government. This may be because the commissioners are usually appointed by public officials, and because they aren't able to connect their constituencies to the work of the commission. The role and reputation of human relations departments and commissions must be recast if these groups are going to play a significant part in government efforts to address race.

The credibility deficit faced by many local governments is particularly acute when it comes to citizens of color. Cultural barriers make it especially difficult to recruit African Americans, Hispanics, and recent immigrants for democratic governance efforts. Even the organizers who have accomplished this feat often look for a better way to do it—they wonder whether neighborhood associations, churches, or other groups with a more natural connection to communities of color might be transformed into democratic arenas for addressing race and other issues. In essence, these organizers are inclined to "go where the people are" and hold meetings on their turf, rather than bringing them out of their neighborhoods and congregations to meet with people in other parts of the city. But there they are confronted with another dilemma: that most of these grassroots groups are not run in participatory ways and have difficulty themselves in mobilizing a wide array of people. Even if these groups were to change the way they operate, many local leaders worry that such an approach would lead to a balkanization of local politics, with citizens talking only with others like themselves rather than working with people who are different. The terms and implications of this strategic choice—between community-wide recruitment and neighborhood-based organizing—have yet to be fully explored by the local pioneers of democratic governance.

The way that local governments address race internally seems to imply that cultural differences can be made to disappear. In most places, public employees go through a one- or two-day diversity training or "sensitivity workshop" once a year (sometimes just once in a career).[47] The hope is that employees will acknowledge and banish their biases in the training, and then be able to operate without prejudice from that point onward. Organizers of local civic experiments have learned that race is more effectively addressed if it is part of an ongoing dialogue in which people can share experiences, learn more about race as an idea, and partner on projects of mutual interest. Most city departments have not found a satisfactory answer to this strategic question of how to incorporate race work in more comprehensive, ongoing ways.[48]

The changing geography of race presents one final strategic challenge. Even though the United States is growing more diverse with every census, our cities and regions also seem to be growing more and more segregated.[49] Racial disparities are more regional than ever before, with poorer people of color concentrated in cities and first-tier suburbs. The sheer distances between people of different backgrounds threaten to outstrip the organizational capacity of local governments to bring those citizens together for diverse discussions. Without this kind of metro-wide civic infrastructure, communities may become less able to deal with difference at the regional level, where it matters more and more.

Race is Here to Stay

In all kinds of places, in all kinds of contexts, race remains a critical issue. The idea that it will soon disappear may be seductive, perhaps because that would make things simpler—but when ordinary citizens discuss the persistence of racism and the wealth of our cultural diversity, they often gain a new appreciation for race as part of the rich complexity of American life. Eric Glover, a student at Blair High School in Silver Spring, Maryland, took part in a democratic small-group meeting on cultural differences among young people. "This is touchy stuff that we tuck in the back of our minds, hoping that the 'I Have a Dream' speech will take care of it," Glover says. "But it won't. Racism is a wide, dirty, complex, and painful subject that deserves to be talked to death, and that's just what we did in our group."[50]

Discussions of race may sound difficult and uncomfortable, and they often are. But one interesting development in local civic experiments is that citizens don't want to stop talking. Most democratic organizing efforts are intended to be temporary projects, with the small groups meeting for only a handful of sessions. Yet in Springfield, Fort Myers, and other places, there are some groups that stayed together, continuing to meet long after the organizers expected them to conclude. Many of these citizens started out with an impatience for the dialogue to end and the action to begin—but they keep meeting even after some of the more tangible changes have taken place. Apparently, the group members have come to value the relationships they have built, the lessons they have learned from listening to people who are different from themselves, and the opportunity to plan more work together as ideas and challenges arise. The democratic organizing effort in Lima, Ohio, began in 1994; over ten years later, some of those original groups are still going.[51]

Race also seems to be emerging more than ever in the context of other issues, such as education and police-community relations. When the school board of Decatur, Georgia, involved hundreds of citizens in deciding how to redistrict its elementary schools, the racial segregation of the city's school system came into sharp focus. When the Inglewood (California) public schools mounted a large-scale effort to boost parent involvement, they uncovered longstanding tensions between Hispanic and African American parents in that city. In any meaningful project focused on police-community relations, issues of race and difference are sure to surface.

Even if race were to recede somehow, other kinds of differences might not: ethnicity, religion, sexual orientation. "What first made me aware of the divisions between us was the fact that my brother is confined to a wheelchair," says Jim Hunt, the Clarksburg city councilman. "From there, I began to understand how all kinds of differences play out in my community. For the sake of our cities, we have to learn how to be truly inclusive."[52]

When people come together in democratic arenas, they are quickly confronted with their differences. They learn to deal with them, and value them, in order to succeed. Democratic governance, therefore, inevitably raises issues of race.

By the same token, it may be that race inevitably raises issues of democratic governance. Cultural differences can be adequately addressed only when certain conditions are present: the opportunity to share personal experiences, the chance to learn by considering theories and arguments, and the possibility of partnering with someone from a different background in order to create tangible changes in your community. These are the same conditions created in the new wave of local civic experiments, and so it is no accident that racial progress and the evolution of democracy are wrapped up in one another, pulling each other and pushing forward together.

5
Washington Goes to Mr. Smith
The Changing Role of Citizens
in Policy Development

In the movie *Mr. Smith Goes to Washington,* our innocent leading man, played by Jimmy Stewart, becomes a senator almost by accident. He has only one legislative priority: setting up a summer camp for boys in his home state. In order to accomplish his goal, and ensure that the voices of his constituents are heard, he is forced to shout above the din of big media and corrupt politicians. During a dramatic filibuster, the strength of his conviction shines through, and he wins the day.

For a variety of reasons, a growing number of public officials and other leaders are reversing the roles in Frank Capra's script. In order to keep public decisions from turning into political debacles—and in order to make their own voices heard over the din of activists and the media—they are bringing those decisions directly to their constituents. They want citizens to take on an intermediary role in policy development, somewhere between utter ignorance and absolute control, where ordinary people become more informed about the issues, settle some of their disagreements, and appreciate the tough choices that officials are forced to make. Increasingly, Washington is going to Mr. Smith.

When they turn toward Mr. (and Ms.) Smith, public officials are motivated partly by the need to feel respect and validation from their constituents. As they begin reaching out to citizens, officials learn that their constituents have the same need. The organizers of these efforts have pioneered new tactics for giving ordinary people a sense of "political legitimacy"—the promise that our opinions and actions carry weight with elected officials and other citizens, that we have a certain status in our communities, and that each one of us has public privileges and responsibilities only we can honor and enjoy.

Organizers don't always advertise these psychological aspects of their democratic governance work: their projects tend to list more rational, objective goals, such as educating the public or gathering input from citizens. But having watched these citizen-government interactions, it seems to me that the emotional need for validation, felt by officials and constituents alike, is a critical motivation driving the shift from expert rule to shared governance.[1]

So far, attempts to incorporate citizens into policymaking are far more common at the neighborhood, local, and county level than at the state and federal level. (A more accurate title for this chapter might be "City Hall Goes to Mr. Smith.") The federal agencies with the most experience in citizen involvement tend to be the ones which make local decisions—how to manage a toxic waste cleanup, for example, or whether to protect an old-growth forest—and their interactions with citizens usually focus on those local policies rather than national ones.[2]

However, democratic governance projects dealing with state and federal policies seem to be on the rise, partly because some officials at those levels of government are now feeling the same kinds of pressures as their local counterparts. If these large-scale civic experiments succeed, then citizens may soon play the same kind of catalytic role in state and federal policy-making that they are now beginning to play in local arenas.

In this attempt to "scale up" democratic governance, other key members of the cast include major foundations and national civic organizations like the League of Women Voters, the National Civic League, America*Speaks,* and the Kettering Foundation. Some of the most ambitious statewide and national civic experiments have been initiated and staffed by them, at the urging of public officials. Leaders of these civic groups are motivated not only by the desire to resolve policy dilemmas, but by the impulse to strengthen their own organizations and to revitalize old notions of citizenship: many of these organizations were founded a century ago during the Progressive Era, and they are stalwart champions of "good government" and civic duty. The League of Women Voters, perhaps the most historically minded of these groups, has been particularly effective at honing the rhetoric of political legitimacy and convincing citizens that their talents and opinions matter.

Because states and nations are much larger than neighborhoods and cities, however, these large-scale civic experiments face much greater obstacles. Some fail to resolve the foremost challenge: the need to assemble a sufficient critical mass of citizens. Overall, the projects that survive and succeed are the ones that validate people not only as voters but as members of powerful, democratic institutions. By connecting citizen voices to state and federal policymaking, they are giving us glimpses of what the next form of democracy may look like when it reaches a truly massive scale.

Walk a Mile in My Shoes

Many public officials are unsure what citizens are actually thinking. They are tempted to assume that if people don't turn out at city council sessions and other public meetings, they must be satisfied with the performance of government and the state of the community. But at some point, most public officials eventually find themselves in a situation where large numbers of citizens do turn out—and they are yelling as loud as they can. This is a common, unsettling, even scarring experience for local leaders, and it is one of their main motivations for seeking out different ways to involve citizens in policymaking.

This dynamic is beginning to affect all kinds of public officials, but it is still most evident at the local level, in the experiences of people like Doug Rutan, the superintendent of schools in Kuna, Idaho. Rutan is a dedicated, hands-on local leader: he drives a school bus several times a month so that he can talk to students and parents. In fact, when the school board purchased a new bus several years ago, Rutan saved the district some money by picking up the bus directly at the plant in Tennessee and driving it 2,000 miles back to Kuna. He has faced his share of challenges as a superintendent, many of them related to the explosive growth of his district. From 1990 to 2004, Kuna grew from a small town of less than 2,000 people to a booming Boise suburb of almost 10,000.[3]

In 1998, as the number of students in the system was skyrocketing, Rutan and the Kuna school board made a loan agreement with a bank so they could purchase a plot of land for a new high school. An article about the impending purchase went out in the school newsletter, but Rutan got no responses, so the board went ahead with the deal. Citizens didn't flock to the school board meetings to criticize the plan. Then the board put a school bond issue on the ballot to fund the land purchase and construction of the school. They may not have intended to, but Rutan and the board had chosen a "decide, announce, and defend" approach.

The bond issue alerted residents to the land purchase made by the school board, and many of them weren't happy. In this kind of situation, citizens usually express their anger in several ways. Some claim that the policy decision was clouded by corruption; others say that the political goals of public officials came before the interests of the community. Often, citizens don't understand the decision, simply because they never understood the facts of the situation. Finally, some people express frustration not because of ignorance or suspicion, but because they feel the public official should have consulted with them first. In many cases, the majority of the citizens who have been following the decision "tune out" in resignation and disgust, leaving the field to the people who are just too angry to stop yelling.

Some of those typical responses were apparent in Kuna. The most obvious result was the defeat of the school bond in the September 1999 municipal election. Soon afterward, when Rutan helped involve citizens in discussions on the future of the school system, many of the dialogues began with participants venting about the decision. "With regard to the land purchase," one group wrote in its report, "the school board's communication was perceived as a means to justify their actions." "Absolute, complete honesty is necessary," said another. "Some residents have lost confidence in the school board because of the land purchase putting the public into debt," wrote a third group. "We feel that we need an apology from the board . . . We don't need a rude and arrogant School Board."[4]

Once the Kuna participants had finished venting and were able to assess the land purchase, the bond issue, and the future of the district, they were able to make recommendations for how the school board ought to proceed. Some of those suggestions had to do with the school board's relationship with the community—they urged the board to treat them as partners and neighbors. "Board members and city officials should give straightforward answers and if they don't know the answer—say so. Don't try to give an answer to something you don't know. It's OK to say, 'I don't know but I'll find out.' "[5] Though some of these residents had felt empowered enough to attend meetings before—primarily to express their frustrations to Rutan and the school board—they had not felt legitimized as a part of the district's decision-making process.

In the past, it was probably easier for public officials to get away with making major policy decisions without involving citizens. By announcing their verdict confidently, and presenting it as the product of expert research, they could often avoid hearing people's frustrations.[6] But many officials feel that twenty-first century citizens are more skeptical—and seem to have the skills and confidence to act on that skepticism. There may be a number of reasons for this change: people are more educated than they ever were before; they have access to the Internet as a source of information and a way to connect with other concerned citizens; they receive more attention from the media and are able to exploit those opportunities. In any case, local leaders are increasingly afraid of these "instant activists"—mild-mannered senior citizens or soccer moms who suddenly come screaming out of the woodwork when a controversial decision is made.

In these meetings, some officials get defensive while others keep their cool. But no matter what they show on the outside, officials often admit privately that they are doing a great deal of soul-searching. Some say that these policy fiascos have caused them to rethink the reasons they ran for public office. "It isn't an easy transition to make," says Steve Burkholder, mayor of Lakewood, Colorado. "You figure you were elected by citizens in order to govern the community—and that if you aren't effective, citizens will let you know by not re-electing you. The longer you serve, the more you realize that you'd better involve citizens in ways that go far beyond voting."[7] Many officials are deeply hurt by the accusations hurled at them by citizens. "Citizens don't always realize that elected officials are human beings too," adds Henrietta Davis, a city councilwoman from Cambridge, Massachusetts. "When the public is screaming at you, it does make you question why you chose a career in public service."[8]

Roger Bernier, an official for the Centers for Disease Control (CDC), began to rethink his role in 2001, when he had to defend a number of controversial policy decisions related to vaccines and autism. "An advocate told me that our research was 'dead on arrival.' That startling phrase was not really a criticism of the science. . . . It was a reflection of the lack of trust between government and some segments of society. . . . If I were to wear a button to capture this, it would say, 'IT'S NOT JUST ABOUT THE DATA,' or better still, it would say, 'IT'S THE RELATIONSHIP, STUPID!' "[9] For officials like Rutan, Burkholder, Davis, and Bernier, the decision to involve citizens more intensively is a personal one, not just a political move or an objective desire to gather more data. These leaders want citizens to understand how government operates, to recognize the trade-offs inherent in policymaking, and to validate public officials as caring, committed human beings.

Getting the Ball Rolling

Even before his bond issue was defeated, Doug Rutan could tell that his relationship with the public was off on the wrong foot. Intending to start over, he called together a small group of community leaders who decided to form the Kuna Alliance for a Cohesive Community Team, or Kuna ACT. The members of Kuna ACT wanted to foster discussion on school priorities like the bond issue, but they wanted to address other concerns as well. Kuna's senior citizens were upset about the number of cars speeding through the streets; they blamed the town's booming population of teenage drivers. Parents and teachers were concerned that the roads from Boise were also carrying big-city problems such as drug abuse and teen pregnancy. Rutan was open to these other topics. "Doug had a vision for the community that went far beyond the schools," said Arnette Johnson, a soft-spoken, resolute school volunteer who became the coordinator of Kuna ACT. "He convened the first meeting and pulled the group together. Without that big entity [the schools] behind us, I don't know how we would've gotten the ball rolling."[10]

Like their counterparts in many other communities, the Kuna ACT members had to make some careful decisions about the role that public officials like Rutan would play in their process. On one hand, people want to know that their input will affect policy, and having decision-makers involved in the meetings gives people some confidence that it will. On the other hand, when citizens know that public officials are involved, they often wonder whether those leaders are only pretending to welcome a range of views—and are in fact using the project to push their own political agendas. People want political legitimacy, but they worry that officials are trying to co-opt them, taking advantage of their participation to push through a pre-determined agenda. In the Kuna case, many people probably suspected that Rutan would try to bias the process so that he could promote another bond issue. Rutan had initially served as the president of Kuna ACT, but he and the board members realized that this sent the wrong impression to some residents, and he stepped down.

They also realized that by recruiting a wide range of people for the board, and by soliciting the endorsements of many different groups and institutions, they could show that Kuna ACT was not skewed toward any particular agenda. Once the organization had incorporated itself as a non-profit, the board included local pastors, a sheriff, a representative from the senior center, and a city councilwoman named Laurale Neal. Unlike similar coalitions in many other communities, the board also included four high school students. The students chafed at what they saw as unfair accusations by adults in the community, and welcomed the chance to dispel those stereotypes.

But though it included a wide cross-section of leaders, Kuna ACT did not enjoy universal support. The mayor, Greg Nelson, had been in office for sixteen years, and he was publicly opposed to the project. "Public officials in Kuna never asked for input—that just wasn't part of the way they did business," said Neal. "Decisions were made in a vacuum."[11] After the initial enthusiasm, the project began to bog down. They tried to distribute the organizing tasks among the various members of the group, but the follow-through was lacking. As Rutan recalls, "It soon became evident that we were all very busy with our own organizations and didn't have the time necessary to devote to this."[12] They needed a coordinator, and that meant they needed money. Over the mayor's objections, Neal and two other council members voted to allocate some city funds to Kuna ACT; the mayor subsequently began campaigning for Neal's defeat in the upcoming city council election. Eventually, the board raised enough money to pay the coordinator by soliciting small donations from virtually every organization in town, including the sheriff's department, the school board, the electric utility, and the trash removal company.

As the fundraising went forward, the teenagers in Kuna ACT began to get impatient. Being asked to serve on the Kuna ACT board validated their status as community leaders and gave them a sense of urgency. The students took the high school segment of the project, which they called "Teen Talk," into their own hands. They held a kickoff meeting during a school assembly, and recruited over 100 students for small-group dialogues on the future of Kuna.

Feeling inspired, and perhaps a little embarrassed, by the rapid progress of their younger colleagues, the other members of Kuna ACT pushed forward with the adult side of the project. They mapped out a four-session process where participants would discuss issues relating to education, public safety, livability, and citizen-government collaboration. Because of the success of Teen Talk, many of the "adult" groups that began meeting in the fall of 1999 included students as well.

Helping Your Neighbor

The participants in the Kuna ACT meetings generated over 100 action ideas. One group devised what it called "Project Citizen," a social studies program at the high school that would mix classroom study with community service activities. They saw it as a way to "integrate school and community, encourage adult volunteers, and provide citizenship training." Another group suggested a "Volunteer-to-be-a-Deputy" program to "raise citizen awareness of problems the police face."[13]

The ability of parents to work with students in trouble was a prime topic for many of the groups. "Teachers need to solve student difficulty with parent intervention rather than dump troublesome students into remedial classes," wrote the members of one circle in their report.[14] One participant even suggested that teachers have cell phones so they could call parents immediately when a problem arose.

Other groups focused on ways of raising input and accountability in the schools. "We don't have PTAs," complained one circle report. "There are only parent-teacher conferences. We hear what our kids are doing, but don't have input into course content, schedules, etc." Another group proposed building-level accountability committees, citing a program in Colorado as an example. "The committees should include parents, patrons, teachers, administrators, and students. They would identify building-level goals, and assess success."[15]

The school board got both criticism and praise. Many people were still upset about the board's handling of the land purchase. One group cited the board's tendency to adjourn to an executive session when a controversial issue arose, forcing people to "sit and wait for a public meeting to be re-convened." Another group decided that "a balance can be struck between controlling meetings via the agenda and giving people opportunities to participate."[16]

Many groups came up with ideas to give Kuna a more unique reputation. Since the area is known for its high number of birds of prey, there were many suggestions for incorporating this resource into Kuna's image. Others suggested that the community "get organized" in other ways: adopting a theme and mission statement, drafting a disaster preparedness plan, opening up communication between government and community institutions, and coordinating volunteer service activities. All the groups seemed to agree that Kuna shouldn't give up its small-town character. "People here help each other out," one participant said. "When I was getting ready for a camping trip, a front bearing went out on my pickup. At 11 p.m., I called a local mechanic. He opened his shop and helped me fix it. I want to see this 'help your neighbor' attitude remain as we get bigger."[17]

The Decision-Making Routine in Kuna

Since Teen Talk had pre-empted the other meetings, the high school students were the first to move from words to action. They wanted to show how Kuna ACT was changing their relationship with the rest of the community. "This process put adults in the position where they have to listen to the students, and vice versa," said Holly Keller, then a junior at Kuna High.[18] A set of students who had participated in the program began planning a "senior prom" to bring young people and senior citizens together. The dance was held at the senior center, with both teenagers and seniors dressing up in formal attire and dancing the night away. For many it was a powerful symbol of what was happening in Kuna. "In a trying time for our community, people started talking again," says Neal.[19]

Over the next few months, public officials incorporated the citizen recommendations into a number of city plans and documents, including a new comprehensive land use plan. The Chamber of Commerce embraced the idea to designate Kuna as a "Birds of Prey Area" and launched an initiative to attract tourism and protect the stunning scenery of the nearby Snake River Gorge.

Arnette Johnson and the Kuna ACT board members realized that for some of the action ideas to work, however, a great deal more discussion was needed. In some cases, the groups had suggested new topics rather than new solutions. To meet this need, Kuna ACT developed a new model: every month or two, they hold an informational forum combined with small-group discussions. For the first hour of each forum, attendees hear brief, factual presentations on the policy issue or decision being addressed. For the second hour, they split up into small groups to compare notes on their experiences with the issue, assess the various policy options, and formulate recommendations. Since one hour usually isn't sufficient to get through the steps, the groups are asked to meet a second time, on their own, within the next week. They then submit their reports to Johnson. The records are collated into a report that is shared at a subsequent forum.

The leaders of Kuna ACT have worked hard to show public officials that the organization is trying to help them, rather than pushing a specific agenda or fanning the flames of local controversies. To safeguard its status as a neutral intermediary between citizens and government, the Kuna ACT board adopted a policy that only community institutions could submit topics for the forums. The school board, planning and zoning commission, city council, and other bodies now regularly ask Kuna ACT to convene citizens around particular issues and decisions.

Over the last five years, Kuna ACT has used this format twelve times. Each forum and set of small-group sessions has attracted from 30 to 120 people. The decisions and issues addressed include: city planning priorities; school planning priorities (particularly in regard to the possibility of a bond issue); disaster preparedness; downtown development (including whether to build a downtown auditorium); regional development; substance abuse among young people (including the possibility of drug testing at the high school); juvenile justice issues; fire and public safety (including hiring priorities and whether to shift from a volunteer to professional fire department); and the wastewater treatment system.[20]

From Rutan's perspective, Kuna ACT remedied his past mistakes and changed his relationship with the public. In September 2000, the bond issue to build the new high school passed by a 73 percent margin. Rutan then set up a process by which students worked with the architecture firm to design parts of the building. "What I see happening is our community developing new processes for working together," Rutan says.[21]

The development of Kuna ACT was not a painless process, however. Laurale Neal and another city council member were defeated in the September 1999 election—after they had voted to help fund the project, but before the first set of meetings were held. The fact that the mayor campaigned so actively against them presumably had an impact on the outcome. "Getting a local government to support this kind of effort is a tremendous challenge," Neal acknowledges. "You have to get to the point where they aren't afraid of hearing what people think. It is difficult to get officials out of the mode of 'I was elected and I know best.' "[22]

In fact, Mayor Nelson began to change his stance a year later. He even began working closely with Arnette Johnson and submitting forum topics to Kuna ACT. "I think it's nice that people have started talking to each other more about their community," he said at a public meeting in late 2000.[23]

In the 2004 city council election, Nelson was defeated by a candidate who had been a regular small-group facilitator for Kuna ACT. The president of the Kuna ACT board, Zella Johnson (no relation to Arnette), resigned her post before the campaign began and also won election to the city council.

In an interview shortly after his defeat, one of Nelson's allies said they had decided how to maintain their clout in the community: by continuing to attend the Kuna ACT forums and recruiting their supporters to join them.[24] Ironically, the same people who had opposed the project so vehemently now saw it as a neutral venue for making policy decisions, a democratic arena where every voice could be heard. Kuna ACT had reached a point where it provided political validation to citizens and public officials alike. Some of this aura may have rubbed off on other community institutions as well: Zella Johnson reports that "five years ago, my husband and I were often the only attendees at city council meetings. Now, if you don't get there early, you don't get a seat."[25]

Avoiding Train Wrecks

Even in a town the size of Kuna, it can be very difficult to convince people that their participation will make a difference. This is especially true when experiences like the land purchase have corroded the trust between citizens and government. When it comes to state and federal politics, there is an additional deterrent: policy decisions at those levels seem so remote and difficult to affect that trying to somehow "get involved" in the process sounds like a hopeless waste of time. The distance between Mr. Smith and Washington seems very far indeed.

It is probably no coincidence, therefore, that most attempts to engage people in state or federal policymaking rely heavily on the language of democracy and civic duty. Organizers hope that by casting their project as a chance to revive citizenship and connect the American people with their elected representatives, they can overcome the added alienation people feel about state and federal policy decisions.

This approach comes naturally to the League of Women Voters. From its inception, the League has been a caretaker of the political process, upholding the rights of citizens and safeguarding the integrity of the system. Leaguers have built that reputation by registering voters, holding informational forums, providing clear and unbiased written materials for voters, and moderating candidate debates.[26]

By the early 1990s, however, League leaders were beginning to see that their institution was in trouble. Membership levels were dropping and the organization was failing to attract younger faces; as voting became less compelling to ordinary citizens, so did the League. Many other historic civic organizations have experienced similar difficulties in the last ten to twenty years.[27] "The public remains active, but its public activities are moving away from traditional political institutions," writes John Gastil, a communications professor at the University of Washington.[28] It became clear that suffrage, which was so much a part of the League's history, was not enough to guarantee it a future.

Some League leaders began searching for new roles that would help the organization thrive. "Back when the League was working to pass the motor voter law, we supported it as a way to make politics more engaging and convenient for busy citizens in a busy world," remembers Carol Scott, a former president of the Oklahoma League of Women Voters and board member for the national League. "After it passed, we started looking for that next step, that next project or activity that would grab people out of their hectic lives and get them involved. We knew the League couldn't survive if it kept organizing the same old debates and issue forums it had always done. We needed a way to bring politics to the people."[29]

Scott started her own experiment in 1996, when she realized that the political process wasn't helping Oklahomans address one of the most important issues in the state. "Oklahoma's criminal justice system was in a constant state of crisis management during the '90s," recalls Trish Frazier, who was the executive director of the League in Oklahoma at the time. "The cost of the system was skyrocketing and public confidence in it was dwindling."[30] At the time, Oklahoma had the third-highest incarceration rate in the country, and was spending $247 million of a relatively small state budget on corrections. Meanwhile, prosecutors were preparing to try Timothy McVeigh, the terrorist responsible for the deaths of 168 people at the Murrah Federal Building in downtown Oklahoma City. The image of McVeigh in an orange bulletproof suit and handcuffs, being led to a police vehicle through a crowd of shouting people, symbolized an intensely emotional, multifaceted issue.

The League had put the corrections issue higher and higher on its legislative agenda, but in the 1995 and 1996 sessions of the state legislature, corrections reform legislation failed amidst raucous debate. "Every session, the legislature tried to pass a reform bill," Frazier says, "and every session it ended up in a train wreck."[31] Even the most basic facts were in dispute: corrections and law enforcement officials were unable to agree on how many offenders were in the system.

To help avoid future train wrecks, Frazier and Scott took an unusual step. Rather than lobbying the legislature on a new reform bill, they would involve hundreds of citizens and legislators in discussions on what priorities they thought the justice system should uphold. Scott and Frazier embarked on an ambitious statewide project, striving to recruit 1,000 people all over Oklahoma.

To reach this goal, they enlisted the help of many state and local organizations. At the state level, they were joined by the Oklahoma Conference of Churches, the Oklahoma Academy for State Goals, and the Citizen's League of Central Oklahoma. At the community level, local League chapter presidents recruited a host of organizations to help attract a large and diverse set of participants: PTAs, chambers of commerce, churches, community-action groups, court systems, police and sheriff's departments, corrections employee unions, victims' groups, inmate support groups, colleges and universities, and local government officials, as well as chapters of the Christian Coalition, the American Association of University Women (AAUW), the National Association for the Advancement of Colored People

(NAACP), and the American Association of Retired Persons (AARP). They called the project "Balancing Justice in Oklahoma."

Trying to Correct Corrections

Oklahoma was not the only state in turmoil over corrections: what we should do about criminals has been one of the most pressing policy questions in the last fifteen years. It has been a controversial, emotionally charged issue in political campaigns all over the country.

Several factors have contributed to the controversy:

- Tough new sentencing laws enacted during the 1980s, particularly for drug offenders, greatly increased the number of inmates in the corrections system.
- Public officials started scrambling to win prisons—and the jobs they bring—for their communities.
- Crime became more and more sensationalized, even though crime rates have been falling steadily since the 1970s.[32]

As prison populations and budgets grew during the 1990s, some states and counties turned to other ways of dealing with nonviolent, low-risk offenders, particularly those convicted on drug charges. They began to try alternatives to prison or probation, such as restitution, boot camps, intensive supervisory probation, substance abuse treatment, work release, community service, house arrest, day reporting, and halfway houses. These kinds of sanctions are often lumped together as "community corrections," because they rely on community members and organizations to help with the corrections process, and because they keep prisoners out of jails. Nearly all of them are less expensive than constructing new prisons. Many experts also claim that they are more effective at preventing criminals from committing new crimes after they have served their sentences.[33]

Today, both Republicans and Democrats are recognizing the limitations of a corrections policy that is based primarily on prison construction. "We've got a broken corrections system," says Senator Sam Brownback (R-Kansas). "It needs to be reinvented, much as we found with welfare in the 1990s. Recidivism rates are too high and create too much of a financial burden on states without protecting public safety." In 2002, Americans spent $60 billion on corrections, up from $9 billion twenty years ago.[34]

Back in 1996, many Oklahoma legislators were already convinced—privately—that community corrections made sense, but many of them were equally convinced that redirecting money to community corrections was political suicide.[35] Since every candidate for public office wanted to appear "tough on crime," they were afraid that opposing prison construction would cost them at the polls. To Scott and Frazier, it was clear that if the project was going to have any kind of impact on legislators, it would first have to allay their fears.

A League of Legitimacy

In the fall of 1996, Balancing Justice got underway. Over the next six months, 972 people participated in thirteen communities, ranging in size from Tulsa and Oklahoma City to small towns throughout the state. The success of the League's recruitment efforts was partly due to the level of controversy surrounding the legislative debate, but the Leaguers also gave people a sense that their participation would matter, and that sense of legitimacy may have boosted the turnout as well.

The League used a number of tactics to provide this sense of legitimacy:

1. They organized a kickoff event in Oklahoma City to inaugurate Balancing Justice at the state level, and encouraged the local organizers to hold their own kickoffs. These kickoffs typically included high-profile speakers, an explanation of the program, and testimonials from people who had participated in pilot dialogues. By providing some pomp and circumstance to announce and begin the program officially, organizers were able to convey the expectation that the meetings would be a legitimate political activity through which citizen voices would be heard.

2. Many of the kickoffs and small-group meetings were attended by public officials, including legislators, judges, sheriffs, mayors, and even some candidates running for elected office. Some participants remarked that this was the first time they had been able to have a meaningful conversation with an elected official or candidate. Many officials said the same thing: this was different from their talks with stakeholders, their confrontations with citizens at public meetings, and their chance encounters with people in the supermarket or on the street. It was a more methodical, evenhanded experience, in which the presence of facilitators and a structured agenda kept the officials from dominating or manipulating the dialogues.

3. The meetings included a wide range of people and views. Some of the local organizers made special efforts to recruit citizens who hadn't typically been involved in public meetings. The organizers who assembled

the report of the small groups meeting in Weatherford, Oklahoma, were particularly proud of their turnout: "Those involved included lawyers, law enforcement officers, public service agencies, church leaders, city officials and administrators, private business people, university students/staff/faculty, retired persons, candidates for elected offices, homemakers (male and female), and more. There were victims, offenders, and observers of the criminal justice system. Every political persuasion seemed included: Democrats, Republicans, independents, conservatives, moderates, and liberals. In short, citizens."[36]

4. The organizers relied on their own experience with the League's internal issue study process. Like their counterparts in other states, the Oklahoma Leaguers had used structured, intensive small-group meetings to determine the organization's stance on important policy questions. The Leaguers were therefore well-practiced at facilitating these kinds of sessions and experienced at assembling nonpartisan background information and statistics. When they were talking about the Balancing Justice sessions to other Leaguers, Scott and Frazier called them "League meetings for the public." They created a special "Fact Book" for the project, and gave each participant a guide called *Balancing Justice: Setting Citizen Priorities for the Corrections System.* The guide's three sessions were designed to help citizens set priorities for the justice system, consider various options for addressing the corrections dilemma, and talk about how they might implement some of their ideas and recommendations. All of these elements helped give the program an air of competence and credibility.

These techniques seemed to complement the natural assets of the League in Oklahoma. The League's tradition of studying policy decisions carefully and intensively had given the organization a great deal of political legitimacy. By applying some of these tools in their democratic governance efforts, the Leaguers were able to offer citizens a valid public role—in essence, showing participants that they were part of something larger than themselves.

The Color of Dirt

Interstate 35, Central Oklahoma, 1996
I look out the window at the countryside as it flies by, and I remark that the dirt in Oklahoma is an unusually bright shade of red. Trish Frazier, who is driving the car, is startled and even somewhat indignant; she is convinced that red is the normal, natural color of earth. As a newcomer to the state—

an outsider sent to meet with organizers and train facilitators—this had never occurred to me. I wondered if other Oklahomans shared this view.

Once the Balancing Justice sessions had concluded, it was clear that Oklahomans in different parts of the state were coming to some shared, unexpected conclusions about criminal justice and corrections. The legislators who attended the sessions or read the results in their local newspaper were confronted with arguments quite different from those presented by law enforcement professionals and prison industry lobbyists. They found that their constituents were alarmed at the rising cost of corrections; interested in sanctions other than prisons; frustrated with the lack of resources allocated to crime prevention, especially for young people; and convinced that the legislature was not in tune with citizens on this issue.[37]

On the topic of crime prevention, the reports identified three main areas of emphasis: prevention early in life, prevention by improving the juvenile justice system, and prevention of recidivism by the use of rehabilitative programs early in offenders' careers. The Muskogee report stated that "the groups agreed that early intervention is probably the key to preventing crime." "Load the front end with prevention, early childhood education/development," urged the report of the groups meeting in Norman. In Oklahoma City, the consensus was that "intervention should commence the very first time a child is identified as a dropout, ditching school, poor attendance, abused at home, ill-clothed, etc. At-risk people are identified much too late."

The communities gave specific suggestions about rehabilitation. The participants in Norman decided that each offender should have an "improvement plan," agreed to by the judge, offender, and parole officer. The plan would serve as a framework for the offender's sentence, restitution, and rehabilitation, and progress on the plan would earn the offender new privileges such as work release or weekend visits home. The need for more opportunities for substance abuse treatment, education, and job training was echoed in almost every community. To help judges customize sentences to maximize the possibility of rehabilitation, the Stillwater participants recommended that "judges should be provided with more/better presentencing information regarding offenders, such as prior offenses in other counties or states." By and large, these were not new ideas, but they were not being implemented on a large scale in Oklahoma.

Across the state, the Balancing Justice participants were concerned that the vast majority of offenders served only a fraction of their sentences. "There was great concern for system accountability when even judges cannot tell how long an offender will serve after he or she is sentenced,"

Frazier wrote in the final report. "There should be 'truth in sentencing.' Five years should mean five years," wrote the Oklahoma City participants. Some groups felt that the uncertainty of most sentences impeded rehabilitation efforts, since offenders moved in and out of the corrections system so quickly. On the other hand, there was no consensus among the groups about whether judges should be asked to operate within sentencing guidelines. Some citizens were appalled that sentences for a particular crime could vary so much from judge to judge, while others were pleased that judges had the freedom to decide the best sentence in each case.

Finally, in many of the communities, participants acknowledged that, in order to work in a cost-effective, community-oriented way, the corrections system needed the support and active involvement of citizens. The report from Tulsa called for "more community involvement at all levels of the corrections system, both to cut costs and to increase effectiveness. Volunteering, support groups, mentoring programs both in prison and to support reintegration into the community (as well as prevent crime), were recommended."

These were not the kinds of outcomes that state legislators had expected: the Balancing Justice participants didn't just want to "lock 'em up and throw away the key." They reserved the right to decide how criminals should be sentenced, just as they deserved the right to their own opinions on the natural color of earth. I realized that in Oklahoma, the dirt is red; state legislators learned that their constituents wanted criminal justice policy to be grounded in the needs and assets of their communities.

"An Atmosphere Where We Could Try New Things"

In April 1997, the Oklahoma House passed one of the most sweeping revisions of the criminal justice system in the history of the state, House Bill 1213. By the time it passed the Senate the next day, HB 1213 had been approved by the combined vote of 140–2. The two main policy ideas to emerge from Balancing Justice, community corrections and truth in sentencing, turned out to be the two main components of the legislation.

Though Balancing Justice was a statewide project, the Leaguers were able to assemble a critical mass of participants in a way that allowed each legislator to interact with his or her own constituents. State Senator Cal Hobson, the bill's sponsor, said that "Balancing Justice made a huge difference because it helped to create an atmosphere where we could try new things." Frazier and Scott had expected that the final report would make the most impact, but the bill actually passed before the report was finished.

"Three factors were far more important than the report," said Tony Hutchison, a legislative aide. "First, a lot of legislators took part in the small groups. Second, other public officials—people legislators talk to about policy, like judges and sheriffs—attended as well. Third, there was good media coverage for the meetings, so without attending a session you could pick up a newspaper the next day and find out what people's main conclusions had been."[38]

" 'Balancing Justice' brought together people from many different walks of life to think hard about this issue," said Jacqueline Duncan, a judge in Oklahoma's Second Judicial District who attended the discussions in Weatherford. "The process engendered respect—so, even though the participants didn't always agree, the discussions were civil and productive. Most importantly, the program helped the community as a whole generate ideas on how to handle the prison population and how to sentence offenders in a meaningful way."[39] For legislators, the experience of working directly with their constituents in a respectful way, plus the knowledge that citizens in other communities were coming to similar conclusions, may have helped them avoid another "train wreck" in the legislature.

In addition to upholding the main recommendations of Balancing Justice, the Oklahoma Legislature gave citizens a larger role in implementing corrections policy. HB 1213 delegated the responsibility for dealing with many low-level offenders to local governments. The bill included a mandate for community input, requiring that decisions about local implementation be made by community boards with citizen representation. This sentiment mirrored some of the statements made by the participants in their reports. Members of an Oklahoma City group wrote that "we would like for the Balancing Justice groups to be effective 'change agents,' and in helping to set policies that are balanced. . . . Our group and others like us, as concerned citizens taking time to work on these things, should have a say."[40]

The controversies over state-level legislation had drawn citizens to the project, but once they began examining the issue, many participants discovered that they could make a difference in their own backyards. At the local level, Balancing Justice led eventually to drug courts, teen courts, mentoring programs for inmates and parolees, church outreach programs for former offenders, and job-training partnerships between local businesses and corrections facilities. Participants didn't just want to recommend solutions to their state's corrections crisis; many of them were ready and willing to be part of those solutions.

Bringing Politics to the People

Balancing Justice also had a far-reaching impact on the League of Women Voters itself. Carol Scott's mission to "bring politics to the people" inspired Leaguers all over the country to organize similar projects, including statewide efforts in Minnesota (with roughly 1,000 participants) and New York (2,700 participants) and local programs in places like Claremont, California; Raleigh/Durham, North Carolina; and Dover, Delaware. Kay Maxwell, the national president of the League, says, "Our role as a 'trusted convener' has been instrumental in creating balanced forums where citizens can learn about issues, share their perspectives, and have an impact on decisions made in their communities."[41] The idea of democratic governance has given state and local Leagues the chance to expand beyond the narrow focus on voter registration and candidate debates.

In the way that it validated active citizenship, Balancing Justice recalled the attitude of the suffragists who founded the League over eighty years ago. In arguing for the Nineteenth Amendment, the suffragists pointed out that women were already doing a great deal of public work. Women not only had the primary responsibility for raising children and running their households, they had built campaigns and institutions to deal with the growing urban problems of hunger, housing, sanitation, and education. They deserved the vote not only because they were responsible adults with "inalienable rights" in the grand republican tradition, but because their efforts, ideas, and energy were essential assets to our democracy.[42] The suffragists would have been familiar with many of the roles taken by Balancing Justice participants: deliberating, finding common ground, collaborating with public officials, making decisions, taking action.

So for the League, showing people the valid roles they could play in democratic governance was a way to combine their recent history as an organization with their pre-history in the suffragist movement. They went beyond the assumption that legitimacy clings to people who write letters to the editor, call their Congressman, study the issues in internal League meetings, and, above all, vote. What many of them have found is that calling people to more active roles can help them reach new audiences. They are broadening their definition of citizenship, merging republican rights with democratic work in a way that matches the needs and ambitions of twenty-first century voters.

Some of the newer civic organizations have discovered similar ways to give citizens a place on the public stage. The most interesting examples may be the groups who work with recent immigrants—helping them understand our political culture, preparing them to take the citizenship test, mobilizing them to affect the political process. These may seem like straightforward tasks, akin to the League's traditional focus on voting, but the immigration organizations seem to be embracing a much broader definition of citizenship in order to achieve them. "When we started trying to mobilize Latinos in Massachusetts, we came up against a difficult realization: the American political system is boring!" says Maria Alamo, an organizer for ¿Oíste?, a nonprofit Latino civic group based in Boston. "Recent immigrants from Latin America are used to a much more musical, colorful political tradition, full of banners, marches, and songs. People wear the official color of their party; they feel a real sense of belonging. We realized we had to recreate some of that here."[43]

¿Oíste? has found a number of ways to provide a similar sense of belonging, including special "graduation" ceremonies for people who have passed the citizenship test. By writing radio jingles about voting and electoral reform, organizing parades and caravans, and giving Latinos an opportunity to take advocacy roles on issues like campaign finance reform, redistricting, and bilingual education, the organization has been able to " 'Latinize' Massachusetts politics."[44]

The Jane Addams School for Democracy, located in St. Paul, Minnesota, has taken this approach even further, connecting recent immigrants with college students, high school students, and other local residents in ongoing "learning circles" and learning pairs. Two straightforward goals of these activities are to help people learn about each other's languages and cultures, and help them attain the knowledge and English skills they need to pass the U. S. citizenship exam. However, the discussions have led to a number of other projects and outcomes over the last nine years, as participants compared experiences and generated ideas for improving the St. Paul's West Side neighborhood.[45]

The learning circles are organized according to languages (at least four languages are spoken at the school in any one evening), with English translation in each circle. Bilingual college students serve as language translators and cultural interpreters, to allow people to discuss issues of concern in their native languages. A part of each session is devoted to a more formal cultural exchange where participants discuss current issues, explain cultural traditions, or engage in storytelling. "Valuing the knowledge resources that come from all cultures is key to the Jane Addams School philosophy," says Nan Kari, one of the school's founders.[46] "Students and other non-immigrants learn about their own cultures, and new immigrants teach college and high school participants lessons that are not offered in the academic setting."

Hundreds of participants in the neighborhood learning circles have since passed the federal citizenship exam.[47] Participants in the learning circles have also created a community farming project, a mural, a parent involvement partnership with the local schools, a health project, and an annual community-wide celebration known as the West Side Freedom Festival. And even though most of the emphasis of the circles is on improving the local situation, Jane Addams participants have not stopped there. Concerned about human rights abuses in Laos, they successfully petitioned the Minnesota legislature to pass a resolution urging Congress to negotiate with the Laotian government for more humane treatment of the Hmong population. Participants also acted on their concerns with the way the U. S. citizenship test is administered. They forged a partnership with the regional director of the Immigration and Naturalization Service (INS), who agreed to allow English-speaking partners to accompany Hmong applicants during the citizenship exam and interview.[48]

The "Potentially Concerned" Public

The INS director in St. Paul is one of many federal officials who are beginning to interact with citizens in new ways. In some agencies, notably the ones that deal with environmental issues, this shift has actually been going on for some time. But it has been a difficult transition, and even the most experienced agencies are just now moving from a defensive approach to a more proactive, productive relationship with the public.

In this work, employees of the environmental agencies have a head start on their counterparts in other parts of the federal government, primarily because so much of their work is local. The Environmental Protection Agency (EPA), the National Park Service, the Bureau of Reclamation, the Fish and Wildlife Service, the Forest Service, and other agencies have to make decisions, on a site-by-site basis, that balance the need to protect the environment with the desire for economic development. Once the environmental movement gathered steam in the 1960s, those decisions started to become much more controversial. In some cases, officials encountered opposition from environmental activists; in others, they faced pro-development community members; and in yet others, they were caught in an angry crossfire between the two.

The responses of these agencies were rooted in the need to avoid tense conflicts and help opposing parties (government, industry, and activist groups) reach consensual agreements. "We got into this kind of work out of desperation, really, out of a frustration with what had happened before," says Kama Dobbs, a staffer for the Federal Highway Administration who has helped engage residents in the early stages of highway construction planning. "Getting people involved earlier, changing their perceptions, and getting their buy-in helped head off the challenges we faced in the past."[49] In many cases, these projects seemed to produce better, fairer, more informed decisions, with broader public support.

On the other hand, the defensive mindset that federal officials brought to these projects often placed major limitations on their work with the public. First, since they were focused on the most passionate citizens and activist groups, agencies seldom saw the need to connect with citizens who were less knowledgeable about the issues. Compared with public involvement efforts by local governments, federal officials have done very little recruitment. "On most of the issues, we let people come to us," says Robert Black of the Bureau of Reclamation.[50] Second, federal officials were often so focused on the policymaking process (and potential threats to the process) that they didn't consider the possibility that citizens could help those policies work.[51] Third, the defensive mindset led to the assumption that federal officials must always be present and in charge of any public meeting—thereby drastically limiting the number of meetings that could take place, since there are only so many officials to go around.

Finally, most public participation opportunities offered by federal agencies tended to be either on small, highly structured, "stakeholder" committees or at hearings that were open to the general public. While some agencies have experimented with different formats, most of the large-group meetings follow a traditional format of panel presentations followed by questions or comments from the audience. This bipolar world of intense committee work and perfunctory hearings bears the imprint of the defensive mindset because it reflects two basic impulses: the desire to get experts and activists to invest in the decisions, and the need to hold public hearings to meet the requirements of federal laws on citizen participation.[52] Some of these agencies use a phrase that captures their rationale perfectly: they refer to citizens as the "potentially concerned" public.[53]

Over the last thirty years, this defensive style of citizen involvement has been codified in a number of federal laws. At first, environmentalists and other activists welcomed the public participation requirements enacted in the National Environmental Protection Act (NEPA) and other pieces of legislation, but many now see those strictures as part of the problem. "While studies evaluating the effectiveness of involvement techniques consistently show that participants prefer informal, face-to-face techniques, NEPA and its implementing regulations mandate formalistic and impersonal approaches," summarized one report. "Consequently, the available [communication] techniques tend to be one-way, while the most desirable techniques tend to be two-way."[54]

This plotline is not entirely unique to the environmental agencies. In federal entities such as the Department of Housing and Urban Development, the Federal Highway Administration, the Department of Energy, the Defense Nuclear Facilities Safety Board, and the Advisory Council on Historic Preservation, bad experiences with local activists inspired laws and practices that embody the same kind of defensive engagement.

In some cases, small stakeholder committees seem to reduce the likelihood of controversy, and on extremely technical decisions, they may be more appropriate than broader forms of involvement. But defensive engagement efforts rarely engage large numbers of citizens in meaningful two-way communication, and they do not seem to build a critical mass of citizen support for policy priorities, as was the case in Oklahoma. In those increasingly common situations where the stakeholders aren't adequately representative of the citizens they claim to serve, officials are often confronted by the kinds of controversies they hoped to avoid in the first place. Though all kinds of national policies are managed at the National Institutes of Health (NIH), the incident which had the most profound effect on the agency's citizen involvement work was a profoundly local matter: the agency's plan to expand its campus in Bethesda, Maryland, called for a large old tree to be chopped down.[55] By complaining publicly about the decision, a single neighborhood resident who wanted to save the tree was able to embarrass the agency and delay the plan for months. NIH had appointed a neighborhood advisory board to consult on the building plans, but the resident had either ignored that group or wasn't aware of it. "We thought that by setting up an advisory board, we were creating an 'open door' for the rest of the neighborhood," says Jan Hedetniemi, the lead community liaison for NIH at the time. "We realized that open doors don't work. You've got to go where the people are, and proactively engage them in the decisions that affect their lives."[56]

At agencies like the EPA, which has one of the most extensive track records in citizen involvement, repeated civic experiments have convinced federal officials that there are other benefits to working proactively with citizens. The most visible sign is the growth of "environmental stewardship" organizations, which mobilize thousands of citizens in preserving natural resources: planting trees, cleaning up lakes, bays, and rivers, even monitoring water and air pollution levels to ensure that nearby factories are meeting federal regulations.[57] "The EPA finally understands it can't do everything alone," says the EPA's Patricia Bonner. "Protecting the environment requires the help of citizens, nonprofit organizations, professional associations, universities." She adds, "We are much better off helping people to make responsible decisions than trying to force things on them."[58]

Taking Aim at Federal Policy

The interest in democratic governance is also expanding to the agencies that focus primarily on national policy decisions. Perhaps the most important reason for this is the emergence of a new category of citizen activists; Barbara Loe Fisher, president of the National Vaccine Information Center, is one example. Fisher's interest in vaccine policy stems from her experience with her son, who began to suffer from learning disabilities and attention deficit disorder soon after receiving his diptheria-tetanus-pertussis (DTP) vaccination at the age of two. Fisher, the daughter of a doctor, began investigating how vaccines were developed, tested, and approved. Finding what she felt were alarming problems with the process, and the DTP shot in particular, she co-authored *DTP, A Shot in the Dark* and helped to build an international movement for vaccine safety.[59]

Over the last twenty years, Fisher and other parents have made their voices heard in the vaccine policy debate. They lobbied Congress for the National Vaccine Injury Act, which regulates the administration of vaccines and provides compensation to people who experience severe reactions to vaccines. They pressured the Food and Drug Administration (FDA) to acknowledge the risks presented by thimerosal, a substance used as a preservative in vaccines, and convinced the agency to discourage manufacturers from using it.[60] The most prominent concern the activists are raising now is the possibility that certain vaccines can cause autism in young children. "We are the canary in the coal mine—the warning for others," says Rick Rollens, secretary of the Autism Society of America and father of an autistic son.[61]

Today, the battle lines in immunization policy are clearly drawn. On one side are the parent activists, many of whom have been through deeply traumatic ordeals with their children. Some feel that the federal government has brusquely dismissed their concerns; others believe that officials have been negligent and downright deceitful in their handling of vaccine decisions. On the other side are the officials of the FDA, Centers for Disease Control, and other federal agencies involved in vaccine testing, approval, and distribution. Many of them are doctors or scientists, and they see the claims of the activists as attacks on their professional integrity. Some have experienced the rage of grieving parents at public meetings and hearings, and have come to see the activists as disrespectful, irresponsible, and ignorant of the larger implications for public health.

This situation has resulted in several harmful dilemmas. The anger and distrust between the two groups often gums up the policymaking process, delaying the decisions about vaccine approval and distribution. People like Fisher and Rollens claim to represent thousands of concerned citizens, and they try to bring the moral weight of that critical mass to the table, but officials are unsure just how many people really support the activists. At the level of the average parent, there are few widely trusted sources of basic information about vaccine safety. When people are trying to weigh the risks and decide whether to immunize their children, they may not know which side of the debate to turn to—and millions of parents are probably unaware that there is a debate going on at all. Finally, the outcomes of all those policy choices and individual decisions can have a dramatic effect on public health. If a certain percentage of people are not vaccinated against a disease like whooping cough, the risk of an epidemic becomes much higher.[62] "The relationship between the immunization program and the people it serves is broken," says Roger Bernier, the official who found himself caught between the activists and his colleagues at the CDC. "To be of real service requires that government and citizens interact in authentic ways so that we come to know and understand each other more fully. In immunization, this is not happening. . . . We pay the price for this as a society every time we make an immunization policy decision which is not as sound or as supportable as it could be with more meaningful public input."[63]

Trying to "Scale Up" Democratic Governance

When officials like Bernier begin to plan their own projects, they look for helpful precedents—other attempts to "scale up" democratic governance to the state or federal level. Though these truly large-scale projects are still rare, there are five lessons that can be learned from their successes and failures:

1. Though the logistics are daunting, it is possible to mobilize large numbers of citizens across great geographic expanses. "Oregon Health Decisions," which emerged in the mid-1980s, was one of the first of these projects. Initiated by a partnership of officials and health activists, the program involved over 7,000 people in deliberative community meetings and statewide forums.[64] In the first few years, the discussions focused on access

to health care, cost control, allocation of health resources, and enabling patients to make end-of-life decisions. Partly in response to this input, the legislature enacted the Oregon Health Plan in 1989, expanding health care coverage, mandating that employers contribute to health care benefits, and changing the way that health services were prioritized. The project has also helped to develop living will legislation, health care practice guidelines, and a "scorecard" to help Medicaid clients select among plans. Oregon Health Decisions has since been imitated in a number of other states, including Georgia and California.[65]

Another project, spearheaded by the Arkansas School Boards Association, has mobilized almost 10,000 Arkansans in democratic small-group meetings on education issues since 1998. A number of Arkansas communities, including tiny towns like Alread (population 400), have involved residents in improving the quality of local education.[66] In 2002, the association also held "Speak Up, Arkansas! on Education," in which 6,000 Arkansans met simultaneously across the state to decide what priorities they thought the state's education system should strive to achieve. Many state legislators took part in these discussions. The top three concerns that came out of the Speak Up sessions were teacher salaries, parental involvement, and early childhood care and education. Since then, the legislature has raised teacher salaries from a minimum of $21,800 to $27,500, enacted a new law requiring schools and school districts to develop and implement parent involvement plans, and passed a bill allocating $60 million to early care and education programs.[67]

One of the most ambitious attempts at nationwide democratic governance took place in Canada. Spurred by a "public backlash" against Canada's immigration policies, the Minister of Immigration and Citizenship launched a national "consultation" on immigration in 1994.[68] The resulting "Canadian Immigration Review" used a wide variety of processes to foment discussion, including "town hall" meetings in seven cities and a total of fifty-eight democratic small-group meetings in six metropolitan areas. Over 1,600 Canadians participated in the public meetings, of which 1,100 took part in the small groups. To help ground the sessions, participants were given a document outlining the Department of Immigration's policy goals, a history of Canadian immigration, a sheet of statistics on immigration, facts about who provides services to immigrants, and a paper presenting the arguments on the different sides of the immigration debate. "Following the consultations, immigration policy was changed," claims one report on civic engagement in Canada. "Some changes reflected what government had heard from the public during their consultations, while other changes were ultimately political. The consultations did, however, allow the government to assess which changes would be accepted by the public and which changes would not."[69] For example, when the minister was forced to implement a 20% spending cut mandated by the federal government, he followed the recommendations of project participants and instituted a landing fee for immigrants to defray the cost of some services.

2. The second lesson to be learned is that technology can help to overcome the challenges inherent in creating a truly national discussion. A 1998 initiative called "Americans Discuss Social Security" engaged thousands of people through teleconferences, opinion polls, and face-to-face forums in twenty-five states. America*Speaks,* the national civic group that coordinated the effort, used keypad polling technology in the forums to help citizens summarize their opinions. The $12 million project, which was funded by the Pew Charitable Trusts, "brought data to Washington showing that raising Social Security revenues (by increasing the cap on payroll taxes) was a favored option among informed citizens. As a result, this option began to appear in national polls, and the Congress refocused on it."[70]

The EPA used the Internet extensively as part of a nationwide effort to revise its public participation policy. After years of learning how to interact more productively with citizens, and embracing democratic principles in this work, EPA officials like Patricia Bonner figured that they couldn't formulate an agency-wide participation policy in an autocratic manner. Instead of trying to bring people together face-to-face, they organized a set of online discussions in July 2001 entitled "The National Dialogue on Public Involvement in EPA Decisions." The project was funded by the Hewlett Foundation and coordinated by a civic group called Information Renaissance. People took part by posting messages to a website, either in response to questions posed by the agency or as a reply to another citizen's comment. A total of 1,166 people registered to take part, though only 320 of them actually posted comments.

There are clearly some limitations to a project that utilizes online meetings only; most of the participants seemed to be already quite knowledgeable and involved in environmental decision-making, and one evaluator wondered whether "moving participation online may have distanced EPA even more from those who have historically had little interaction with the agency." However, evaluations showed that participants were satisfied with the process and felt they had had some impact on agency decision-making. The EPA reached a much larger and more geographically diverse group than could ever have participated in person. The precedent has helped other officials contemplating large-scale projects to see how they might use on-line opportunities to support and connect face-to-face meetings.[71]

3.   These projects can indeed lead to local outcomes as well as statewide policy changes. In fact, successful large-scale projects have taken place in situations where there were no high-profile legislative decisions on the table. The Minnesota League of Women Voters launched "Changing Faces, Changing Communities," a statewide effort on immigration issues, in 2000. A total of 961 people took part in seventeen communities. The effort was inspired by Balancing Justice in Oklahoma, but it was not organized with legislative priorities in mind. The focus was on local outcomes, and in a number of communities, the Changing Faces discussions led to diversity festivals, new job training opportunities for recent immigrants, and wider access to English as a Second Language classes. In one town, Pelican Rapids, a new community center was built.[72]

One of the key questions raised by these examples has to do with the nature of "critical mass." Organizers know they need to give people the sense that they are part of something that is large and powerful, but even at the local level they can't predict with confidence just how many citizens it will take. In a town like Kuna, forums of 100 people have made a great impact; in Oklahoma, it took 1,000. For organizers designing federal projects, it is hard to know how to apply this formula to a population of 260 million. It is partly a question of accountability: first and foremost, officials must answer to the voters who elected them, so they have to decide whether the input gathered by a democratic governance effort is adequately representative of the electorate as a whole.

4.   The diversity of the turnout is a critical factor in how a project is perceived. The League of Women Voters of New York State organized "Balancing Justice in New York" in imitation of the earlier Oklahoma project. The New York Leaguers ended up with 2,700 participants in seventy-one communities all over the state. The project helped to develop a number of local initiatives, including new drug courts and youth courts, new programs for mentally ill inmates in Rochester and Albany, more educational opportunities for inmates, and the creation of the Department of Community Justice Services in Tompkins County. However, it didn't seem to have an impact on the state legislature. One reason may be that the network of left-leaning activists on criminal justice issues is much stronger in New York than in Oklahoma, and that set of people flocked to the project so quickly that citizens with more conservative views felt less inclined to participate.

Unlike the earlier Balancing Justice, many of the small groups seemed homogeneous and fewer legislators took part. The state's dominant newspaper, the *New York Times,* paid almost no attention to the project. It is clear that critical mass by itself is not always enough to affect policy. The New York experience suggests that the diversity of the turnout—and the way that diversity is presented in the media—is just as important as the total number of participants.

5.   Finally, two of the state examples demonstrate one of the key limitations of these projects: since they are temporary, their impact on policymaking is temporary as well. It has been almost ten years since Oregon Health Decisions mobilized thousands of citizens in health care discussions, and since that time, key elements of the Oregon Health Plan have been dismantled. Among them was the employer mandate to contribute to health care benefits, which was repealed in 1997.[73] Oklahoma legislators scaled back on corrections reform in 1999, removing some offenses from the truth-in-sentencing requirements and turning the community corrections initiative into a ten-county pilot project. It may be that citizens would have approved these changes had they been intensively involved in the decisions, but that is impossible to tell. Both projects seem to have had a lasting impact on their states—for example, Oklahoma is now one of the national leaders in community corrections—but it is also clear that the invitation they offered citizens was a temporary opportunity rather than an ongoing role in policymaking. "My main regret is that we lost track of the process," says Judge Duncan. "We didn't realize that the way we got people involved was as important as what they said in those discussions. We should've recognized the true value of Balancing Justice—that citizens and government were working together—and found ways of making that a regular, permanent part of the way we made decisions and solved problems."[74]

Getting to Mr. Smith

The need to connect Mr. and Ms. Smith to the policymaking process may become an increasingly important priority in the next decade. There will continue to be parents and other citizens who transform into instant activists in the heat of a controversial public decision, and some of them will become expert and emboldened enough to make an impact on state and federal policies. In the eyes of officials, we may shift from a "potentially concerned" to a "probably frustrated" public.

Some officials will no doubt respond by battening down the hatches and using defensive modes of citizen involvement. Others will make the conceptual transition evident in the thinking of Doug Rutan, Roger Bernier, and Patricia Bonner, and decide to engage the public in more proactive, democratic ways. Bernier himself has helped create a nationwide effort to engage citizens in the decisions related to the prevention of influenza and the possibility of a flu pandemic.[75] In 2005, the League of Women Voters mounted a similarly ambitious project focusing on civil liberties and homeland security.[76] It is too soon to tell what the impact of these projects will be, but their very existence shows the continued development of democratic governance at the federal level.

All of this suggests a shift of scenes in the policymaking drama. In certain situations on certain issues, the deliberation over public decisions will move from city hall to school cafeterias, from the legislature to the living room. Only time will tell how prevalent this plotline becomes, but the best projects seem likely to be the ones with several common characteristics.

- First, they will establish genuine two-way communication among citizens, and between citizens and officials, that informs people about the issues and lets elected leaders know what their constituents are thinking. Those conversations will begin with basic questions that allow people to build trust and connect their own experiences to the policy debate.
- Second, organizers will present information in a clear and balanced way, describing all the main policy options on the table. Their approach will acknowledge that all "facts" must be interpreted, that there are many valid viewpoints, and that common ground can only be reached through deliberation.
- Third, they will find ways to help citizens, community organizations, and other groups contribute their own time, energy, and resources to implementing policies and attacking the fundamental public problems the policies are trying to address. In this way, they may actually expand the notion of policy—from an uppercase "P" to a lowercase "p"—beyond its purely legal, legislative meaning, so that it reflects the thinking of the whole community and marshals the resources of the whole community. One reason why these tactics will continue to emerge is that they tend to produce more informed, supported, and effective public policies, but perhaps an equally important reason is that they make citizens and officials feel respected, validated, and legitimized by one another.

The more this trend continues, the more officials and other organizers will be confronted with the challenges of timing and scale. While many democratic governance projects are temporary efforts—particularly the ones dealing with state and federal decisions—the wheels of the policy-making process never stop turning in city hall, the state legislatures, and the Washington Beltway. If they want to keep the trust of citizens and continue to give and receive political legitimacy, officials will have to find ways of keeping people engaged, either by reconvening them periodically or by re-configuring official public meetings so that they provide valid roles for citizens. The Kuna ACT process achieves this goal for local decision-making, but it remains to be seen how that model could be applied on a statewide or federal scale. In addition, no matter what recruitment methods or meeting formats are used to mobilize citizens across large geographic expanses, the challenge of incorporating interest groups will become more apparent. Lobbyists and organized interest groups will presumably still play a role in the next form of democracy, but it is unclear just what that role will be.

One safer prediction may be that policymaking, even at the state and federal level, will rely increasingly on a foundation of local and neighbor-hood institutions. That is where Mr. Smith lives, and groups like Kuna ACT and the Jane Addams School for Democracy have shown that they can reach him—no matter whether he wears a cowboy hat or a turban. Success-ful organizers have proved that they can connect these groups through the "high touch" recruitment methods used by the League of Women Voters, as well as the high-tech innovations demonstrated by America*Speaks* and the EPA.

The next three chapters will focus on attempts to create more of these kinds of institutions: structures for shared governance within nonprofit so-cial service organizations, within schools, and within neighborhoods. Politi-cally, if not geographically, these groups are halfway between Washington and Mr. Smith, and they will be critical for bringing democratic governance to scale.

The straightforward moral messages in movies like *Mr. Smith Goes to Washington,* which was made in 1939, often seem out of step with twenty-first century politics. How could Jimmy Stewart, wearing his naïve smile and Boy Scout pin, survive on the floor of the Senate? But the basic im-pulses shown by Senator Smith—the need to win approval from his new colleagues, and the desire to remain a part of his community back home—are just as evident in the behavior of constituents and public officials today as they ever were. Federal policymaking still seems remote to the average citizen, but whenever the terms of that mutual validation are fulfilled, the possibility of dramatic national change exists.

Section 3

Building Shared Governance

6
The Strange Career
of Chuck Ridley
Drug Abuse, Community Organizing,
and "Government by Nonprofits"

Chuck Ridley's grandmother lived in Delray Beach when the only thing black folks could do there was harvest sugar cane. Every day, every black man and woman, fathers and mothers and uncles and cousins, went into those sugar cane fields to work all day under the hot sun. And every day, every one of those parents and grandparents brought their children into the fields with them, to play while the adults worked. There were snakes and rats and dogs and all kinds of flying, swooping, biting bugs in those fields, and sometimes the children got bit or stung or scared, but that is where the children played.

One day Chuck Ridley's grandmother saw a young child get bit by a snake. She saw the snake coming, and she yelled as loud as she could, but it didn't matter.

That day Chuck Ridley's grandmother told everybody else, all the mothers and fathers and aunts and uncles, that she was staying home and not going into the fields. She told all those parents and grandparents to leave their children with her, and she would look after them at home.

Every day after that, all the black folks in Delray Beach left their children with Chuck Ridley's grandmother. Every day they brought her food from their kitchens, and firewood and old clothes, and sometimes money, for her to take care of their children. And Chuck Ridley's grandmother raised a neighborhood.[1]

The southwest side of Delray Beach, Florida, might seem like an odd place to observe some of the latest developments in the continuing evolution of democracy. It is a pocket of poverty in the affluent Gold Coast, a neighborhood where most of the adults do not have a high school diploma and over half the children live in single-parent homes. The residents, primarily African Americans and recent Haitian and Mexican immigrants, represent over 80% of the people of color in the city as a whole.[2] But the

sheer desperation of this community has in fact propelled its political innovations: since the traditional political process has served Southwest Delray
so poorly, leaders and residents there have had even greater cause to work
together in new ways.

One of their innovations is part of a larger shift that is helping to reshape
the relationship between citizens and government: the change in tactics by
traditional community organizers. Since the time of Saul Alinsky, who first
began mobilizing residents in 1940s Chicago, the practice of community
organizing has diversified into a broad spectrum of strategies, including
"faith-based organizing," "consensus organizing," and other variations.[3]
This dissemination was driven by the experimentation of local organizers,
who reacted to changing conditions by modifying various aspects of their
approach. The organizers themselves have also diversified, partly because
people who were trained in the Alinsky tradition have gone on to serve as
public officials, nonprofit directors, program officers at foundations, and
in other roles. These leaders have adapted the skills and philosophies of
traditional community organizing to fit the perspectives and needs of their
new positions.

Some of these organizers have reached an important threshold: rather
than pressuring public officials to give citizens what they want, they have
created arenas where citizens, decision-makers, and other stakeholders can
sit down and make policy together. In some places, they have taken this
a step further, establishing nonprofit organizations that oversee neighborhood decision-making and manage the delivery of most public services.
Instead of always mobilizing citizens to *affect* the political process, these
organizers are finding new ways to *incorporate* the process.

These entities are practically governments in themselves; they are probably more autonomous and comprehensive than the structures for shared
governance now emerging in schools (see Chapter 7) and neighborhood
councils (Chapter 8). But, they also call out a long list of difficult new
questions about accountability, power, and the purpose of community
organizing.

In Southwest Delray, a skilled, veteran community organizer named
Chuck Ridley has been at the center of all of these changes. He is the heir
to a family tradition of local leadership: his grandmother organized the first
day care center in that part of the city, and his father was a prominent local
pastor. He is an eloquent speaker and a tireless fundraiser, and the warmth
of his personality allows him to connect with all kinds of people.

Ridley also draws on his own hard-won experience as a cocaine addict in that same neighborhood. "For a while there, I was snorting half of

south Florida," he admits. "I give thanks to God, and to my wife—who has kicked down the doors of more crackhouses in my neighborhood than anybody—and to the sheriff, who was looking for someone to help him deal with the crack epidemic in Delray Beach. When I started to straighten out, he got me to start helping others."[4]

It is fitting that the leader of this transformation in Delray Beach was a former addict, because the scourge of drug abuse in urban neighborhoods is a dramatic illustration of how the state of democracy affects our lives. Most addicts do not belong to cohesive communities that validate their positive qualities, that help them deal with their problems, and that put their skills to use. Some live in neighborhoods where the social norms encourage crime rather than condemning it—where dealers are role models, where drug abuse is considered normal, and where people are afraid to make eye contact on the street. Finally, many addicts have come to the disheartening conclusion that our political and economic systems are stacked against them. The decision to abuse drugs, which insulates the body and mind from the natural stimulation of friends, family, and community, is an extreme expression of alienation from society.

At first, Chuck Ridley made progress on his own drug problem, and that of his neighborhood, by fighting dealers and finding treatment. Then he transformed himself and his neighborhood by building institutions that foster citizenship, strengthen community, and allow citizens and government to share the powers and responsibilities of governance. "All along I needed something to belong to, a neighborhood that could solve its problems and shape its future," he says. "Finally I realized that other people need that too."

MAD DADS with a Plan

In 1993, Ridley and one of his neighbors founded the local branch of MAD DADS, which stands for "Men Against Destruction, Defending Against Drugs and Social disorder." Most of the initial members had played on the same high school football team. At first, it was an informal volunteer group that conducted daily patrols in an attempt to discourage the thriving drug trade in Southwest Delray. Then they began branching out, creating youth programs and fostering neighborhood associations.

In 1999, MAD DADS entered a new stage in its development. Ridley and his allies had proven they could raise money and "rally the troops" to fight drug dealers and other local problems, but they weren't tapping the full citizen potential of their neighborhood. They wanted residents to analyze problems for themselves, considering all the various options. They wanted to forge productive relationships between citizens and the public employees who did the actual work of policing the streets, educating children, and running the city. They wanted residents to contribute their ideas and efforts, not just their voices and votes, to solving local problems. They wanted to include public officials in the process of building consensus among citizens, instead of forcing them to react to the demands of the neighborhood. "We wanted to create a political environment that would bring out the best in everybody, that would allow people to claim power for themselves and responsibility to others," Ridley says.

Two other longtime activists were instrumental in this transition. Chuck's wife, Cynthia Ridley, was always at the center of the organizing work, quietly recruiting residents, making sure their questions were answered, and dealing with the logistics. The Reverend Sharon Hogarth, a faith leader who says her "ministry is the community," helped MAD DADS access ideas and resources from outside the neighborhood while ensuring that the ideas and resources *inside* the neighborhood always took center stage.

The most logical first step, it seemed to Hogarth and the Ridleys, was to make a plan for the neighborhood. In the past, MAD DADS had been a typical grassroots organization: whenever someone had a good idea, that person would rally a few neighbors and try to implement it. MAD DADS had never involved the residents of Southwest Delray Beach in a more deliberate, comprehensive planning process—there had never seemed to be enough time. But the three activists decided that, if they wanted citizens to help implement the plan, they had to give those residents a chance to help create it. To lay the groundwork, they assembled a representative set of citizens, including young people, members of all the different ethnic groups in the neighborhood, and public employees who had a professional connection with the neighborhood.[5]

As they began their planning, the core group of twenty residents and outside stakeholders wanted to involve more of their neighbors before trying to implement any particular project. But there was one overarching idea that the residents consistently and emphatically supported: a new school. Thirty years before, there had been a high school in Southwest Delray Beach, but it had been shut down as part of the desegregation efforts of the 1970s. Carver High School had been a center of the community in that part of Delray, and residents still talk fondly of the teachers who worked there and the state championship football team that took the field every Friday, representing the pride of the neighborhood. By 1999, the children of the neighborhood were being bused to seventeen different public schools in other parts of the county. The students of Southwest Delray scored much lower than their peers on standardized tests, had much higher suspension and dropout rates, and exhibited many other signs of failure in the mainstream educational system.[6] The residents in the core group were adamant about the need to take charge of their children's education; for the moment, they put aside their plans to involve more citizens in order to focus on this idea.

The residents also wanted a very unusual kind of school. Through long planning sessions and a great deal of research, they came up with an innovative format for what they began to call "the Village Academy." This school would operate on a year-round schedule and remain open twelve hours a day, six days a week. It would be a "total system," incorporating social, educational, civic, and vocational opportunities. It would have extensive health and medical services, and social workers on staff. There would be one teacher for every fifteen kindergarteners, and one for every 20–25 teenagers.[7] Parents would work directly with teachers, staff members, and the principal to make decisions about priorities such as the curriculum, teaching practices, and school safety. They would also volunteer their time to help implement ideas and improve the school. Students would attend this school from the time they were toddlers until they went off to college. And the residents were more resolute about this point than any other: those kids had to get to college.

Having envisioned the Village Academy, which at times must have seemed like an impossible dream, the MAD DADS core group set out to make it a reality. Through the local United Way, Chuck Ridley met Arthur Kobacker, a local philanthropist with a desire to help "break the cycle of poverty" for children in Delray Beach. Kobacker's interest was piqued by the Village Academy plan; he and Ridley even went on research trips to several innovative schools in other parts of the country. Kobacker joined with the Annenberg Foundation to provide the additional funds the school would need to maintain its expanded schedule and services. A scant five months after the core group had made it a priority, the new school had been approved by the Palm Beach County School Board. Construction got underway in the spring of 2000, and the following August, the Village Academy opened its doors.

Co-opting the Decision-Makers

One aspect of the MAD DADS planning process shows how some community organizers have changed their approach: Ridley and his allies were able to involve public officials and other decision-makers from the very beginning of the effort. This was a key reason for the success of the Village Academy plan.

The idea that citizens and decision-makers should be kept apart from one another was one of the original precepts of community organizing. Alinsky worried that if outsiders were part of the initial discussions with residents, they would dominate, manipulate, or co-opt the process. Instead, organizers tried to build a separate base of power by interviewing citizens, identifying their common interests, and then recruiting them for "house meetings" and other events that would solidify their commitment to a shared cause. They sometimes also recruited other allies, outside the neighborhood or community, who were already receptive to that cause. Once the people had turned out and the group was formed, the organizers and participants could begin to broadcast their priorities in the corridors of power. From that point, community organizers might confront the decision-makers ("us" vs. "them") or they might work together with public officials ("us" working with "them"), but they still assumed that citizens and decision-makers were two very distinct sets of people.[8] Residents had to hold officials accountable to the interests of the community.

Some community organizers now use a broader definition of "us." This is partly because organizers are much more likely to negotiate and partner with public officials than in the more confrontational days of the '60s and '70s. More recently, in places like Southwest Delray, organizers began to realize that if they structured the sessions well, and offered additional leadership training opportunities for residents, they could change the dynamic between citizens and decision-makers and include both sets of people in the discussions.[9]

In Ridley's eyes, the "us" included not only the people who lived in his neighborhood, but the people who worked there, provided services to its residents, or had some other stake in its success. Bringing some of these people together was a difficult challenge: in fact, the very first meeting of the "core group" was unproductive because the neighborhood residents didn't speak up as much as the outsiders. The three organizers put the planning on hold; in the interim, they gave the residents some leadership training and more opportunities to "gel" as a group. Then they brought the residents and outside stakeholders back together. There still had been no decisions made by that point: before any priority had been established, before any cause had been embraced, citizens and decision-makers sat down together, talked about their backgrounds and personal experiences, and shared their hopes and concerns for the neighborhood. By bonding in this way, the participants created a unifying glue that helped them deal with conflicting interests or opinions without having anyone storm out of the room. They built trust and confidence first; by the time the idea of the Village Academy had taken shape, it was a vision they all shared.

This allowed MAD DADS to practice a very facilitative kind of leadership in pushing the plan forward. Once the Village Academy plan was down on paper, they began sharing it with decision-makers who hadn't been involved in the planning sessions, and seeking support for it outside the neighborhood. The power in their approach came from two sources: 1) both neighborhood residents and outside stakeholders felt some ownership of the vision, and 2) because the "core group" represented all the various sets of people within the neighborhood, public officials and potential funders could expect that the Southwest Delray residents would do their utmost to back the new school. Whereas community organizers have traditionally been concerned about decision-makers co-opting citizens, it may be fair to say that MAD DADS helped citizens co-opt the decision-makers.

After the school had opened, the residents of Southwest Delray made good on their promises. They supported the school and the students who attend it, volunteering in many ways to develop the facility and help it function. The students quickly benefited from their new environment: when the school opened in 2000, only 18% were reading at grade level, but by 2004 that number had risen to 52%.[10]

Broadening the Base

As the work to build the school went forward, the Southwest Delray core group began assembling a larger critical mass of neighborhood residents. "If you want to build trust, empowerment, and support across an entire community, you have to reach a large number of people," says Cynthia Ridley. "We needed to bring in the people who are most at risk," Hogarth adds. "The drug dealers are out there all day, harvesting lives, so you have to be just as persistent if you want to save lives."[11] In a calculated move, they gave their ambitious project a friendly, unintimidating, downright unassuming title: "Community Chat."

Because of their experience with traditional community organizing, Ridley and his allies knew the value of personal recruiting, the power of sharing experiences in small-group meetings, and the galvanizing effect of larger forums. But like many other organizers in recent years, they added some important adaptations, such as impartial facilitators, ground rules set by the group, and a guide that introduced a range of viewpoints.

They also wanted to increase their capacity to attract and retain people who weren't normally considered "pillars of the community." Ridley and Hogarth hoped that by starting with personal experience, by ensuring civility, and by valuing participants for their potential contributions rather than their prior offenses, they could create a welcoming environment for people who hadn't felt welcomed before. "People who abuse drugs are acting out the pain of their communities," says Hogarth, "and we wanted to strengthen the community web so that it caught them and supported them." Keeping current and potential addicts in the room required that the groups get beyond stereotypes and begin to value the unique contributions of each member. As Hogarth puts it, "Many people at risk are already the scapegoats of their families and the community. The process has to help them—and the other participants—see their own potential."

In the summer of 2000, as the paint was drying on the walls of the Village Academy, well over 100 residents of Southwest Delray Beach were taking part in small-group discussions about the challenges facing their community. Many of the concerns and priorities mentioned by the participants were things MAD DADS had been working on for years: crime and drug activity in the neighborhood; misunderstanding and mistrust between African American, Haitian American, and Hispanic residents; the need for more job training and job opportunities; the need for more youth activities and programs; tensions between residents and police officers; and the threat of gentrification from the South Florida housing boom.

There were also some conclusions that surprised Hogarth and the Ridleys. For example, some young people were upset about the Village Academy, because the best set of basketball courts in the neighborhood had been appropriated as the site of the new building. Because MAD DADS shares office space with a community policing substation, some of the young people also assumed that MAD DADS was an arm of the police force. The organizers found that there was more tension than they had thought between different generations of people living in Southwest Delray Beach.

Many residents who were recent immigrants from Haiti felt that the police and social welfare workers were undermining parental authority. They described a common scenario where unhappy Haitian teenagers (who themselves go through a difficult cultural transition in relocating to the U. S.) call the police to accuse their parents of child abuse. Acting partly on misconceptions about traditional Haitian culture, representatives of the courts and social service agencies seemed more likely to place the children under state custody. Many recent immigrants also expressed great fear of deportation. The Community Chat discussions uncovered a total lack of communication between public employees and residents who were recent immigrants.

Another surprise for the Community Chat organizers was that the residents of Southwest Delray didn't want to wait for the action forum to take action. After talking about the challenges faced by single parents in the community, participants in one Community Chat group formed a parent support group that has been meeting regularly. When the young people in another group complained about the lack of recreational opportunities, the participants organized a youth basketball team that has since qualified for a state tournament (MAD DADS has also built a new set of basketball courts to replace the ones displaced by the Village Academy).

Some of the participants also began attending—and making themselves heard—at public meetings of the local Community Development Corporation and the Delray Beach City Council. Recognizing the surge of interest on the Southwest side, the planners working on the city's Vision 2010 initiative held a special forum in that part of the city. The forum got a large turnout, and the planners were impressed by what they heard. "It was the most successful visioning meeting we've had," said Lula Butler, the city's Director of Community Improvement, "because the people came in so prepared—and because they weren't just concerned about fixing potholes."[12]

In its early days, MAD DADS regularly organized prayer vigils in front of houses where drug activity was going on. One of the Community Chat groups decided to revive this practice, and they organized a vigil where groups of residents pounded on the doors of known drug houses. After the first vigil nearly led to violence, the police department began assigning officers to attend; over 150 people, including several police officers, attended the second vigil. "When people connect, there's power in that," Cynthia Ridley says. "They take the initiative to do things they wouldn't ordinarily do." The small-group discussions reconfirmed residents' commitment, and emboldened them to recapture their streets. For Chuck Ridley, "It felt good to see other people take the same kinds of risks for their neighborhood that Cynthia and I took when MAD DADS first began. And this time, we didn't have to lead the charge."

Residents also recognized some of the neighborhood's existing assets, and built on them. One example is the "Delray Divas," a step group and drill team for young women that has been expanded dramatically. There are now over 100 girls and young women, ages 6 to 18, involved in this music program, which also gives them access to tutoring and counseling opportunities at the Village Academy. The Divas have become a source of intense neighborhood pride and a very useful organizing tool—people turn out for neighborhood meetings and events when they know the Divas are going to perform.

One group focused on the impact of gentrification on senior citizens. As rising rents and property taxes put a strain on their finances, many seniors find themselves unable to meet the maintenance costs on their homes. The participants who discussed this problem included a roofer, a house painter, and a man who runs a landscaping service; they decided to devote some of their time to help rehabilitate houses lived in by seniors. Other members of the dialogue group also had roles to play in the rehab plan: they began raising money from local churches and businesses to offset the cost of supplies, and scheduled meetings with public officials to enlist their support. A local Home Depot store agreed to donate building materials, and the city provided some funding. The group has since completed rehab work on twelve homes.[13]

"One of the most exciting things is that the people getting involved aren't just the same faces who've been on the front lines before," Hogarth says. In fact, the Community Chat leaders began to feel more like followers. They did their best to keep up with the participants, helping them organize youth summits and set up dialogues to help Haitian-American parents work with social service providers. But other projects raced ahead without them: several participants who had been active in neighborhood associations created the Westside Neighborhood Presidents Council to further develop new leadership and give the area a more unified voice. Others helped defeat a developer's plan to turn an historic African American hotel into a halfway house. "The residents of that neighborhood have become a powerful political force in a very short period of time," says Delray Beach City Councilwoman Alberta McCarthy.[14]

From Community Organizing to Organizing Communities

As the Delray Beach experience shows, it is difficult to define a field as diverse and fluid as community organizing. Most good organizers are driven primarily by practical considerations, rather than philosophical ones, and so labels like "faith-based" or "consensus-based" don't fit very well anymore. "Most community organizations are complex and multifaceted and cannot easily be placed into neatly defined boxes," says Kristina Smock, a consultant who has worked extensively with community organizers.[15]

In order to define their work and find their place within the field, community organizers are beginning to reconsider a number of important questions:

1. Who are the people being "organized"? Alinsky focused his original efforts on urban neighborhoods where the injustices were clear and the residents were obviously disempowered. The "faith-based" organizing that gained steam in the 1960s and 1970s began to expand the sense of who should be at the table. By appealing to core religious values, organizers were able to bring together people of different congregations and cultural backgrounds.[16] Organizers like Chuck Ridley have taken this inclusiveness one step further, recruiting public employees and public officials to take part in their projects. To make these more inclusive conversations work, some organizers have created environments where participants can examine many different sides of an issue, weighing all the major policy options. In so doing, they are raising the second major question:

2. What constitutes an "issue?" In Alinsky's world, " 'issue" was roughly synonymous with "objective"—organizers would conduct scores of one-on-one interviews, asking people about their concerns for the neighborhood, and how those concerns could be addressed. One example of an "issue" that might emerge from this process is "building more affordable housing." The list of "issues" compiled from the interviews would often be narrowed down on the basis of whether they were "winnable." Brenda Easley Webb, a longtime community organizer in Buffalo, changed her approach after taking part in house meetings where she "felt railroaded by organizers to pick an actionable issue."[17] Instead, many organizers today are bringing people together before the solutions have been determined. The Kansas City Church/Community Organization, for example, now involves residents and decision-makers in examining the larger problem rather than moving quickly to specific goals or demands (see Chapter 2).[18] These organizers are taking a more deliberative, problem-solving type of approach, in which an "issue" is a broadly stated topic with a range of possible solutions.

3. Who is responsible for taking action? In Alinsky's parlance, "action" referred to a demonstration where large numbers of people showed their support for a particular cause or policy change. But even then, community organizers were helping citizens act in more tangible ways, from street cleanups and crime patrols to lending circles and land trusts. Today, it is clearer than ever that action is occurring at a number of levels, and that it is being accomplished by residents, not just decision-makers.[19] Much of the work in Southwest Delray, for example, was carried out by citizens themselves. By ensuring that action and advocacy efforts are associated with the participants rather than the project itself, organizers can also maintain their stance as conveners, rather than being seen as activists for particular causes.

A closely related development is the increasing willingness of community organizers to build long-term relationships between citizens and public employees like teachers, police officers, social workers, and city planners. Many of the action efforts that emerged from Community Chat were propelled by the fact that the small groups contained these kinds of practitioners, whose expertise helped the group brainstorm ideas and then figure out how to implement them. The traditional approach of building a separate power base and then communicating with government was more likely to create collaboration at the top—between organizers and public officials—than at the rank-and-file, rubber-hits-the-road level of social workers and Haitian parents, police officers and prayer vigil organizers, teachers and volunteer hall monitors at the Village Academy.[20]

4. How should organizers think about power? Alinsky assumed that there were basic conflicts of interest between decision-makers and citizens, between the rulers and the ruled. This outlook influenced the rhetoric used by organizers: their language often pinned the blame for problems on government, overlooked or devalued neighborhood assets, and suggested to residents that the system was stacked against them. "Who has the power to redress our grievance?" is a question that has long been used by community organizers.[21] In this view, power is something to be seized and used by citizens.

    The strategies and rhetoric being used by community organizers today seem to suggest a less limited definition of power. Organizers like Warren Adams-Leavitt, director of the Kansas City Church/Community Organization, are more concerned with building power than taking it from others. "We are more co-creative with local government," he says. "Some of that is the result of our own growing sophistication as an organization. Some of that is the growing respect that we have earned in town, i.e., people see their interest in partnering with us because we get things done."[22]

    This language about power seems to suggest that, while there may be some important differences between citizens and decision-makers, their roles can be complementary and they have many goals in common. Rather than a "togetherness against the system," this mindset is open to the possibility of a "togetherness that *is* the system."

There is more variety in the way community organizers answer these four questions than at any time in the last fifty years. There is a lively debate inside and between national organizing networks like the Industrial Areas Foundation, the Pacific Institute for Community Organizing, and the Gamaliel Foundation.[23] The diverse assumptions of local organizers reflect the fact that they have tried so many different strategies in order to be effective. In some places, they have achieved breakthroughs by going beyond Alinsky's desire to influence power and establishing new democratic arenas where power can be exercised by a wider range of actors. It is no coincidence, then, that community organizers are more likely to recruit all kinds of people, welcome all kinds of views, value all kinds of action, and understand all kinds of power, since those seem to be important preconditions for democratic governance. In situations where organizers cross this threshold, and incorporate political processes rather than affecting them, it may be that the title of "community organizer" no longer fits. In those cases, we should probably call them "democratic organizers" instead.

This doesn't mean that traditional community organizing has somehow outlived its usefulness. There are certainly situations where organizers can make more headway by trying to affect policy decisions from the outside, using a separate power base to confront or negotiate with decision-makers. Some of the most dramatic changes occur when different kinds of strategies are used at the same time—it may be that strong "outside" advocacy efforts help convince decision-makers that they ought to participate in new "inside" arenas for policy-making.[24] Furthermore, some of the techniques first developed by Alinsky, and refined by other organizers over the years, should perhaps be used more widely: employing intensive one-on-one interviews, publicizing outcomes heavily, coaching and mentoring new leaders, and providing stable jobs for professional organizers.

The fact that community organizing has become a much larger tent, with mayors and police chiefs as well as neighborhood activists, makes some veteran organizers nervous. "Some of them still adhere to a more traditional model and don't see anything else as legitimate organizing," says Kristina Smock.[25] But when people cross the threshold into democratic governance, that doesn't mean they are ignoring questions of power or abandoning muscular radicalism for a softer, more conciliatory, and ultimately more co-opted approach. It is simply a different approach, embodying different ideas about how to ensure accountability and justice, with different implications for the future of politics. "Organizing chauvinism and the myth of pure or 'real' organizing has not served our movement well," says one researcher. "Not every organizer will be or needs to be another Saul Alinsky. Organizing has to be seen less as a sacred priesthood and more as a set of skills that can be learned and practiced by all kinds of people, in a variety of organizational settings."[26]

If we concentrate too much on the differences among community organizers, we may also miss the real point of interest: how the strategic innovations of community organizers have paralleled the discoveries made by other kinds of local leaders. Practitioners and public officials in fields like race, education, and law enforcement have developed similar approaches, because they are dealing with similar breakdowns in local politics. This can help communities create new kinds of public institutions, as we will see in Southwest Delray. It also sets the stage for new forms of democracy.

From Defying Governments to Designing Them

By 2001, it was clear that MAD DADS had utterly transformed its role and had actually taken over many of the traditional functions of local government. At the same time, they had run out of money for Community Chat, Ridley was consumed with overseeing the Village Academy, and they were unable to respond to all the requests for advice and support from neighborhood associations, public agencies, and potential organizers all over South Florida. Delray Beach even won a coveted All-America City Award, given by the National Civic League, partly because the city's nomination highlighted the work of MAD DADS.[27] The organization was having an enormous impact on several major policy issues, on the professional lives of scores of practitioners, and on the quality of life of thousands of citizens—and it was operating out of several rooms in an old police substation where the septic system flooded like clockwork every two weeks.

To meet these challenges, the leaders of MAD DADS decided to transform the structure of their organization. They changed the name to the "Village Foundation," feeling that it was a more holistic and accurate title. It would raise money and coordinate the work of the school, Community Chat, the youth activities, and the crime prevention efforts. It would also serve as the hub of a new "Village Alliance" of nonprofits that work on other issues in the neighborhood, such as housing, hunger, and parenting. They intended the Village Foundation to act as a convener for all kinds of public dialogue and problem-solving efforts. Chuck Ridley became the director of the organization and the unofficial mayor of the neighborhood.

The Village Foundation represents a new type of quasi-public institution, a kind of "government by nonprofit." This transformation was not the result of any master plan; MAD DADS stumbled into it, led by the successes and ideas generated by their organizing work. They started out, years ago, by appropriating law enforcement roles for themselves, holding prayer vigils, and closing down drug houses. When they built the Village Academy, they created not only the first educational institution in Southwest Delray in thirty years, but a relatively autonomous entity—a school district for the neighborhood. By working more intensively with neighborhood associations, they set up a network of block-level organizations that any local government should envy. The residents who stepped forward through Community Chat have made a major impact on planning, economic development, and housing, not only by providing input to decision-makers but by carrying out much of the work themselves.

Ridley's desire to build a stronger institutional base is in keeping with the Alinsky tradition. Traditional community organizers have always created "permanent power organizations" to articulate neighborhood interests in city politics. These tended to focus on lobbying and advocacy, but over the years, some of the most successful groups added programs and services for neighborhood residents. Some of these organizations have become established political actors in their communities, while others are more like the Village Foundation in their focus on services instead of politics, and still others combine the two roles.[28]

The Village Foundation also mirrors a much larger trend that is apparent in communities all over the country: creating holistic new structures that address a range of policy issues in a specific neighborhood. Some "community development corporations" (CDCs) now fit this description. Many CDCs were spun out of community organizing efforts in the 1960s and 1970s, and some received their initial funding from the federal Office of Economic Opportunity. Most started out with a broad social agenda, but with the federal housing cutbacks of the 1980s, they began to focus more on the construction of low-income housing. This work intensified, to the point where CDCs have now built hundreds of thousands of housing units. In the last fifteen years, some CDCs swung back to a broader focus, spurred by the realization that, while housing was critical, they couldn't adequately support residents if they didn't also address social issues like child care and crime prevention. Many have branched out, as seen in Chapter 2, taking on roles that go far beyond housing construction.[29]

"Comprehensive community initiatives" (CCIs) take this idea a step further, trying to revitalize neighborhoods by addressing all the major factors that influence persistent urban poverty, including housing, child care and education, crime, transportation, job training, and economic development. Major funders like the Local Initiatives Support Corporation, the Neighborhood Reinvestment Corporation, and the Rockefeller, Surdna, and Annie E. Casey Foundations have devoted hundreds of millions of dollars to these multipronged initiatives.[30] The Clinton Administration brought the federal government into the mix by introducing the Empowerment Zone/ Enterprise Community program. Over $1.5 billion over a ten-year period was allotted to 137 EZ/EC neighborhoods.[31] All of these efforts focus on distinct neighborhoods and try to account for every obstacle that might keep residents from pulling themselves out of poverty. By 2000, there was a CCI operating in at least one neighborhood of every major American city.[32]

The comprehensive approach to fighting urban poverty has a long tradition, beginning with the settlement houses of the late nineteenth century and continuing through the War on Poverty in the 1960s. In the late 1980s, it was reinforced by academic research showing that social services, housing and economic development, and political and cultural activities were increasingly carried out in isolation from each other, and that this segregation limited their overall effectiveness. During the same time period, governments have been cutting back on their anti-poverty work: George W. Bush added force to the trend by proposing that "faith-based organizations"—a label that fits many nonprofit social service groups—take a larger role in providing services to the poor.

CCIs arose to confront these challenges. These multipronged, neighborhood-focused nonprofit initiatives are based on three main assumptions: that poverty tends to be concentrated in city neighborhoods, that the network of groups and personal relationships in a neighborhood is critical, and that residents need a range of assets and services close by in order to improve their lives.[33]

Comprehensive anti-poverty work has also drawn inspiration from a less likely source: drug dealers. Dealers are a daily presence in urban neighborhoods, interacting with residents, enforcing their own codes for behavior, and occupying a central role in the economy of that area. The Reverend Eugene Rivers, who helped found "the Ten-Point Coalition" to revitalize low-income neighborhoods in Boston, conceived of the plan after talking with a drug dealer named Selvin Brown. When Rivers asked Brown why the church was unable to counteract the lure of drugs, Brown explained that "when Johnny goes past my corner on the way to school, I'm there, you're not. When he comes home from school, I'm there, you're not. When he goes to the corner store . . . I'm there, you're not. When he goes back home, I'm there, you're not. I win, you lose." Rivers realized that the church groups and social services available to children and teenagers in Boston were simply too distant from their lives and too disconnected from one another. The Ten-Point Coalition, like other comprehensive community initiatives, offers an array of programs and services in a way that is coordinated, highly visible, and reinforces the network of responsible adults and institutions in that neighborhood.[34]

To strengthen community networks and to compete with drug dealers, neighborhood leaders have joined forces with foundations and public officials to create institutions like the Village Foundation. What makes this work so difficult and intriguing is that by combining and coordinating the major public services and functions, they are essentially recreating local government, one neighborhood at a time. Many of the people now leading, funding, and planning these institutions started out as traditional community organizers. The shift in organizing tactics has changed their relationship with governments: rather than defying them, these longtime activists now find themselves designing new ones.

Ridley Resigns: Lessons in Democracy and Accountability

What happened next in Southwest Delray raised some interesting concerns about the model of government by nonprofits. In 2003, Chuck Ridley decided to hire an assistant director and raise his own salary, based on the expectation of a large grant from a national foundation. The grant was delayed, a budget shortfall loomed, and the Village Foundation board members were furious that Ridley hadn't cleared the decision with them (Ridley claimed he had done so informally). The board suspended Ridley, and in the furor, he resigned. Two presidents of neighborhood associations in Southwest Delray claimed that the board was disregarding the wishes of neighborhood residents.[35]

Regardless of what the truth might have been in this whole affair, the fiasco does suggest some difficult questions about the accountability of nonprofit governments. Though the Village Foundation might have been just as important to the quality of life in Southwest Delray as the City of Delray Beach, neighborhood residents couldn't vote for the director as they would for the mayor or city council. Ridley and his successors were accountable only to the Village Foundation board members, most of whom did not live in Southwest Delray. In important decisions like the one about Ridley's conduct, the neighborhood did not have a say.

Questions about the lines of accountability have arisen in other comprehensive community initiatives as well. Some directors don't answer to the residents because they make no distinction between their organization and the neighborhood itself. "As long as a community-building organization sees itself as the community, it cannot work effectively to improve its representation of the community," says William Traynor, who directs a CCI in Lawrence, Massachusetts.[36] Some of these projects have resident advisory boards or committees, and have residents serving on their boards of directors, but in many of those cases it is open to question whether those citizens possess any real authority. Even when foundations urge the organization to "ask the community" rather than looking to program officers for approval of major decisions, the culture in these nonprofits has been very difficult to change: perhaps understandably, the organization directors want to appease their funding sources.[37]

The Village Foundation then faced other difficulties, challenges that may also pertain to nonprofit governments in other places. Though it was coordinating and providing public services, the organization did not receive tax dollars directly, and so was greatly dependent on foundations. The United Way pulled back other grants it had made to the Village Foundation, citing sloppy management and bad bookkeeping. Finally, in the summer of 2004, the Village Foundation closed its doors.[38]

Even if the Village Foundation had been a model of good management, its fate suggests that nonprofit governments are by nature going to be on tenuous financial footing. If local governments had to rely on foundations and charitable contributions to meet their operating expenses, they would probably go bankrupt just as quickly.

The Village Foundation's greatest weakness may have been that it wasn't designed in a way that reflected the democratic, participatory organizing that created it. It lacked processes and procedures that would involve residents in dialogue, decision-making, and action to govern the organization and improve the neighborhood. "[Ridley] didn't have anyone else involved in the decision, and he bore the responsibility himself," said the co-chair of the Village Foundation board.[39] One has to wonder: would Ridley have stumbled had he been involving large numbers of residents in key decisions like how to prioritize the organization's budget?

Other CCIs have the same shortcomings when it comes to mobilizing citizens. Some of these efforts experience the same kind of dynamic that plagues many neighborhood associations and parent-teacher organizations: a small group of citizens manages to gain a powerful role within the organization and then begins to shut out other residents. When citizens have worked hard to gain a place at the table, they don't always see the need to then make room for their neighbors. As one resident in an Empowerment Zone put it, "It was like trying to take a lollipop from a child who has been waiting for it for weeks."[40]

Many CCIs characterize their work as "resident-driven" but fail to involve large, diverse numbers of people in their planning, decision-making, and implementation work. Some EZ/EC sites were able to mobilize citizens in order to apply for the funding, but weren't able to sustain that involvement once they were past the planning stages.[41] Kathy Bailey trains CDC and CCI employees in her work for NeighborWorks America; she says that "when I get more specific with our training institute participants about what it means to do 'resident-driven' neighborhood revitalization, they realize that their programs really don't fit that definition. They are still giving far too much control to planners and other outside practitioners, at the expense of the residents and stakeholders inside the neighborhood."[42] It may be that the challenge of constantly bringing in new people, reaching out to different sectors of the neighborhood, and involving those residents in regular, routine, ongoing ways is turning out to be more difficult than CCI founders had anticipated.[43]

The experience of the Village Foundation, as well as CCIs in other places, suggests that issues of governance are bound to arise even when the official government is not in the picture. If anything, shifting from public agencies to faith-based organizations or other nonprofits will make these questions more critical and more obvious. Just like local elected officials, the directors in charge of these initiatives struggle to inform residents, gather meaningful input, and tap the potential of citizens and their organizations to help implement policy. No matter whose side you take in the classic debate between liberals and conservatives about big government versus small government, you still have to deal with questions of democracy, accountability, and power.

The Strange Career of Chuck Ridley

The fields where Chuck Ridley's grandmother and her neighbors used to cut sugarcane are no longer crawling with snakes. The South Florida development boom ran over them, obliterating the tall grass and turning their habitat into parking lots and subdivisions.

But there are still snakes in the streets of Southwest Delray. These new serpents roam through that neighborhood, tempting children and adults with a fruit that promises escape, oblivion, a way to opt out of a life that is stacked against them. While Chuck Ridley and others try to build up their community, the drug dealers—who are themselves products of isolation and hopelessness—offer a venom that, by further isolating one person from another, threatens to tear it down.

We used to treat our nation's drug problem as if it were either a war (fighting drug suppliers at home and abroad) or a disease (treating individual addicts to decrease the demand for drugs). Over the last twenty years, we have begun to realize that drug abuse also represents an institutional failure: where drugs are rampant, it means that the parents, grandparents, aunts, and uncles do not have control of the schools, street corners, police departments, and public services that demarcate their neighborhoods. Comprehensive initiatives like the Village Foundation will probably continue to proliferate, because they bring multifaceted resources to bear on multifaceted problems, and because they can connect those external resources to the internal assets of neighborhood leadership and activism. They may not succeed in the long run, however, unless they can reach out beyond those initial sets of leaders and involve all kinds of residents in meaningful, ongoing ways.

Intertwined in this development is the continuing evolution of community organizing. Projects like Community Chat will probably continue to proliferate because they are often effective for meeting one of the original goals of Saul Alinsky: giving people a chance to wield power in their neighborhoods, their communities, and their lives. Some organizers will continue to take the political system in their communities as a given; they will try valiantly to make citizens—and low-income people in particular—a force in that realm. Others will continue trying to create parallel political arenas where the range of players is much more diverse, including "powerbrokers" and poor people alike. In some places, they will be able to give citizens the opportunity to take part in governing, rather than simply influence those who govern.

The strange career of Chuck Ridley may represent a twisting, tortuous road, but that path promises to become increasingly well-trodden as people try to solve the challenges of democratic governance in low-income neighborhoods. Ridley himself will be glad of the company; though he resigned as director of the Village Foundation, he says he "did not resign as its founder." He continues to play an important role in the revitalization of Southwest Delray, serving on the board of the city's Community Redevelopment Agency and in other capacities. His neighborhood's greatest achievement, the Village Academy, seems to be thriving: test scores are rising, and the school's social service programs have been sustained under the management of other nonprofits.[44] In some ways, the school has taken over the kind of holistic role that the Village Foundation was designed to fulfill.

When Ridley thinks about how to help the young people of his neighborhood avoid drug abuse and find ways to contribute to their community, he reflects on the lessons he learned from his own experiences. "When I was on drugs, one of the things that finally got to me was that the adults I had looked up to as a kid were now afraid to come out of their houses. And I was one of the main reasons! The leaders and role models the neighborhood needed—that I still needed—were barricaded indoors because they feared me. That got me thinking about what I was doing with my life."

In the midst of Ridley's addiction, it took people like his wife and the sheriff to recognize his talents and true qualities, and that helped him change his course. What has kept him on his current path is the chance to build institutions that he could belong to and lead. In that sense, his work is not so different from that of his grandmother: he is trying to raise a neighborhood.

7

"Marrying" Schools and Communities

Endless Love or Affair to Remember?

Kelly Butler is frustrated. As the executive director of Parents for Public Schools (PPS), she spent ten years helping citizens and educators work together to improve their schools. She helped build the first PPS chapter in Jackson, Mississippi, and grew it into a national alliance that now spans twenty-six states. She has seen what can happen when parents, teachers, and administrators work together in public engagement efforts, and she is always looking for ways to formalize that relationship in the way that schools operate, but the constant courtship between schools and their communities never seems to settle into an agreeable long-term pattern. Butler feels like a prospective mother-in-law: with a mixture of hope and consternation in her voice, she asks, "Why won't they just get married?"[1]

This question is being asked, in different ways and with varying degrees of concern, in school districts all over the country. It is actually a new twist on a very old question: a long line of public thinkers, starting with Thomas Jefferson, continuing through John Dewey, have argued that citizens should be constant contributors to the great project of education. In fact, one of the distinguishing ideas in the American political tradition is that a democracy requires thriving public schools, and vice versa: public schools require a supportive democracy. Some current observers worry that our education system is no longer producing capable, responsible citizens.[2] Others argue that our education system is crumbling because citizens no longer feel that the public schools are a priority. David Mathews, president of the Kettering Foundation, worries that "Americans today seem to be halfway out the schoolhouse door." One of his books, *Is There a Public for the Public Schools?*, has become required reading for public engagement pioneers.[3]

But though these civic observers are fundamentally correct about the interdependence between democracy and the public schools, they are not telling us why democracy and our schools are changing together today. Parents and educators are being drawn toward one another, not by a mutual interest in the state of civil society, but by a range of more immediate concerns that are rooted in their daily lives. In the process, they are finding that their roles have changed: as the veil of expertise is lifted away, it is clear that educators no longer enjoy the blind faith of parents or the unquestioning support of the community. Teachers and administrators have to approach parents and other citizens on a more equal basis. In some communities, what follows is a difficult negotiation—sometimes subtle, sometimes explicit—about how to share power, responsibility, and governance between the schools and the community. Citizens and educators need each other, and they are trying to make the relationship work.

They're So Good Together

Democratic governance goes by different names in different fields, and in education, the idea that citizens and educators should work together more closely is usually called "public engagement." When the term gained prominence in the late 1980s and early 1990s, it seemed straightforward and fairly innocuous: education experts began to point out that students were more likely to succeed when their parents and other role models were closely involved in their schooling.[4] Experts like Joyce Epstein, James Comer, and Deborah Meier began to argue that schools should reach out more proactively to their communities.[5] For many schools, the first step was to foster stronger connections between parents and teachers, encourage parents to volunteer in schools, and train parents to work with students on their homework.

At first blush, most parents and educators probably didn't realize what a big step this was. The initial assumption behind public engagement seemed to be that citizens ought to play a stronger *supporting* role in education. Educators didn't intend to give parents greater influence over curricula, funding, or other school policy decisions. Once they had been invited in, however, many parents realized that they wanted more of a say in some of the core aspects of education.

Meanwhile, many school administrators began to feel pressures that forced them to open the door even further. The most basic reason was money: in many districts, superintendents and school boards faced budget shortfalls and overcrowded schools.[6] They realized, often through hard experience, that if they wanted school bonds or other funding measures to pass, they first had to strengthen the relationship with the community. To get this kind of support, some of them launched initiatives like the one in Kuna, Idaho (see Chapter 5), where they involved large numbers of people in school funding decisions, provided all the facts and figures about the financial situation, and mobilized parents and other school advocates to help get out the vote. This kind of approach led to successful bond measures in Reno, Nevada; South Kitsap, Washington; Delaware City, Ohio; and many other places.[7] The financial relationship between citizens and educators is becoming even more direct and entrenched: many school districts now rely on parents to make donations and raise outside funds even for basic needs, like textbooks.[8]

Other school districts faced controversial decisions about redistricting and desegregation. These scenarios often played out as Not In My Back-Yard (NIMBY) dilemmas: the possibility that their child's school might be closed, or that their child might be bused to a different school, brought angry parents out in droves. School leaders in cities like Decatur, Georgia, and Portsmouth, New Hampshire, organized large-scale public engagement projects in order to minimize the tensions, allow people to analyze the situation thoroughly, and decide which of the redistricting options would be most beneficial and least disruptive.

Some educators welcomed these changes. School public relations officers, who had often been at the center of battles between parents and administrators, were among the first to see public engagement as something more than a communications strategy. "If we are to realize the improvements we desire in education, we need to do *more* than ask them to support school-related projects," wrote Karen Kleinz of the National School Public Relations Association. "We need to engage the public in thinking through the challenges schools face and helping them to make decisions on how to solve them."[9]

Many school board members also saw public engagement as a way to fulfill their mission. "School board members often feel like they're caught in an awkward position between the parents and the schools," says Paul Thomas, former president of the school board in Tulsa, Oklahoma. "We run back and forth, trying to help parents understand the educators' side of things, then trying to help educators see the parents' side. Sooner or later, you realize how important it is to bring these people to the same table." The National School Boards Association and several state associations have trained local board members to do public engagement. "To build a great school system takes long term, systematic commitment to community participation," says Anne Bryant, the Association's director. In places like Westminster, Colorado, school boards are using these techniques to develop new programs for students.[10]

In the late 1990s, many districts also began to feel pressure from parents and community groups over the persistence of "achievement gaps" between the test scores of white students and students of color. This provided yet another mandate to reach out to citizens, help them understand the data, and enlist their help in boosting the achievement of students of color. The school districts in three Maryland counties—Harford, Calvert, and Montgomery—have mobilized large numbers of people to address these issues.[11]

More pressure came from state legislatures and, eventually, from Congress: new laws that set standards for schools, measured by how students fared on their standardized tests. Some of this legislation simply forced schools to provide more information to parents than ever before; other laws, such as the federal No Child Left Behind Act (2002), imposed sanctions on schools that do not make the grade.[12] Some administrators backed away from their public engagement work, claiming that the emphasis on standards forced them to focus solely on the core mission of helping students pass their tests. Others began to do more public engagement, because they saw it as a way to boost student achievement; they may also have realized that when parents are more involved, they can see for themselves how hard it is to meet the standards. In states like Rhode Island, which enacted a mandatory annual School Report Night in 1997, many administrators have used the recruitment tactics and small-group discussion techniques of democratic organizing in order to help parents process the student achievement information and understand how schools are performing.[13]

Issues of student relations and "school climate" also became rallying points for public engagement efforts. Alarmed by racial tension and segregation on campus, educators and citizens began to engage students in small-group discussions designed to address issues of race. The "Mix It Up" program is probably the largest single example; this dialogue format, developed in 2002 by the Southern Poverty Law Center and the Study Circles Resource Center, has been used at 9,000 schools to get students talking about cultural differences and other kinds of divisions.[14] Bullying has also emerged as a vital concern, partly because of incidents like the 1999 massacre at Columbine High School in Littleton, Colorado. Communities like Essex Junction, Vermont, and Portsmouth, New Hampshire, have involved parents, students, and other citizens in dealing with violence among young people.

Finally, the movement toward "school reform" in the last fifteen years has advanced public engagement in a variety of ways.[15] School reformers advocate ideas like smaller schools, stronger teamwork between educators, and more professional development for teachers. They promote public engagement partly because it has a direct effect on student success, and partly because they see it as a vehicle for mobilizing the resources and support necessary to implement other school reform ideas.

In Stillwater, Oklahoma, the school district engaged large numbers of parents in addressing key challenges to the system. One of the conclusions the participants reached in their discussions was that teachers needed more time and money for professional development. "People came in [to the sessions] saying teachers get too much money and too much time," says Brenda Bose, president of the local League of Women Voters, "and now they understand the need for more money and time." New professional development opportunities have since been put in place for Stillwater teachers.[16]

The initial proponents of public engagement and school reform tended to be education experts and other school "insiders," but in the larger cities, many community organizers now use these ideas to help their constituents change school systems from the outside. Groups like the Cross City Campaign for Urban School Reform and the Bay Area Coalition for Equitable Schools are using traditional community organizing tactics, mixed with some of the newer approaches associated with democratic governance. For example, the Logan Square Neighborhood Association in Chicago used a combination of one-on-one interviews, community meetings, and old-fashioned advocacy to get new schools built in their neighborhood.[17] Community organizers are equipping citizens to articulate their interests in the school reform debate and mobilizing them to put pressure on school administrators.

In some communities, school reform is being advanced by administrators and teachers inside the school system, as well as by parents and community organizers on the outside. A few school districts have taken advantage of this energy by adopting a two-pronged approach: internal discussions among educators on how to improve the way schools and classrooms function, along with discussions between parents and educators to gather input and figure out how the community can better support the schools. For example, student test scores in Kansas City, Kansas, rose dramatically over a five-year period as the schools implemented a district-wide restructuring called First Things First, and the local United Way mobilized thousands of citizens in the KCK Study Circles (see Chapter 2).

The attraction between citizens and educators can begin, therefore, in all kinds of ways, and lead to all kinds of benefits:

• increased funding for schools;
• less acrimony over major decisions;
• more volunteer effort to support students and provide them with enriching activities;
• less violence between students;
• greater agreement and less tension over standards and school performance;
• stronger communications and accountability between educators and citizens;
• more opportunities for school reform ideas to be proposed and embraced; and, at the most basic level,
• higher levels of student achievement.[18]

In her role as matchmaker, Kelly Butler might say that schools and communities are "so good together."

But, though public engagement gives us tantalizing glimpses of wedded bliss, in most cases it doesn't meet Butler's definition of a true marriage between schools and community. Most of these projects are temporary: they lead to worthwhile short-term gains, but they don't seem to create permanent changes in the structure and operating procedures of schools, school boards, local school councils, or parent-teacher associations (PTAs).

Citizens and educators may simply continue this intermittent romance, coming together only when they need one another for a specific reason. However, as in most love affairs, the longer these people work together, the more they are confronted with long-term questions about what they mean to each other. Citizens who have been involved in one major decision will wonder if they are going to be consulted on the next one; educators who receive new community resources need to know if they can plan on receiving more in the future; both sides wonder who is ultimately in charge of the public schools. It may be that if you keep doing public engagement, sooner or later you have to decide whether to get engaged.

Educators Court Citizens: Inglewood, California

When McKinley Nash became superintendent of the Inglewood Unified School District in 1994, he knew he had inherited a challenging job. Inglewood is a first-tier suburb of Los Angeles, and several of the schools sit under the flight paths for the Los Angeles International Airport. The district was dealing with low test scores, deteriorating school buildings, and frequent violence between Latino and African American students.[19]

Any one of these problems might have merited some kind of public engagement effort, but Nash knew he wanted to engage parents in a way that could address all of them. In a previous job he had instituted "Quality Circles," a process used in business to help employees give input to managers. In this approach, teachers, administrators, and staff would meet regularly to discuss problems and come up with solutions.[20] Nash envisioned his public engagement program as a way to bring the principles of quality circles to bear in engaging parents and other community members.

One of the primary assets Nash had at his disposal was a network of community liaisons in the district. Each Inglewood school has a community liaison who is responsible for helping educators work together with Parent Teacher Associations and other parent groups and community organizations. Nash asked the community liaisons to organize at least one series of democratic small-group meetings at each school. Over 700 parents took part in multiple-session meetings at twenty Inglewood schools in late 1997 and early 1998.

The educators quickly noticed that the discussions seemed to help improve relations between Hispanic and African American parents. Inglewood's students are roughly 60 percent Hispanic and 40 percent African American, and the schools had experienced violence between the two groups almost every year on *Cinco de Mayo*. "Before, there was not much interaction between Hispanic and African American parents," said one of the community liaisons. "The cultural sharing that happened during the process at my school helped form more positive relationships, and I can see that now in all the activities we do."[21]

The schools gained credibility by following through on many of the recommendations made by the parents and community members. At one school, parents suggested that the principal needed an assistant; Nash gave the approval to hire a new staff member who serves as a "teacher coach" and coordinator. At the same school, participants recommended a new team teaching strategy for the fifth and sixth grade classes; the strategy has since been implemented.

The level of parent involvement also rose in the immediate aftermath of the project. Participation in PTA meetings, donations to schools, and volunteer participation at schools all increased.[22] At Daniel Freeman Elementary, participants made a formal pledge to help implement all the action ideas they generated. Parents at Oak Street Elementary donated their time to programs for gifted students, after-school tutoring, and community service opportunities for high school students. After-school programs and activities for parents (such as English as a Second Language classes and computer courses) were also implemented.

Some of the community liaisons concluded that they needed be more aware of parents' schedules than they had in the past. One liaison realized that the parents at her school work long hours and many different shifts. When she enlisted parents' help in painting school buildings, she asked one set of parents to do the preparation for painting so that another group could finish the job. Many parents volunteered their time for cleaning school facilities and taking care of the shrubbery and school gardens.

In other school districts, many educators have reservations about this kind of volunteerism: some worry that school maintenance work done by volunteers may not meet health and safety codes, while others are concerned that parents' willingness to help out might actually weaken the bargaining position of school employee unions. Whenever citizens take on tasks that would normally be done by employees of the school district, it raises these kinds of questions about the role of professionals vs. amateurs. In Inglewood, the community liaisons—a rarity in most districts—probably helped address this question, since they could ease the concerns of educators and provide some supervision for volunteers.

As Nash had hoped, the public engagement work helped parents see the need for greater resources at the district level. For some time, the Inglewood schools had been experiencing a shortage of funds for capital improvements. In many schools, the roofs leaked, asbestos was still present, and space was so limited that libraries and staff rooms had been converted into classrooms. The participants in the small-group sessions gave substantial input on what improvements should be made. They rallied behind a proposed $131 million school bond, called "Measure K." Parents and students volunteered time at the campaign headquarters, created phone trees, sent out mass mailings, and set up various means of outreach to educate others about the measure. Measure K passed with 88 percent of the vote.

Inglewood's public engagement work, and the stronger parent-teacher communication it has fostered, may also have played a role in the academic achievement of students. At the same time that he was reaching out to the community, Nash rolled out a set of ambitious elementary school reforms based on the practices employed at the two best schools in his district. The reforms featured "an intense focus on basic reading skills, constant testing to detect students who fall behind, and relentless teacher training."[23] By 2000, the Inglewood schools were getting national recognition for elementary students who excelled on standardized reading and math tests. "The city's elementary schools . . . are filled with poor students who qualify for free lunches and who learn English as their second language," reported the *Los Angeles Times*. "Yet they have leaped to the top ranks of California's new Academic Performance Index, defying the rule that equates poverty and minority status with low achievement in the classroom."[24]

Tragically, McKinley Nash did not live to witness all of these achievements: he died of a heart attack in 1998, at age 65. With Nash's passing, the impetus for public engagement in Inglewood began to fade. There have been no major district-wide efforts to recruit parents and other citizens in the last few years, despite the fact that the school system still faces a number of challenges—including poor test scores at the high school level—that the community could address. It is harder to tell what the long-term impacts are at the school level, but it appears that while some community liaisons continue to enjoy strong relationships with some parents, they do not involve parents with the same regularity and intensity that they did under Nash's tenure. At most schools, participation in PTA meetings and other school activities has dropped.[25] Citizens and educators in Inglewood have won some great victories by working together, but they don't seem to have formalized or sustained their partnership.

Citizens Court Educators: Winston-Salem, North Carolina

There are some key questions that will have to be answered in order for Inglewood, or any other community, to embed public engagement into the way that the schools function. Some of these questions are apparent in Winston-Salem, North Carolina, a city of 153,000 in the western half of the state.

The Winston-Salem case also shows that not all major public engagement efforts are initiated by educators.[26] It isn't easy for groups outside the school system to create this kind of community focus on education: sometimes it takes a real crisis, like a high-profile lawsuit or the takeover of a district by a legislature. But some community groups have been able to initiate meaningful, far-reaching public engagement efforts even when a crisis is not apparent. Some of these organizations are community-organizing groups that have a track record on other kinds of issues. Others are parent associations, like the ones belonging to the Parents for Public Schools network. Still others are Local Education Funds, nonprofit community organizations that assist and promote the public schools but are independent from them.[27] The Winston-Salem project was led by an LEF called the Community Alliance for Education in Forsyth County.

In most cases, LEFs play an "outsider" role in education: convening stakeholders, raising money, gathering data, and enlisting volunteers. Some LEF leaders have become frustrated with the limitations of their work; they recognize that teachers, administrators, and other education "insiders" still monopolize the key tasks of meeting student needs, raising the quality of teaching, and establishing an environment conducive to learning. So they turn to public engagement as a way to help insiders and outsiders work together more effectively.

This is what happened in Winston-Salem, where the Community Alliance mobilized hundreds of parents, educators, and other citizens in 2003. Four main action teams, all staffed by volunteers, emerged from those discussions: communications, school board, school climate, and teacher recruitment and retention. "From the beginning of this project, we saw ourselves as a bridge between the community and the schools," says Amber Brooks-Norman, who coordinated the public engagement campaign for the Alliance. "We wanted the schools to understand better what people wanted them to do, but we didn't just want to present a laundry list of recommendations for educators to try to implement."[28]

When they began planning the effort in 2002, the Community Alliance board decided that they wanted to recruit large numbers of people representing many different viewpoints and backgrounds. They also felt that the participants would need plenty of time in small-group discussions in order to fully understand the issues, develop sound action plans, and feel empowered to help implement them. By reaching out through various community networks, the Alliance recruited a diverse turnout of 220 people. After the small-group sessions ended, participants attended an action forum where they shared their conclusions and formed teams to work on particular solutions.

Many of the participants in the small-group discussions noted the rifts between students of different racial and ethnic backgrounds. A "school climate action team" was formed at the action forum to address this challenge. The team organized a Mix It Up dialogue project on two high school campuses in which over 600 students joined in small-group discussions on issues of race, diversity, and other social boundaries.

As they talked about issues on campus, the students learned about each other and formed new relationships. They also came up with recommendations for improving the atmosphere in schools that they asked administrators to implement. In this process, students assumed some of the rights and responsibilities of adult citizens. Students, parents, and educators must now consider how they may be redefining the role of young people in school decision-making.

Another action team was formed to tackle issues of trust and communications between schools and community. That team conducted a major survey on parent-school relations, with the assistance of public administration graduate students at Wake Forest. The survey found that parents of younger children were more trusting of the school system, and that parents felt that the information they received directly from teachers was more credible than other kinds of information coming from the schools. It also showed that distrust correlated with income level, so that parents of higher incomes were less trusting of the system and school board.

The team has since focused on a project that will provide training for parents to work with educators. "They want parents to feel like 'the system belongs to you' and 'you have a role in it,' " says Brooks-Norman.[29] One of the featured events is a full-day workshop entitled "No Parent Left Behind." Winston-Salem's PTA Council, which is a partner in this initiative, sees it as a way to broaden the PTA's role as a catalyst for getting parents involved in school governance. "So many PTAs are stuck in the mode of simply holding the annual book fair, the carnival, the candy bar fundraiser—they aren't helping parents become better advocates for their children," says Nancy Griffith, the director of the Community Alliance.[30]

This is a challenge for many communities: PTAs and other similar groups are viewed as the primary venue for parent-teacher collaboration, and yet most of them aren't very effective at recruiting parents or giving them a chance to be heard. In Inglewood, the PTAs alone were unable to sustain the momentum of the public engagement efforts there; by working with the PTAs, the communications action team in Winston-Salem hopes to create more inclusive, participatory, powerful structures for parents.

The third action team to emerge from the forum focused on teacher recruitment and retention. That team discovered that, while Winston-Salem has three different universities with degree programs for prospective teachers, the three programs didn't seem to be working together at all. The team has helped the colleges collaborate on a scholarship program, called the Forsyth Futures Fund, that would allow some teachers to go back to school and help recruit new teachers who are currently in college. New teachers would make a commitment to teach for several years in Winston-Salem in return for their scholarships. As part of the fundraising campaign for this program, the action team is asking every family in Forsyth County to contribute one dollar to the fund.

By helping recruit teachers and support their development, citizens on this action team have assumed a more active role in improving the quality of instruction. This is the kind of task that would normally be done by employees of the school district. So far, their help has been welcomed by school administrators—but if volunteers continue to take on more tasks that would normally be done by school employees, citizens and educators will have to continually renegotiate their respective roles in the system.

Finally, a school board action team was formed to examine the board elections process and research the possibility of shifting from a partisan to a nonpartisan board. The team found that Winston-Salem is one of only three school districts in the state where school board candidates must identify their party when running for election. Making the elections nonpartisan would require a vote by the legislature, so the team began interviewing school board members and state legislators about the proposed change. The team is also working on a recruitment drive for prospective board candidates and developing a training program for new board members.

The nonpartisan elections proposal points out the questions of accountability that often arise from public engagement efforts. It is hard for public officials to decide how much weight to give this kind of policy recommendation. The Winston-Salem action team received no official charge from government; its power depended on whether it included a broad array of people and whether it represented the ideas of an even larger and more diverse group (the participants in the project as a whole). Perhaps the team also gained credence from the time they spent in a structured, deliberative process, which forced them to do their research and examine a number of different viewpoints as they developed their recommendation.

Public officials in Winston-Salem didn't think the school board action team had passed these tests. They showed no support for the nonpartisan election proposal; critics claimed this was because the current school board had a Republican majority, and the local delegation of state legislators, which was also primarily Republican, wanted it to stay that way. The election proposal was just one idea among the many that emerged from the Winston-Salem discussions, but it showed that decision-makers don't always feel accountable to participants in a public engagement effort—especially if the officials weren't involved in setting up the project in the first place. In order for the Winston-Salem school board to support the nonpartisanship proposal, the action team would probably have needed the strong support of a much larger number of people—in other words, enough voters to sway an election.

The four Winston-Salem teams receive some logistical support from the Community Alliance, but they are fueled by volunteer energy; they are also maximizing resources by developing collaborative projects with universities, PTAs, and other local leaders. Once they have accomplished their goals, however, the teams are likely to disband. It is also unclear whether the Community Alliance can continue mobilizing large numbers of people in small-group discussions and action forums. "We knew going in that this would be a very labor-intensive project, and we were right," says Katy Harriger, a Wake Forest political scientist who is the Board Chair for the Alliance.[31]

Even if the Community Alliance can continue this work, simply repeating what they have done before may have some limitations. The discussions so far have dealt with district-wide priorities and concerns; to attract more participants and make a greater impact on what happens inside the classroom, the project will need to focus more on the building level, so that parents and other citizens are working more closely with educators at each school. This may lead to yet more complications down the road: if people identify more and more with their own school, it may become harder to maintain strong connections between different schools. Parents and teachers may lose their sense of the "big picture," their opportunities to meet with people who are culturally different from themselves, and their sense that they are part of a much larger effort with the potential to create lasting change. Public engagement is difficult to maintain; it may be even harder to control.

The Winston-Salem experience shows how the developing relationship between citizens and educators leads to long-term questions about accountability, the role of students, the structure of parent organizations, and the interaction between professionals and amateurs. These are tough questions, but the fact that they are considering such interesting dilemmas is probably a good sign. "We have stayed true to our original vision," says Amber Brooks-Norman, "but we have grown up in our awareness of what it takes to achieve that mission." [32]

Opposites Attract—But Can They Live Together?

The political scientist Clarence Stone argues that communities need a high degree of "civic capacity" to advance school reform and improve the quality of education. The public engagement efforts in Inglewood and Winston-Salem demonstrate the possibilities and difficulties implicit in this concept. "Reform never comes from people who are engaged in running routine operations," Stone claims. "It comes, instead, only when [people] acknowledge that they have a problem in need of the attention of the community as a civic body." This kind of civic capacity cannot be achieved simply by creating school-business partnerships or blue-ribbon panels of local leaders: it requires the kind of chemistry between citizens and educators that only occurs when large numbers of people sit down to air their concerns and propose new solutions. "The highest levels of civic capacity," says Stone, "rest on an ability to engage not just an array of strategic elites but also a broad base of ordinary participants."[33]

What makes this civic chemistry so difficult to generate—and even harder to sustain—is that citizens and educators tend to have such different motivations, assumptions, and styles. The culture clash between them is apparent in two main ways:

1. Citizens and educators have differing responsibilities. Whenever they work together, they are making a commitment to each other, but they are also accountable to others outside the room. Administrators, teachers and other school personnel must report to their superintendents, principals, or other supervisors; they may also have to maintain good relations with school board members and union presidents. Educators involved in public engagement must be conscious of how their efforts are perceived by other players in school politics, and have to answer skeptics who charge that working with parents simply creates unwanted interference and unrealistic expectations. Parents and other citizens who do public engagement usually have more room to maneuver, but they still have to be aware of how their involvement with the schools is perceived by others in the community.

   Educators and citizens therefore have different fears about what can go wrong in a public engagement project. Educators may worry that they are "over promising"—that the project itself may require more resources than the school system can provide, or that the action ideas that emerge from the discussions may simply be unrealistic. Citizens may worry that they are being co-opted—that the "powers that be" in the school district will not actually be listening to what the community has to say, and that no tangible changes will occur as a result of the project.

2. Citizens and educators adopt different standards of behavior in the way they work. When approaching a community organization, educators are more likely to consider the chain of command in that group, and make formal requests to the president or director. Having received a commitment of some kind, educators will then avoid "poking their noses in" to find out how the community group will fulfill its promise. Parents and other citizens may take a different approach, especially if they have years of experience as volunteers or activists: asking for help from whatever contact they have at the organization, and then checking in constantly to see that the group understands the request and is able to deliver on its commitment.

This divergence in styles is sometimes even evident in the way people talk. Educators are more likely to choose their words carefully, to qualify their statements, and to give credit to others. Parents and other community members are more likely to talk brashly, to "vent" about their concerns, and to describe their knowledge and connections as a way of establishing their credibility.

In many ways, these differences are typical of a situation where one set of people feels more powerless and less legitimate than the other. Educators have the official status given to them by their profession and their position as employees of the school system. They may not exactly feel powerful, but they have a more defined, legitimate, and authoritative role in the education of young people. They are conscious of their membership within an institution, and they act accordingly when they come into contact with other institutions. Citizens are aware that they stand outside the educational institution, so they are less comfortable playing by institutional rules. Their attitudes, their speech, and their styles of working reflect their sense of comparative powerlessness.[34]

Jeff Kimpton, who directed a major study on public engagement for the Annenberg Institute for School Reform, claims that these overtones of power fade as educators and citizens build trust, help each other, and work together on shared concerns. "In successful engagement," Kimpton writes, "the word 'power' is replaced with responsibility and accountability."[35] This claim seems credible, at least in the short term: in Winston-Salem, Inglewood, and many other places, the citizens and educators most involved in public engagement efforts seem to feel a greater sense of legitimacy and a greater awareness of their civic responsibilities. Some citizens and some educators will probably remain "married" forever after. But for others, the feeling of power and purpose begins to ebb after the most immediate goals have been accomplished.

The negotiation about power, accountability, and responsibility lies behind the other long-term questions about the citizen-educator relationship. Perhaps this would be the central, defining characteristic in any "marriage" between schools and community: large numbers of parents and other citizens would feel that they had an official, meaningful, legitimate role in their educational institutions.

School Councils: True Love or Shotgun Wedding?

In a few cases, the same pressures driving public engagement have led to official changes in the power relationship between citizens and educators.

In Chicago, Illinois; Plainfield, New Jersey; and at Hudson High School in Hudson, Massachusetts, public engagement has been formalized and institutionalized—but in three very different ways.

The most prominent example is Chicago, which instituted a district-wide system of local school councils in 1988. The Chicago schools had hit rock bottom after a lengthy teachers' strike and a long period of dismal test scores. Significant forces outside the school district, including political figures like Mayor Harold Washington and community organizations like Parents United for Responsible Education (PURE) and Designs for Change, mobilized broad support for a radical restructuring of the school system. The Illinois legislature obliged them by passing the Chicago School Reform Act, which took many school operating decisions away from the school board and handed them over to a newly established system of local school councils. Each council consists of six parents, two teachers, two community representatives, and the principal; other than the principal, the council members are elected by the citizens of that school's catchment area. The high school councils also have one nonvoting student member. The councils have the ability to hire and fire their principals, develop annual school improvement plans, and oversee school budgets. Other school districts use similar kinds of "site-based management," but many of them put non-educators in an advisory role or place major limitations on their authority.[36] Every year, the 5,000 Chicago residents who serve on the 560 councils wield a significant degree of power over school finances and personnel.

A 2002 study showed that most of the councils are viable, active, responsible organizations. Some skeptics worried that the groups would infringe on the professional autonomy of teachers and principals, but there seems to have been little tension between the educators and non-educators on most of the councils. (However, the relationship between the councils and school officials at the district office has often been rocky.)[37] Archon Fung, a Harvard public policy professor who has studied the Chicago schools, argues that this kind of "regular and structured" setup can create "channels of accountability" in which citizens monitor educators "and press them to do their jobs." In this respect, the Chicago system—precisely because it is a system and not just a temporary engagement effort—may be more effective than the Inglewood and Winston-Salem projects.[38]

But while the total number of people serving on the Chicago school councils is impressive, that is partly because Chicago is such a large city. Each council enjoys a great deal of authority over its school, but ten people is a small sliver of that school's community, and most of the councils don't seem to involve large numbers of other parents and residents. Council members are given training in budgeting, planning, principal selection, and group process techniques, but not in public engagement. This lack of a broader base of support seems to be emerging as a major weakness of the system. The first danger sign is that fewer people want to serve on the councils: in 1989, there were three times as many candidates as there were council seats, but by 2002, almost half of the seats could not be filled. Some observers blame the district, which has cut back the funds for recruitment and support of school council members.[39]

Student test scores have improved in Chicago, but the system still has many failing schools. The district is now in the midst of another major restructuring, a move toward smaller schools that will result in the closure of sixty schools and the opening of 100 new ones.[40] About a third of the new schools will be run by the district; the rest will be charter or contract schools run by independent organizations. It is not clear how many of the new schools will have local school councils, a fact that has prompted a great deal of criticism from the city's current school council members.

Archon Fung writes that "participatory democratic forms can easily be subverted by haughty officials or powerful, narrow interests when people fail to participate effectively because they are unaware, unequipped, or un-mobilized."[41] Some Chicagoans claim that the new restructuring is the work of haughty officials; others argue that if the school councils had reached more people, the district would have improved to such an extent that the re-structuring would be unnecessary. In either case, the fact that the new plan is being put into place over the objections of the councils may be a sign that they lack the broad base—and therefore, the political power—to survive in Chicago politics.

One reason for this weakness may be the way in which the local school councils were created. The system was not the product of negotiations be-tween citizens and educators: it was enacted by the legislature in an at-mosphere of great tension. This "shotgun wedding" created a permanent framework that guaranteed representation for parents, but it didn't encour-age or prepare parent leaders or school administrators to involve larger numbers of people. Like other purely "republican" systems, it is heavy on structure but light on the democratic elements of recruitment and group process. It is probably much better than having no public engagement at all, but the learning, brainstorming, and support are restricted to a relatively small circle of people at each school. In that sense, it is still a very limited kind of partnership.

Hudson High School, in Hudson, Massachusetts, has established another kind of formal relationship: an extensive system of student self-governance. Hudson is just outside Worcester; the high school's enrollment is roughly 1,000 students. The district's superintendent, Sheldon Berman, was one of the founders of Educators for Social Responsibility, and he came to Hudson with a strong commitment to civic education. Berman argues that "public education serves a larger civic mission . . . to preserve democracy," and yet in most high schools, the only preparation for adult citizenship comes from dry civics classes and superficial student governments.[42] In order to produce better citizens, Hudson High reorganized its ninth and tenth grade curricula to focus on civic judgment and education. The school has adopted a systemic approach to "service learning"—the idea that students learn best when their lessons take place in the real world. Hudson chemistry teachers help students test water quality of local streams; social studies classes host multicultural events; students in technology classes teach senior citizens how to use computers.

The most unusual aspect of the Hudson system is the creation of school "clusters," which are the major governance units in the school. Each cluster meets one hour a week to discuss school issues, develop new service learning projects, and make recommendations on how to improve the school. Under the new school constitution developed by students and teachers, recommendations made by the clusters are given to the "community council," an elected body of students and educators. "Students have recommended changes in our food service program, the parking policy, the attendance policy, the dress code, and the strategies we use to integrate students from other countries into Hudson," says Berman. If the principal chooses to veto a recommendation that has been approved by the community council, the issue is referred to a "board of conciliation" consisting of the superintendent, a school board member, and an individual selected by the council.[43]

Since the Hudson system was implemented, Berman and his colleagues have learned some lessons about how to make it work better. First, they realized that the younger students needed more preparation in order to feel comfortable in the decision-making roles. They've changed the curriculum to give eighth and ninth graders a better foundation. Second, both students and educators recognized that self-governance is not just a nice privilege, but difficult work as well: they now receive course credits, and are graded on a pass-fail basis, for their participation in the clusters. Just like the participants in so many other kinds of civic experiments, the Hudson students felt that their time and effort should be valued and legitimized by the school.

The Hudson High School experience does not represent public engagement as most schools practice it, since parents and other community members aren't part of the process. In that sense, it is an even more limited partnership than the one in Chicago. However, the service learning projects generated by Hudson students are having an impact on the community in addition to enriching their education. Plus, the students themselves may be considered a kind of bridge between educators and citizens, one that more school districts should recognize. Within the school, the system combines elements of both republican structure and democratic strategy.

Collective Responsibility in Plainfield

Perhaps the next step beyond public engagement is some kind of contractual obligation between citizens and educators; if so, then Plainfield, New Jersey may represent the future of public schools. The district's official Accountability Plan certainly reads like a marriage license: it describes how the commitments between parents, teachers, and administrators are embodied in the Leadership, Innovation and Change Councils (LINCCs) which govern each of the thirteen schools in this city of 48,000. The plan lays out goals for each school, not just in areas like student achievement and teacher certification, but in community engagement and governance too; these include quantified benchmarks like attendance at school meetings and percentage of parents regularly engaged in school activities. Just in case the reader fails to grasp the central point of the document, "Accountability = Collective Responsibility" is emblazoned at the bottom of each page.[44]

Perhaps the district is so explicit about the terms of the school-community contract because of the hard work, commitment, and shared pain it took to create it. On Larry Leverett's first day as superintendent in 1995, he walked into a student protest over insufficient recognition of Black History Month. Leverett was beset by complaints over the district's low test scores, high dropout rate, and high turnover in administrative positions. "Many people were tired of being shut out," Leverett wrote, "and wanted to make sure that the 'new kid on the block' got that message right from the start. . . . All of them insisted on a better partnership between the schools and community and wanted change immediately." Leverett made the discussion even more painful—but also more open—by disclosing a great deal of information that had previously been withheld from the public, including the district's financial difficulties and weaknesses in the physical infrastructure. "Telling the truth drew a lot of heat from inside the district," says Leverett, but "full disclosure was an important early step in establishing credibility [with the] community."[45]

At the same time, the district began convening small-group dialogues with parents and other community members. Administrators and representatives from the school unions went through conflict resolution training together, and the unions became full partners in the public engagement process. Nearly 250 people took part in a planning effort that led to Plainfield's Blueprint for Educational Excellence in 1996. Many others now serve on the LINCCs, each of which includes the principal, parents, teachers, support staff, family members, community members, and (in the high school) students. There is also a district-level LINCC that connects the school councils and helps to formulate district policy.

Leverett and his allies have experimented with many different formats for public engagement over the years, including small-group discussions on standards and school finances, and issue forums on topics such as social promotion, the board's policy on school uniforms, and the development of the district's budget. They have learned the value of structure and training in this work, developing their own "toolkit" of meeting formats, facilitation approaches, and decision-making techniques. They also constantly use language that reinforces the idea that parents have a powerful role in the system: even the training seminars for parents are called "Saturday Parent Power Conferences."[46]

Plainfield's approach seems to have paid off in a number of ways. Student attendance and parent participation in school events have both risen. Action teams of citizens and educators have established a Local Education Foundation, and designed a district report card that is now part of the accountability system.[47] Existing youth programs in the community were strengthened and connected more closely with the schools; a collaborative of social service agencies, called the Plainfield Coalition, was formed. The unions and the school district have agreed quickly on new contracts. Community members have also participated in the expansion of comprehensive after-school programs to encompass all of the district's schools. Voters passed a $34 million referendum to build new schools, renovate others, and connect every classroom to the Internet. When the state took away $12 million in aid, citizens organized rallies, letter-writing campaigns, and other lobbying efforts until the legislature restored the funds.[48]

The stronger relationship between citizens and educators in Plainfield was forged in a period of intensive public engagement, and that seems to show in the city's school-community contract. From the first dialogues convened in 1995, it was apparent that parents and other community members were capable of more than just a supporting role in education. The Plainfield system gives citizens a wider range of opportunities—volunteers, political advocates, decision-makers—than in most other school districts. Some education experts refer to this kind of shift as a "distribution of leadership."[49] There has been a similar distribution of leadership within the ranks of Plainfield's school employees: as they adapted to working more closely with the public, Leverett and his colleagues adopted a flatter, less hierarchical, more decentralized staff structure.

The Plainfield experience seems to back up Jeff Kimpton's claim that successful engagement leads to changes in power dynamics. Leverett refers to it as "a shift from the power and control paradigm to one that concentrates on aligning the culture around a set of normative beliefs, attitudes, expectations, and actions."[50] Rather than treating the school district as a static institution which the superintendent, school board, and parent groups all struggle to control, Plainfield is struggling to create an institution in which all those players—and, even more importantly, parents and community members—have legitimate, productive roles. In their republican structures, their democratic strategies, and their language about collective responsibility, Plainfield citizens and educators seem to have established a new kind of bond.

Get Me to the Church on Time

Whether they are temporary projects like the ones in Inglewood and Winston-Salem, or permanent systems like the ones in Chicago, Hudson, and Plainfield, public engagement efforts demonstrate the willingness and capacity of citizens to examine thorny school issues and implement solutions. The result is an arrangement that seems to work for both sides: parents and other community members devote their time and energy to solving school problems, and educators give them a greater say over school policies in return.

This may be the beginning of a long and beautiful friendship—but it also could be nothing more than a series of affairs, producing beneficial short-term outcomes but stopping short of fundamental long-term changes. The short-term attitude may just be too entrenched in the system: school administrators move quickly from one job to the next, jaded teachers wait for the next set of reform ideas to come and go, parents scan the real estate ads for homes in other school districts. With the lure of a better job or a better school always around the corner, many citizens and educators may not have the stomach to stick together and try to work things out.

Eventually, citizens and educators may get tired of their mutual unwillingness to commit, and public engagement itself will begin to get a bad name. Parents will become even more convinced that teachers and administrators don't want to listen to them; teachers and administrators will become even more convinced that parents only want to complain.

In order to avoid this scenario, citizens and educators need to think through the implications of their new civic experiments. The most basic lesson is that, in order for the partnership to last, people on both sides need to feel that their contributions to education are critical, meaningful, and welcomed.

Having established that basic level of trust and understanding, citizens and educators will have to negotiate a number of points if they want to develop a durable school-community contract:

- They will have to develop a system for accountability at the district level, so they can make policy decisions efficiently and so everyone feels that their input is being considered in a meaningful way.
- They will have to decide whether, and how, students should be involved in school governance.
- They will have to create a consistent framework for decision-making at the school and classroom level, so that parents, teachers, and others know how they can have an impact on the way students are educated.
- They will have to coordinate the work of education professionals and enthusiastic volunteers, so that they avoid replication or competition.
- They will have to ensure that local school councils, parent-teacher associations, and other education-related groups are run in ways that are participatory, efficient, and compelling to all kinds of people.

As more citizens and educators decide how to share governance of the schools, they may also begin to connect their work more directly to the governance of the community as a whole. The KCK Study Circles (Chapter 2) allow citizens to address a range of priorities, including but not limited to education; participants in Inglewood and Winston-Salem have branched out into race relations and other issues. Increasingly, schools may become hubs for all kinds of community activities and problem-solving efforts, like the Village Academy in Delray Beach (Chapter 6). Schools may become a vital component of our democratic infrastructure, focal points for decision-making and action on many different issues. This is a development that would warm the hearts of civic observers like David Mathews and Clarence Stone—and the challenges and complications inherent in this shift would give their successors plenty to think about.

Wherever it leads, the trend toward shared governance in education is dependent on the promising, uncertain, complex relationship between citizens and educators. Committing to one another requires fundamental changes by both parties, including sacrifices and adaptations that may feel uncomfortable, at least at first. This is a leap of faith for everyone involved, and it will only happen in situations where people trust one another, have some history of shared work together, and know how to communicate productively. But by sharing school governance, citizens and educators can help fulfill the dream of democratic education advanced by Jefferson, Dewey, and other visionaries. In other words, they will be doing what compassionate, responsible, farsighted adults ought to be doing: helping their children succeed.

8
Sharing the Buck
Communities Rethink Public Finances and Public Responsibilities

Judging by the opinion polls, you would never guess that the residents of Lakewood, Colorado, are questioning the role of government in the modern world. Surveys show that they are overwhelmingly enthusiastic about their elected representatives and city employees. Lakewood residents have a strong sense of public safety, they value the public services they receive, and they are excited about the new downtown rising up in their midst (see Chapter 3). Going by the survey results, you might think that Lakewood is some kind of first-tier suburban utopia.[1]

The public finances of Lakewood, however, have reached a crisis point, partly because city residents have voted down sales tax increases on every occasion since 1971. These ballot measures were not proposed for major new expenditures; they were intended only to offset the declining tax revenues from a sagging retail market, and to support the current level of government services and operations. Without the ability to maintain revenue, the city has endured years of cutbacks, laying off key personnel and terminating popular programs. Lakewood now has the lowest level of tax revenues per capita in the Denver region, despite the fact that it rates higher in citizen satisfaction than almost all of the neighboring communities. In 2005, as the city council prepared to put yet another sales tax increase on the ballot, Lakewood seemed to be the utopia no one wanted to pay for.

Lakewood's predicament is actually quite typical. Many other cities have experienced a similar disparity, with residents who speak highly of local government performance and yet are unwilling to reward and maintain that performance with their tax contributions. Officials are left with few options: if they make cuts in municipal services, citizens ask why the streets weren't plowed or the trash picked up. Officials may also try temporary fixes like deferred capital maintenance, freezes on hiring and salaries, or shuffling money between funds or departments.[2] Eventually, however, the gap between revenues and expenses grows so large that it cannot be concealed or ignored.

These financial crises in local government are often blamed on the state of the economy, wasteful public officials, or declining aid from state and federal governments. But while those factors cannot be discounted, they also obscure a more significant trend: our sense of who is responsible, and who pays, for the public welfare is now in question. Since the Progressive Era a century ago, we have assumed that the role of government is to provide services, and the role of citizens is to pay taxes for those services. That way of thinking may no longer apply in most places.[3]

No wonder that even our best city managers are hard-pressed to keep their administrations afloat. Public management schools still train them to believe that the main criteria for good government are openness and efficiency, and yet it is increasingly apparent that those Progressive Era values will not ensure citizen support. Lakewood's government is open and efficient, but that isn't enough; people just aren't sure what they want out of government anymore.

Faced with budget shortfalls, public demand for services, and pressing issues like crime prevention, housing, and roads, city managers and other local officials are trying many new approaches—most of which blur the lines between citizens and government. Like the community organizers described in Chapter 6 and the educators of Chapter 7, local officials are trying to build structures for shared governance that will allow citizens and practitioners to work together productively. Like the residents of Lakewood, they are rethinking the connection between public finance and public responsibilities.

They are three main ways in which city managers and other local officials are approaching this work:

1. Participatory budgeting. Some public officials are inviting residents to take a stronger role in the budgeting process, engaging them in public meetings that help people assess the financial picture and decide for themselves how tax revenues should be spent. "To successfully market a budget, a local government must move from monologue to dialogue," says Frank Benest, a former city manager. "That means including the public in the budget process before the actual document is formally adopted."[4] Sometimes the focus is on one particular project, proposed initiative, or section of the budget, and the question to the public is whether this expenditure is necessary, and if so, how it should be managed. In a few other cases, officials have asked citizens to address the local budget in its entirety, and make recommendations about how to balance different priorities.

2. Sharing problem-solving roles with citizens. The second strategy is to involve citizens in doing some of the public work themselves. This is already a common practice in education; it is also becoming a routine part of crime prevention, because residents interact with police officers more frequently than other public employees, and because the effectiveness of citizens in reducing crime is a well-established idea. But in the last decade, governments are relying on citizens to donate their time and effort on a much broader array of public priorities. Residents are doing more than just building playgrounds and painting murals: they are analyzing the quality of drinking water, monitoring court proceedings, and growing produce to feed low-income households. Much of the work to clean up and conserve our streams and rivers has been done by unpaid volunteers, and volunteer ham radio operators are now a vital link in disaster preparedness plans.[5]

3. Neighborhood councils. The third approach is to establish new institutions at the neighborhood level that involve people regularly in planning, decision-making, and action. Examples include the Strong Neighborhoods Initiative in San José (Chapter 3) and the neighborhood associations in Springfield (Chapter 4). These "neighborhood councils," "priority boards," or "strong neighborhood committees" take different forms in different places, but most of them are intended to place a greater share of public resources under the control of neighborhood residents. Some of these systems also give residents an official voice in citywide budget and policy decisions, and some of them encourage citizens to contribute their own time and energy to solving local problems. Because they are more than just temporary exercises, and because they allow people to tackle many different issues, these structures represent a more comprehensive approach to citizen-government collaboration.

All three of these strategies represent new answers to the question of what residents and public employees want from one another. They treat volunteer efforts, the work of public agencies, and collaborations with other groups as different elements of a community's problem-solving capacity. They ask what "we" the community want to do—what problems we want to solve, what services we want to provide—and how "we" are going to pay for, support, and work toward these priorities. This is a new kind of deal: citizens give their consent, their support, and their volunteer time to public activities, in return for the chance to help direct them.

Though this arrangement seems to work for both citizens and government, it isn't clear whether either side will be able to hold up its end of the bargain. Local governments are designed for implementation, not collaboration. In most places, their hierarchical structures aren't flat or flexible enough to respond quickly to people outside city hall. Meanwhile, neighborhood councils and other kinds of citizen organizations tend to be under funded and understaffed. Many of them fail to mobilize large numbers of residents, and they usually aren't able to focus citizen effort and enthusiasm for more than short bursts of time. This imbalance is the major challenge facing shared governance in city administration: governmental institutions are too entrenched, citizen institutions not entrenched enough.

"Communities are Smarter"

These days, local officials facing unworkable budgets and uncertain futures often turn to Ed Weeks, a professor in the public policy school at the University of Oregon. Weeks has become a kind of guru for people interested in adopting a "participatory budgeting" process. Over the last fifteen years, he has helped local governments involve large numbers of people in developing popular, realistic, balanced city budgets. His mantra is simple: "People are smart. Communities are smarter."[6]

Though he is a large, shaggy bear of a man, the unassuming Weeks often melts into the background—until you get him talking about one of the communities he has worked with. His first attempt to implement participatory budgeting was in the city where he lives: Eugene, Oregon, a university town of 125,000 people. In 1991, city finances were complicated by rising health and pension costs, a weak economy, and state ballot measures that capped local property taxes. Confronted with an $8 million budget shortfall, the city used some conventional citizen involvement tools—meetings with stakeholders, opinion polls, a town hall meeting, and a questionnaire that was printed in the newspaper—and got some unhelpful results: instead of recommending ways to balance the budget, respondents asked local government to provide more funding for libraries, police, and social services, all without raising new revenues.[7]

Back at the drawing board, the city council turned to Weeks for help. They needed a democratic governance strategy that was more intensive and deliberative: they wanted to inform citizens, engage them in discussions with each other, and give them a chance to work through the city's budget arithmetic. They came up with an informational tabloid, including a budget worksheet where citizens could see the costs of different programs and services and develop their own balance of revenues and expenditures. The tabloid and worksheet were sent out to every household in the city. A simpler version of the worksheet was used as part of a mail-in questionnaire that was sent to a representative sample of voters. Finally, the worksheet be-came part of the discussion material for a number of three-hour community workshops, in which small groups of citizens discussed the budget options. The entire process was dubbed "Eugene Decisions."

The full version of the worksheet described forty different programs and services—all components of the current city budget. It presented five new services or service enhancements that had been proposed. On paper, citizens could come up with their own preferred mix of reductions and expansions. If people decided they wanted to raise revenues, the worksheet offered sixteen different tax and user fee options for them to consider. Over a thousand people filled out and returned these worksheets. The simpler questionnaire that was mailed to the representative sample of voters had a response rate of over 50%.

At the community workshops, participants met in groups of 7–9 people. Each group had a facilitator who was a trained volunteer, and a city staff person who could answer questions about the budget. Like the city council, the group members made decisions by majority vote. "The city had never before had more than a couple of hundred citizens attend a public meeting," says Weeks, but 682 people turned out for the budget workshops.[8]

The city council then developed three broad strategies, based on the input they had received, to present back to the community as options for the city's economic future. They held a second round of deliberations, with another tabloid/worksheet explaining the three strategies and a new set of community workshops. Everyone expected participation to decline, since the decisions to be made were becoming more difficult. However, turnout at the workshops declined only slightly, and the response rate for the work-sheets actually doubled, to over 2,500 people. Eugene residents felt that the process was valuable, and they kept at it.

The concluding budget deliberations of the city council provided one final surprise. For three days, the council crafted a budget that met the parameters established by citizens in the worksheets and workshops. Then the council abruptly reversed itself, put in $10 million in new services, and enacted Oregon's first local income tax to pay for them. The city's daily newspaper, the *Eugene Register-Guard,* called it a "moment of madness."[9] After three days of public uproar, the council changed course again, and enacted a budget that mirrored the citizen input. The final budget included six efficiency measures, twenty user-fee increases, twenty-five service re-ductions, three transfers of service costs to non-general funds, and three service expansions.[10]

One outcome of Eugene Decisions was that the city gave up the responsibility of administering all the public spaces in the downtown area. This work is now coordinated by Eugene-in-Common, a partnership of downtown businesses. Eugene-in-Common manages the process of licensing and managing street vendors, sidewalk cafés, farmers' market, and special events.[11] The arrangement seems to have saved the city—and taxpayers—some money while giving more latitude to downtown merchants, who probably have the most at stake in maintaining a vital central business district. It is the kind of solution that seems to emerge when people examine city budgets in terms of community needs and capacities, rather than just dollars and cents.

Because of the success of Eugene Decisions, Weeks was invited to design "Sacramento Decisions" in 1996. Sacramento, the state capital of California, is a city of about 400,000. In order to balance the budget, the city had deferred maintenance, raised user fees, and cut services. They now faced decisions that promised to be even more unpopular, so the city council and city manager decided to involve Sacramento residents in helping to make these tough choices.

The overall structure of the Sacramento effort was similar to that in Eugene, with a tabloid, worksheet, and community workshops. Sacramento is a larger and more racially diverse community, however, so the organizers made a greater effort to reach the city's different ethnic populations. Materials were translated into Spanish, Chinese, Vietnamese, Laotian, Hmong, and Russian, orientation meetings were conducted at neighborhood centers, and community organizations helped to recruit participants from among their constituencies. This work seemed to pay off: demographically, the Sacramento participants reflected the make-up of their community.[12]

The *Sacramento Bee* provided a great deal of coverage to the project, and even printed the Sacramento Decisions tabloid at cost. Response rates to the mailed questionnaire were lower than in Eugene: roughly 30%, which is about average for municipal surveys.[13] On the other hand, over 800 people attended the Sacramento community workshops.

The city manager and city council members were so enthusiastic about the participation that they merged Sacramento Decisions with the city's official budgeting process. Under California law, a city must develop its proposed budget and then allow for public comment before the city council can review and ratify the final budget. The Sacramento City Council used the input from the worksheets and community workshops to draft a proposed budget. City staffers then conducted a telephone survey with 400 residents, sent out more mail-in questionnaires, and held several more workshops, to get further public feedback. Mirroring the traditional budget review process, participants in this phase were asked to evaluate the proposed budget; if they wanted to suggest a funding increase in a particular area, they had to propose a way to cover the cost (a budget cut in a different area, for example). In this phase, roughly 1,700 people completed questionnaires on the proposed budget, and 150 took part in the community workshops.

Embedding Sacramento Decisions in the city's budgeting process was a very unusual step. A few cities have official budgeting processes that formally include citizen institutions like neighborhood councils, but these are representative systems, and they don't require large-scale public engagement. Other cities, like Eugene and Washington, DC, have sponsored large-scale citizen involvement on local budget priorities, but treated the project as a kind of extracurricular activity, a way for council members to get better advice from the public. The Sacramento setup incorporated large numbers of citizens in a more formal, legitimate way.

The second phase of the Sacramento process allowed citizens to ratify the final budget, which was then enacted by city council. One aspect of the final budget surprised some observers: a cut in funding for public safety. Many communities allocate a large percentage of their local budgets to police and fire services; in Sacramento, the figure is 80% of the general fund. Public officials are often reluctant to reduce public safety funding because they are afraid of a backlash from citizens. In Sacramento Decisions, participants were able to see that if they didn't cut public safety, they would have to make much deeper reductions in other areas of the budget. Citizens made the tough decisions, and local officials worried less about the political implications.

Madness and Sanity in Eugene and Sacramento

In many ways, Ed Weeks fits the academic stereotype: when making his arguments, he may go into full lecture mode, pacing the floor and waving his long arms around. He could even be considered the mad scientist of participatory budgeting. But the experiences of Eugene and Sacramento, as well as similar experiments in other communities, may be changing the definition of sanity in public finance. When participants in Eugene and Sacramento Decisions had the chance to examine their worksheets and discuss the budget with their peers, they felt like they were part of a sane, reasonable process.[14] When Eugene's city council members proposed a budget that did not match citizen preferences, their mental stability was questioned by the media.

Eugene is not alone: the typical way that budgets are produced in city halls and state legislatures seems irrational to many citizens. This is partly because political campaigns are dominated by simplistic slogans about lower taxes or expanded programs and services. After the election is over, lawmakers try to follow through on these unrealistic promises. In Eugene and Sacramento, citizens and public officials got beyond the knee-jerk demands and made budget decisions based on a careful analysis of the financial options.

Liberals and conservatives carry different kinds of hopes into participatory budgeting exercises. Observers on the left are encouraged that, when citizens take a careful look at local budgets, they become more likely to support higher taxes and government services. In the second round of Eugene Decisions, participants selected their favorite among the three overall budget strategies, and then turned the page to begin calculating their own preferred mix of service cuts and expansions. Those who picked the "no new taxes" strategy ended up creating budgets that included, on average, $3.3 million in new taxes. To Weeks, the explanation for this apparent contradiction is that the worksheet helped people see the full implications of their initial opinions. "The difference lies in the ability to evaluate the consequences of an action," says Weeks. "Behind the slogan of 'no new taxes' is the consequence of losing valued community services—services for which they are willing to tax themselves."[15]

Observers on the right prefer outcomes like Eugene-in-Common, which demonstrate the potential of private businesses and community organizations to take over tasks that would previously have been handled by government, at taxpayer expense. The city council didn't plan for this to happen; in fact, the workshops didn't give the participants time to talk about how they might take action themselves. "We went in with the old assumption that government is the main problem solver and service provider in the community," says Weeks. "In retrospect, we might have allowed for the possibility that people and organizations could 'pick up the slack' for government."[16] Participatory budgeting advocates should perhaps pay closer attention to the lessons about action that have been learned by civic experiments on other issues. A greater emphasis on action might also have boosted attendance at the second-round workshops in Eugene and Sacramento: in both cities, once people had given their initial recommendations, they were more likely to stay home and fill out their budget worksheets than attend the workshops to talk with their peers. If the council had encouraged citizens to look for ways to supplant or enhance public services, they would have had more reasons to get together.

For most local governments, the financial picture has become much more dismal over the last ten years. Even as the state and federal governments shift the burden of funding public services increasingly to the cities and towns, ballot initiatives and state legislatures make it harder for local officials to raise tax revenues.[17] "Certainly, it is risky to truly open up and engage people in the budget process," says Frank Benest, a former city manager. "But it is even more risky not to."[18] Brea, California, the city where Benest worked, has engaged citizens in budgeting; so have places like Davenport, Iowa; Washington, DC; and Toronto, Ontario. In this economic climate, more and more cities may follow suit. The larger question is whether citizens and public officials will treat this form of democratic governance as a long-term solution or simply a kind of temporary sanity.

Making the World Democratic for Safety

The fact that public safety takes up 80% of the city budget in Sacramento, and a similar percentage in many other communities, reflects the fact that crime prevention is one of the most popular public priorities. Collaboration between police and community members, therefore, is more than just a way of improving relations between officers and residents: it can also be viewed as an attempt to redistribute the problem-solving roles of citizens and government.

In 2000, the level of trust between police and residents in Buffalo, New York, seemed to be at a low water mark. The police department had consolidated its eleven neighborhood precincts into five district station houses, and some parts of the community were still feeling the loss of "their" precinct station.[19] Residents were frustrated with the consolidation plan; they also wondered about the level of commitment and morale on the force. "Citizens felt that the police were resigned to a certain level of crime," says Shakoor Aljuwani, who was the director of Buffalo's United Neighborhoods Center at the time. Meanwhile, many officers felt that residents complained too much without doing their part to help prevent crime. James Giammaresi, the police department's chief of staff, was frustrated that residents wouldn't show up at meetings called by the department. "When we tried to be more open, we just couldn't get the community to participate," he says.[20]

These are the kinds of problems that "community policing" is supposed to fix. The concept emerged in the late 1980s and early 1990s; its basic premise is that getting police officers out of their squad cars and onto the street, working face-to-face with residents, is an effective way to increase public support and decrease crime. Advocates of community policing argued that officers ought to be dealing proactively with the causes of crime, like poverty, substance abuse, and a lack of guidance for young people, rather than waiting for crimes to occur. In many cities, the shift toward community policing was accompanied by a crackdown on low-level crimes like graffiti, loitering, and public drunkenness. Residents and criminologists alike felt that these kinds of misdemeanors, which police had often ignored in the past, created a "sense of disorder" that contributed to neighborhood blight; furthermore, these are just the kind of crimes that citizens are well-placed to prevent and counteract.

However, community policing has been implemented in many different ways, with corresponding differences in effectiveness. Simply asking more officers to walk the beat didn't seem to produce the kinds of proactive police-community relationships that people envisioned. Some criminologists began calling it community-*oriented* policing, which seemed to emphasize the responsive role of officers and minimize the contributions of citizens. Officers often grumbled that they were being forced into roles they didn't expect: they found themselves acting like social workers or youth counselors rather than lawmen. On the beat, they mostly interacted with young people, panhandlers, and owners of storefront businesses; when they attended neighborhood association or neighborhood watch meetings, they usually encountered small cadres of long-time residents who wanted to know why they hadn't caught the culprits in the latest crime. They had more face-to-face interaction with residents, but it didn't seem to be making their jobs any easier.

In places where community policing strategies were able to engage larger numbers of residents, crime rates have dropped. In fact, stronger and more active connections between residents, regardless of whether they were created as part of a neighborhood watch strategy or not, seem to have a strong statistical impact on crime. Felton Earls, a researcher at Harvard University, calls this quality "collective efficacy." Earls argues that "the most important influence on a neighborhood's crime rate is neighbors' willingness to act, when needed, for one another's benefit, and particularly for the benefit of one another's children."[21] Perhaps the key to community policing, then, is the degree to which it actually involves the community. Rather than policing strategies that are community-oriented or community-friendly, officers and residents may need crime prevention strategies to be more community-*active*.

In some places, this is a more formidable challenge than others: incidents of bias or brutality by officers, whether actual or alleged, have eroded the trust between police and residents so badly that any kind of collaboration seems impossible. It is a crisis not only for the forces of crime prevention, but for democracy itself, since the police-community connection may be the most common way that citizens interact with public employees. The first step for cities like Cincinnati, Ohio, which witnessed dramatic civil disturbances touched off by a controversial police shooting in 2001, has been to try changing the culture and training within the police department so that officers can deal with issues of race and difference. The second step is to try repairing the police-community relationship, bringing officers and citizens together so that they can understand each other's views and start rebuilding trust. As part of this process, participants can begin turning their attention to how they might work together to prevent crime. Many cities, including Cincinnati; Louisville, Kentucky; and Fayetteville, North Carolina, have organized large-scale democratic governance projects aimed at one or all of these goals.

Though the level of trust between officers and residents of Buffalo was low, it was not complicated by high-profile incidents of police brutality. "People were worried about racial profiling going on in the suburbs," says Aljuwani, "but inside the city the question was whether the police were doing enough to prevent crime."[22] Some life-long residents saw the challenge as restoring the police-community relationship to the closer partnership they had enjoyed years before. "When I was growing up, Buffalo was a city where you knew every policeman, and they knew you," said Johanne Gimbrone, an employee of the United Neighborhoods Center. "If you got in trouble, the police would take you right to your parents' door. Now, that rapport is gone, the familiarity is gone. It's hard on the people, and it's hard on the police. Now when the police get a call, they don't know what they're walking into."[23]

Buffalo's Odd Couple

Shakoor Aljuwani and James Giammaresi are an unlikely pair. Practically the only thing they seem to have in common is an unspellable last name.[24] Aljuwani is a longtime community activist and organizer who was born in Buffalo but has spent most of his adult life in New York City. He is an African American who converted to Islam as a young man. In the mid-1990s, he was lured back to Buffalo to head the United Neighborhoods Center, which serves as a liaison between local government and the city's 300 block clubs.

Giammaresi grew up in one of Buffalo's Italian-American neighborhoods and has lived in the city all his life, working his way up the police department ladder over a twenty-year career. His job made him a central figure in the department; he was constantly managing deployment decisions, dealing with personnel issues, and interacting with community groups, public officials, and angry residents alike.

At second glance, however, the two share many common traits. Both men are earnest, plain-spoken, and almost never defensive—even when they find themselves under attack. Both had been frustrated by long years of conflict between police and community, particularly between white officers and residents of color. Both believed strongly that citizens have a powerful role to play in preventing crime, working with the police, and solving problems that shouldn't require the police in the first place. They decided to work together on a project that would engage officers and residents in structured small-group discussions and collaborative neighborhood-level action efforts.

The difference in the backgrounds of the two leaders turned out to be a key factor in the success of their program. Both by his reputation and as director of the United Neighborhood Center, Aljuwani had credibility with Buffalo's block clubs, particularly in neighborhoods where distrust of the police was highest. Giammaresi's rapport with fellow officers won over many of the skeptics inside the police department, and his support of the project convinced residents that the discussions might actually have an impact on policing decisions. The partnership between the two men was a model for the officers and neighborhood leaders who helped set up the project, and set the tone for the respectful, productive dialogue that took place in the sessions themselves.

This kind of partnership has been a key ingredient in many democratic governance efforts; it combines the authority of government with the capacity to reach out to community organizations. Since these programs rely primarily on one-on-one recruitment efforts by local leaders and organizations, Aljuwani's connection to the block clubs was critical for turning out a large number of people. Since people won't attend unless they think the program has the potential to create real change, Giammaresi's status as a high-ranking police official was equally important.

By the summer of 2001, Aljuwani and Giammaresi had involved 350 people in thirty-two small-group dialogues, concluding with an action forum. The organizations that recruited participants and hosted the sessions included a public housing resident's association, a Nation of Islam faith community, an historic preservation group, several Business Improvement Districts, and many block clubs. Each of the groups was neighborhood-based, involving homeowners, renters, businesspeople, church leaders, young people, and police officers who live or work locally.

Some of the officers who took part were a little worried that the discussion would turn into a shouting match, but once the participants began to see that they all had some of the same hopes and concerns, they began to form a bond. "At first they vented a lot—they definitely weren't intimidated—but then they got to know me, too," says Officer Brian Ross. "Shortly thereafter I started to get calls from them, asking questions, giving me information I needed." Patricia Webb, who serves on the resident council for the Schaeffer Village public housing development, says that the experience "showed neighbors and the police that they could work together," even if they had a long way to go.[25]

Splitting the Bill in Buffalo

Buffalo, New York, 2001

After giving an overview of the project and summarizing the action ideas emerging from the small-group sessions, Shakoor Aljuwani invites James Giammaresi to the podium "to take any questions you may have." The first action forum of the Buffalo project is drawing to a close. Giammaresi comes forward to a round of applause from the audience. At the back of the room, several people raise their hands; they have been talking with the newspaper reporters in attendance, but now that Giammaresi is front-and-center, they want to be heard. "Why have you closed the police substation in my ward?" asks one. "What have you done about the noise problem in my ward?" shouts another. Other audience members can be heard groaning with frustration. For twenty minutes, Giammaresi calmly acknowledges the criticisms and explains how the department is trying to address them.

Aljuwani and Giammaresi had made a common mistake: allowing time for participants to make comments and ask questions at an open microphone. These "open mike" sessions are a staple of traditional citizen involvement, and they are rarely productive. In this case, several of the open mike speakers were people who had not attended any of the small-group sessions—but who were running for city council, and therefore wanted this chance to audition for the participants and the news reporters in attendance.

Because of the open mike segment, the action forum didn't reflect the spirit of police-community collaboration that had been emerging within the project; nonetheless, that feeling would continue to grow. In one neighborhood with several halfway houses for the mentally ill, police officers and small-business owners had complained about ongoing disturbances. In the small-group meetings, people discussed how business owners often called the police about incidents involving halfway house residents. They also pointed out that officers are not trained to handle such situations. A state legislator, the director of mental health services for the county, and several peer leaders who had successfully battled mental illness attended the meetings. The participants came up with the idea of a trained emergency response team—to include business owners, former halfway house residents, and county mental health professionals—that would be on call for every neighborhood in the city.

Graffiti was one common concern in many of the discussions, and a number of groups decided that changes in landscaping and maintenance would help alleviate the problem.[26] In two neighborhoods, residents and police officers shared their concerns about local businesses that weren't doing their part to prevent crime—the places were poorly lighted and lacked adequate security. The business owners in those groups pledged to work with residents and police to improve security, including hiring private guards.

Using the slogan, "Putting the Neighbor back in the 'Hood," participants in one group decided to promote stronger police-neighborhood communication, an end to racial profiling, and a number of new anti-crime measures. The group, which was organized by a block club and Masjid-Nu'Man, a local Nation of Islam community, initiated a citizen effort to identify suspicious "people hanging out on corners" and cooperate with police in monitoring possible criminal activity.

One key to affecting the police department's internal decisions was the fact that, in many of the sessions, citizens got their first chance to form relationships with police lieutenants and inspectors. These middle-ranking officers make some of the most important decisions about how the department operates and how community policing is administered. "They're the ones who make things happen," says Aljuwani, "but the block clubs just hadn't connected with them before." "In the past, lieutenants and inspectors didn't have a big role in terms of interacting with residents," says Giammaresi, "but they are critical for helping the department and the community work together successfully."[27]

The need for more officers on the street was a common theme in all the discussions. Budget shortages and a threatened strike by the police union made this difficult, but Giammaresi and his colleagues came up with other solutions. Starting in the summer of 2001, the entire graduating class of Buffalo's Police Academy spent its first tour of duty walking the beat instead of sitting in patrol cars. Giammaresi also began a "Park and

Walk" program in South Buffalo, where police officers park their patrol cars for part of the day to visit all the businesses and organizations in the neighborhood.

By creating active partnerships between citizens and officers, Aljuwani and Giammaresi were taking the concept of collaboration to new frontiers. Collaboration is a favorite buzzword of public management professors and other government experts, but their definition often seems limited to relationships between heads of organizations—mayors, pastors, police chiefs, and directors of nonprofits.[28] In Buffalo, all kinds of people were offering their support, resources, and volunteer time in exchange for the opportunity to give meaningful input into law enforcement policy. This trade was being made at every level of the system: individual residents with the cops on the beat, block clubs with police lieutenants and inspectors, the community with the police department as a whole.

Over the next two years, the project won some victories that, in retrospect, may have weakened its ability to sustain this level of citizen-government partnership. First, the police department and United Neighborhoods Center won a large grant from the U. S. Department of Justice. The funding supported another large-scale effort to bring citizens and officers together, in 2002 and 2003. However, the grant was directed at racial profiling, so the discussions had to be focused on that issue, rather than larger crime prevention concerns. Midway through, the organizers realized that this orientation was too narrow, and they broadened it to "racially biased policing." In any case, the turnout was lower, and the sessions centered on tensions between particular kinds of people: between police officers and young people of color, for example, or between African American residents and store owners of Middle Eastern descent. The outcomes included: more training opportunities on Muslim culture for officers; more training for citizens on what to do if you are stopped by the police; translating the police complaint forms into Arabic; and an ongoing dialogue process that brings together African Americans and members of Buffalo's growing Yemenite population.[29] These activities have clear benefits for the community, but because the discussions focused solely on cross-cultural understanding, they didn't lead to the more tangible kinds of crime prevention measures.

The input from the 2002–2003 discussions also led the police department to reverse course on one of its deployment decisions. Because of the city's 2002 fiscal crisis, the department had laid off thirty-two officers and reassigned its community policing officers (CPOs) to regular patrol duty. CPOs typically spend more of their time interacting with citizen groups and receive more training in how to work with the public. As a result of the democratic governance project, the CPOs were reinstated and a new system of monthly neighborhood meetings was established, but this too may have been a mixed blessing: having CPOs handle most of the interactions with citizens may actually make it harder for citizens to penetrate the police bureaucracy. Because of the layoffs and redeployments, many regular patrol officers had been assigned to attend the small-group discussions—on their evaluations, participants rated these sessions higher than others because they got a chance to meet "regular cops." The patrol officers gave the discussions higher marks than their CPO counterparts did, perhaps because the experience was more unusual for them, and maybe because they had lower expectations going in. Buffalo's approach to community policing, which is similar to that of many other cities, now results in CPOs attending neighborhood meetings rather than regular patrol officers. It may be that having a small percentage of police officers who specialize in police-community relations, rather than giving all police employees some exposure to the public, further insulates the department from the community.

But if the internal structure of the police department posed one challenge, then the instability of the United Neighborhoods Center presented an even greater one. The United Way of Buffalo and Erie County, which had housed the center, decided in 2003 to concentrate on grant-making rather than administering community programs. The center eventually found another home, at the Community Action Agency of Buffalo, but with a smaller funding base. During this transition, and partly because of it, Shakoor Aljuwani left to pursue other opportunities.

Meanwhile, James Giammaresi retired from the police department, leaving Buffalo's pioneering democratic governance effort without its two original leaders. Angela Jones, who works at the United Neighborhoods Center, says that there have been many requests from residents for more sessions with the police, but the organization hasn't been able to fulfill them. "I am not sure there will be anyone to drive the process," said Pamela Beal, a criminologist at SUNY Buffalo who wrote a report on the project.[30]

In order for Buffalo, or any other community, to sustain this kind of civic experiment, people there will have to address a fundamental imbalance between governments and community organizations. Police departments and other city agencies employ full-time professional problem-solvers. In most instances, the public employees who regularly interact with citizens are a specially trained minority; the structure of the department treats public engagement as a supplemental activity rather than a core component of problem-solving. On the other hand, the block clubs, neighborhood associations, and groups like the United Neighborhoods Center tend to be much less structured, partly because they have fewer employees—in most cases, none at all. They are usually reliant on grants to support the staffing they need to launch democratic governance efforts, and because the funding is temporary, the projects are as well. If local leaders are serious about sharing public responsibilities between citizens and government, they will have to find ways for these very different sets of people, the specialized professionals and the overstretched volunteers, to work together. Otherwise, communities will have trouble splitting the bill for public priorities.

Trying to Tap Neighborhood Potential

In their efforts to find out what citizens want from government, and how residents and public employees can work together, some local officials have latched on to an approach that is more permanent and comprehensive than participatory budgeting or community policing. They have created neighborhood-level citizen structures, new public arenas that are much closer (literally and figuratively) to where people live. In some cases, these systems are designed to gather input on policy decisions *and* embolden citizens to take action themselves. The core idea is that local government shares some of its authority and resources with the new neighborhood structures, in order to expedite public decisions and tap into the volunteer efforts of citizens. "We're sharing power in order to gain power," says Tom Argust, who recently retired as the director of community development for the city of Rochester, New York.[31]

Some of the oldest neighborhood council systems, in places like Dayton, Ohio; St. Paul, Minnesota; and Birmingham, Alabama, emerged from the federal anti-poverty efforts of the 1960s.[32] The system in Santa Rosa, California, was part of a compromise between people who wanted the city council to be elected according to districts, and those who wanted to stay with the current setup, in which all council members are elected at-large. The Neighborhood Commission in Hampton, Virginia, emerged out of controversies related to the city's new comprehensive plan.[33] Other city governments cite a mix of economic and political reasons as their inspiration for sharing power with neighborhoods.

In Los Angeles, the desire to create new neighborhood structures was more political than economic. The aftershocks of the 1992 civil disturbances, and the fact that various parts of L. A. wanted to secede from the rest of the city, convinced local officials that they had to give neighborhoods more power—before they tore the city apart. After lengthy negotiations in city council and two separate city charter reform commissions, the election of Mayor Jim Hahn gave the idea one last push, and the city's neighborhood council system was inaugurated in 2001.

From community to community, these neighborhood structures vary in several ways. Some of them are purely advisory groups that provide input to local government, most commonly to the police and planning departments. Others have the power to make certain decisions themselves. Usually this authority is limited to their neighborhood, but not always: in Dayton, the neighborhood "priority boards" play an official role in the city's budget process. Some neighborhood structures must follow procedures and processes dictated by government in order to be "certified," while others receive advice and assistance from government but are not compelled to manage their affairs in any particular way. Still others are left entirely to their own devices, with no dictates or support from the city. In some places, city staffers are always present at neighborhood meetings, either to facilitate them or to provide information; in other communities, staff are rarely involved.[34]

Stakeholder: Vampire or Hibachi?

The story of the Los Angeles neighborhood councils is now being used as a cautionary tale for what can go wrong with these kinds of structures. The L. A. councils have an advisory role on most policy issues, though the mayor has given them a fairly strong role in the formation of the city budget, and the city has established an Early Notification System to warn each council about policy decisions that might affect their neighborhood. Each council is also allotted $50,000 each year to spend on its own initiatives. After four years, over ninety councils have been established in the city.[35] Some of them have been deadlocked over controversial decisions, driving council members away in frustration; others haven't been able to hold undisputed elections; still others have been extremely unpopular in their own neighborhoods. In a few cases, police have been called to break up violent arguments at council meetings, making headlines for Los Angeles as the city where even democracy can be dangerous.[36]

This level of controversy and disorder seems to suggest that the L. A. councils are plagued by unstructured, undisciplined conversations. But in some ways, the system is very orderly indeed: every council must adhere to innumerable restrictions that govern how it elects its members, conducts its business, and advertises itself to the community. All agendas must be posted in five public places at least three days before the meeting, and nothing can be discussed that is not on the agenda. Council members must disclose their personal financial data, and under open meetings laws, council members can't discuss neighborhood business in private. To be certified by the city, councils must show that they have notified churches, businesses, and other neighborhood groups of the time and date for each meeting. To run the meetings themselves, many councils adhere religiously to the hidebound Robert's Rules of Order.[37]

The most notorious aspect of the system—and the only one that seems totally unrestricted—is that any neighborhood "stakeholder" can vote in that neighborhood's council election. The city has not established a clear definition of the term; one city councilwoman gained fame by saying she didn't know whether a stakeholder was a vampire or a hibachi.[38] The stakeholder voting policy has fanned the fears of neighborhood residents, who don't want "outsiders" to outvote them.

On one hand, the city's willingness to acknowledge stakeholders reflects an admirable desire to include and capitalize on all the assets available to a neighborhood. It makes sense for neighborhood leaders to accommodate all those people who have some connection to the place and who might want to help improve it.[39] On the other hand, the policy is so open that residents can, in fact, be outnumbered by people who don't live in that neighborhood. Churches, construction companies, and other groups have been accused of busing in whole blocs of voters in order to elect their candidates and get their way on a particular decision.

What may be even more surprising is that the neighborhood council elections are so hotly contested in the first place. Los Angeles residents seem to believe that the only way to affect the decisions of their neighborhood council is by being elected to serve on it. They are probably right: with all of their procedural restrictions and Rules of Order, the councils are essentially mini-Congresses—decision-making bodies designed to represent citizens but not to involve them. Greg Nelson, who directs the city's Department of Neighborhood Empowerment (DONE), calls the council members "lobbyists for the people." But the people aren't always happy with this arrangement: in some neighborhoods, councils are fighting it out with community organizing groups and other grassroots organizations over decisions about land use and policing.

One problem is that the L. A. councils are trying to serve populations that may simply be too large for their outreach capacity or staff support. Each one represents, on average, 38,000 people, but most of the councils do not have paid staffers to help with recruitment. DONE, which is the main source of technical assistance to the neighborhoods, employs one staffer for every five councils—one for every 200,000 residents. Ken Thomson, a researcher who has been documenting neighborhood councils for twenty years, suggests that the structures work best when each one has at least one staffer, and when they operate in populations of 3,000 to 5,000 residents.[40]

Some neighborhood leaders also feel as if they're just about done with DONE. Instead of offering sound advice on group process or recruitment, critics claim that DONE staffers focus on forcing councils to meet the bureaucratic requirements mandated by the city attorney's office (which monitors open meetings compliance) or by DONE itself. One council member who was interviewed for a report on the L. A. system said that "we are being empowered into a corner with paperwork."[41] DONE staffers criticize the councils for their weak and passive approach to outreach: posting notices rather than actively recruiting a wide range of people. The city doesn't seem to have sent the message that a larger, more diverse participation will give the councils greater credibility and capacity. However, the low turnouts may have more do with the way that the neighborhood meetings are run: DONE encourages meetings where "parliamentary procedure is respected, and stakeholders are given opportunity to comment." These sound more like the staid proceedings of a city council or school board than a vibrant neighborhood group. Some council members agree that their attendance problem is not because of a lack of outreach, but due to the fact that "people don't come back."[42]

Because the L. A. system pushes policy-making one level farther down, one big step closer to the average citizen, residents may well be better off than before the councils were established. The councils are widely credited with defeating a proposed citywide water rate increase in 2004.[43] Many councils have used their city-allotted funds to plant trees, build playgrounds, and improve parks and sidewalks. In some councils, there is evidence that residents are adding their own sweat equity to the $50,000 granted by the city, conducting street cleanups, creating disaster preparedness plans, helping bring buildings up to code, establishing new anti-crime networks, and helping high school students apply for college.[44] So far, the councils' role in the city budget review process seems to have been productive and noncontroversial.

Though some observers predict their demise, others say that the power of the neighborhood councils in city politics is actually growing. Some local leaders are proposing that councils be allowed to file maintenance requests directly with the city's department of public works; others are asking the new mayor, Antonio Villaraigoso, to give guaranteed spots to neighborhood council members on all city commissions.[45] When the police department was formulating new procedures for responding to burglar alarms, the alarm companies sent their lobbyists directly to the neighborhood council meetings to argue their case. Because the councils are official bodies of government, with the seal of the city stamped on their flyers and agendas, they will presumably have more staying power than other civic experiments. Unlike Eugene Decisions or the Buffalo community policing discussions, the L. A. council system is built to last.

But the L. A. neighborhood councils might be even more powerful, representative, and effective if they tried to be democratic institutions rather than simply republican ones. Perhaps they have too much of the wrong kind of structure: instead of the bureaucratic red tape about personal financial data and open meetings, they need processes and techniques—small-group dialogues, impartial facilitators, ground rules, and discussion guides—that give large numbers of participants a chance to speak and feel heard.[46] Instead of notifying other neighborhood groups of their meetings, they should probably be recruiting more actively, listening to the reasons why residents would want to be involved. Instead of being decision-making bodies only, maybe they should also be groups that mobilize and convene the neighborhood—rather than "lobbying for the people," they could help people lobby for themselves.

If the neighborhood councils were oriented toward mobilizing their neighbors, they could probably produce the kind of volunteer-driven projects so evident in Buffalo. This inclusiveness might also make them more representative, both in the input they relay to the city and in the makeup of the councils themselves. Currently, 63% of the council members are homeowners, even though 70% of city residents are renters. By creating a format where different groups and factions in the neighborhood could talk through their differences, they might be able to achieve a higher degree of consensus, and they might do a better job of fostering new, more diverse leadership.

A more democratic mission for the neighborhood councils of Los Angeles might also clarify what it means to be a stakeholder. Rather than a citizen who uses the council to gain access to city hall, exploiting the lifeblood of the neighborhood, a stakeholder is someone who has something to contribute to the community. Neighborhood councils might be more vibrant if they focused on these intellectual, industrious, conversational, compassionate contributions of ordinary people.

Organic Governance in Rochester

In Rochester, New York, Mayor William Johnson knew that he couldn't afford a system that encouraged citizens to make new demands on local government: in an economic sense, neither the city nor its neighborhoods had any more blood to give. The city's population was decreasing, the housing stock was deteriorating, and the tax base was declining. "The damage that has been done through economic restructuring, the concentration of poverty, and disinvestments is deeply serious and ongoing," said Johnson when he was elected mayor in 1994. "We cannot fix it alone, and we shouldn't have to."[47] Johnson began campaigning for more regional collaboration and more state aid. But the mayor, community development director Tom Argust, city council president Lois Giess, and other leaders felt that they also needed to tap neighborhood potential in a much more dramatic way. The result was a civic experiment called "Neighbors Building Neighborhoods" (NBN).

NBN was designed as a kind of recurring planning process, in which residents would map the assets in their neighborhood, create a plan for capitalizing on them, work with the city and other groups to implement the plan, and then go back to plan some more. There have been three cycles so far: NBN1 from 1994–1999, NBN2 from 1999–2001, and NBN3 from 2001–2003. The individual neighborhood plans were incorporated into a new citywide comprehensive plan, and then, in 2003, a complete rewrite of the city's zoning code. From the beginning, Johnson's rhetoric about the strategy made it clear that this was not simply an input-gathering exercise: neighborhood residents and institutions would be called upon to help implement the plans they developed with their own time, resources, and sweat equity.

The NBN strategy was also a conscious attempt to shake up the relationship between city government and the existing neighborhood groups. Tom Argust and some of the other planners were concerned that the neighborhood associations that were already active—in the sense that they had a small core of committed members—would dominate the planning process for their neighborhood. (This seems to be what has happened in many Los Angeles neighborhoods.) So instead of using the boundary lines of the thirty-six more-or-less distinct neighborhoods in the city, NBN established ten new sectors that brought together multiple neighborhoods. This created more of a blank slate for the organizing process; it forced neighborhood associations and other groups to work with each other as well as interacting with local government.[48]

Each sector team had a great deal of freedom in how it conducted its business, reached out to residents, and made decisions. The NBN literature even goes so far as to call the sectors "self-organizing." This is a bit misleading, however: the city provided a great deal of advice and assistance, but then gave the sectors great latitude in how to apply it. Argust and his colleagues produced a *Citizens' Guide to Community-Based Planning* (known as "the cookbook") that summarized some of the theory and best practices in democratic governance. The city trained sector volunteers in group dynamics and group process, and hired several organizational development consultants to work directly with the sectors. Some public employees, particularly those in the planning department, also went through the training. "We retrained and retooled the entire planning staff," says Argust, "and asked them to serve as facilitators, enablers, resource people . . . This was a tough transition for some of them, because they were champing at the bit to do the planning themselves."[49] They also established a series of training workshops called the NBN Institute. The workshop topics, which have changed and proliferated over the years, include things like meeting management, working with volunteers, budgeting, the zoning process, and database design. Broad-based recruitment was a key theme in all of the advice and assistance, and starting with NBN2, sectors were asked to develop detailed recruitment strategies to think through how they would involve diverse groups of citizens in the planning itself.

One of the first steps for each sector was to make an inventory of all the different kinds of assets in that area. In Sector 10, a low-income area close to downtown, one of the assets listed on the initial map was "amateur gardeners." In Los Angeles, this might not seem like a particularly valuable asset, but in Rochester, which endures the highest average annual snowfall of any American city, the high number of gardeners showed that people in Sector 10 knew how to persevere.

That initial asset mapping exercise in Sector 10 germinated the idea for an urban farming project that has since become a truly large-scale operation. Residents have brought in the United Way, the U. S. Department of Agriculture, and the Kellogg Foundation as partners and funders of the program, which is called Greater Rochester Urban Bounty (GRUB). Using approximately three acres of previously vacant land in the center of the city, GRUB harvests over 12,000 pounds of organic produce every year.[50] Sector 10 residents receive food by purchasing shares in GRUB; the rest is sold to area restaurants and to shoppers at the Rochester farmer's market. GRUB employs several residents, provides apprenticeships for local teens, and attracts hundreds of volunteers. All profits are reinvested in the community.

Other sectors brag about their own citizen-driven outcomes. One NBN progress report lists two new music festivals, a land use study, a number of park and street cleanups, two new neighborhood gardens, three new neighborhood directories, a quilt illustrating neighborhood history, new murals, many opportunities for people to learn about homeownership or renters' rights, and new painting and landscaping at an elementary school. There are many other instances in which residents partnered with other organizations, like banks, schools, and foundations, on more capital-intensive projects to build affordable housing and commercial spaces, a Community Development Corporation, a micro-loan fund for small businesses, a youth center, and new sculptures and other art installations. Over 80% of the action ideas in the original NBN1 neighborhood plans have since been implemented.[51]

Bureaucracy and "Ad Hocracy"

Neighbors Building Neighborhoods was also intended as a vehicle for public input on government policies and initiatives, but this aspect of the system was awkward at first. In one sense, Johnson's administration was completely committed to NBN: the mayor even stipulated that "every allocation of the city's $350 million annual budget must support the NBN plans."[52] Instead of the Los Angeles setup, where each neighborhood council has its $50,000 set aside from the rest of the city budget, Rochester's city department heads had to ensure that all of their operations followed citizen goals. However, city staff had a hard time getting used to this idea. The middle-level managers in city hall who decided how trash was picked up, how potholes were fixed, and how policing was organized weren't always comfortable having residents looking over their shoulders. "We directed this thing into the neighborhoods and forgot to bring our employees along," Johnson acknowledges. Meanwhile, many residents seemed to expect that the city would automatically implement or adhere to any goals set by the sectors, leading Johnson to grumble that "when we empowered the citizens, we didn't disempower the mayor or the City Council."[53]

One of the first major confrontations—and learning experiences—took place over the redesign of University Avenue, a major thoroughfare. City planners wanted to widen the road to ease traffic congestion. Neighborhood residents wanted to make it narrower, more beautiful, and more pedestrian friendly. The city postponed the decision, and sent the planners and traffic engineers onto the street for a day to experience it as a resident might. In the final compromise, the road was widened two feet, but also gained "traffic calming" measures, parking arrangements that were more convenient for shoppers, and an "Art Walk," a stretch of sidewalk decorated with colorful embedded designs, sculptures, and artistic street lamps and benches.[54]

From this and other experiences, Argust and the other NBN leaders learned how to make the decision-making process run more smoothly. For NBN2, they developed a Priority Council, made up of representatives from the school district and all the major city departments, that meets with each sector team before they turn in their plans. To facilitate better citizen-government relationships outside the planning process, they have also established Neighborhood Empowerment Teams, made up of city staffers and police lieutenants working out of six different storefront offices around the city. The Team offices serve as resource centers for all kinds of citizen concerns: you can get a building permit, register a complaint about excessive noise, register for a youth program, or find out about housing codes, all in one location.

Finally, the experiences with citizen-government collaboration drove home the need for more training of city staff and sector leaders. A National League of Cities report on NBN claims that Rochester public employees began to realize that process was as important as results, and their roles ought to be "community centered" rather than simply "job focused." The role of city planners, in particular, was "intentionally shifted from planning on behalf of citizens to facilitating a process through which the community members conducted planning."[55] Residents and public employees now make decisions together in every area of city operations, including code enforcement, signage, public works, historic preservation, crime prevention, parks, and economic development. Many aspects of the neighborhood plans have been codified in the city's new zoning code, which is very unusual in that it dictates design standards but has few restrictions on the use of land.[56]

It soon became apparent that tracking the outcomes of NBN, which ranged from high-profile policy decisions to tiny volunteer projects, would be an enormous task in itself. In order to help citizens quantify their progress, the city used federal funds to create the NeighborLink Network, an information management system that shows, by percentage of goals achieved, how well each neighborhood has been doing on the implementation of its most recent plan. At every public library in Rochester, residents can use Global Information System (GIS) mapping technology, access websites for each NBN sector, find grant sources and available volunteers, and direct questions to the Neighborhood Empowerment Teams.[57] As another way of communicating their plans and progress, several sectors have established their own newspapers, with funding from the Rochester-based Kodak Corporation.

There seems to be a sizable constituency for democratic governance in Rochester. According to the city's most recent estimate, roughly 6,300 people take part in NBN activities every year.[58] However, unlike the Los Angeles neighborhood councils, NBN is not an official government structure: it could be described as a management practice married to a grassroots organizing process. Argust calls it an "ad hocracy" that relies on well-defined timeframes (six months of planning followed by a year of implementation), a constant supply of fresh volunteers, and a great deal of support from the city.[59]

Mayor Johnson has served his final term, and Rochester residents are now wondering about the future of NBN. Argust thinks that "if the support system is ever taken away, then the model will continue for a while, but not indefinitely—some sectors would keep going, but others might atrophy quickly."[60] Giess says, "We need to get things moving again—despite all that NBN has accomplished, the system is in peril."[61] Presumably, the new mayor will embrace the system for both political and practical reasons, but that may not be enough to guarantee its survival over the long term. If the Los Angeles neighborhood councils need to become more democratic, perhaps their Rochester counterparts should become more republican; they might develop a continuous schedule of sector team meetings, more formal connections between sectors and the city council members representing those districts, and an official process through which the sectors could take part in citywide policy decisions. This kind of protective greenhouse might sustain neighborhood planning without crimping its innately organic character.

From the outside, the limits of democratic governance as a purely urban experiment are also clear. Though Rochester property values have risen dramatically, and the housing stock has improved, the city continues to lose population and wealth to the surrounding suburbs. "We're at the bottom of the food chain," complains Johnson, who argues that cities bear all the costs of metropolitan development—social services, policing, infrastructure, homeland security—without receiving adequate support from the suburbs or the state and federal governments.[62] "The exodus of middle class people over the last thirty years was dramatic," says Argust. "The city takes up 5% of the land in the county, but 75% of the low-income people live there. NBN has done a lot of great things, but to put the burden of overcoming that concentration of social ills on a model like NBN may be asking too much."[63] The success of nearby Pittsford (see Chapter 8) proves that democratic governance is *not* a purely urban experiment—but if they cannot find ways to make it a regional phenomenon as well, both communities may suffer.

The Next Life of Great American Cities

Among his fellow mayors, William Johnson still feels like a nonconformist. "I have colleagues who have said to me, 'Have you lost your mind?' " he says, "because in their minds, the powers of government are very clear, finite and not to be shared. The will of the people is an abstract theory."[64] He's either the craziest mayor in America or the sanest. The latest developments suggest the latter: just as more communities are embracing Ed Weeks's theories of participatory budgeting, an even larger number have been setting up neighborhood council and planning systems similar to those in Rochester. The abstract theory is becoming much more tangible, thanks to the hard realities of dwindling city budgets and persistent public problems.

For public officials, it is a world turned upside down. Face-to-face with complaining citizens, defeated tax increases, and secession attempts, they are forced on the fly to reconsider their most basic assumptions about public service. At conferences of the National League of Cities and the International City-County Manager's Association, the panels and side conversations sometimes feel like group therapy sessions, as public managers complain, commiserate, and help each other try to adapt.

Though it may not hit them with the same psychological force, it is a brave new world for city residents too. The question of who provides for the general welfare can't be answered with the old Progressive equation, in which citizens' tax contributions support government problem-solving. The new problem-solvers are a varying mix of citizens, public employees, churches, nonprofit organizations, and other community groups, working in different ways on different issues. People may support public services by paying for them with their tax contributions, paying for them through the organizations they belong to, or paying for them with their volunteer efforts.

This is a complicated relationship, and it is making the public life of cities more and more complex. As a result, we have clearly outstripped the traditional modes for citizen-government communication. It is not enough, anymore, for local governments to produce reports or newsletters on public services and policy decisions—they are lost in the daily media barrage that hits every household. As they try to provide information to citizens, public employees need to focus on quality and not just quantity.[65] Some communities are adopting interactive, Internet-based information systems, like Rochester's NeighborLink Network, in order to help citizens track the decision-making process and monitor public issues. When people have a chance to report on their own work and register their own views, thereby adding to the data themselves, they are more likely to absorb and use the information they receive. This more interactive approach to the evaluation and documentation of public problem-solving might complement the more proactive stance of citizens in the next form of democracy.[66]

The larger challenge facing cities is how to reconcile the structural imbalance between citizen organizations and government departments. Cities need a kind of political architecture that will routinely bring people and public employees together as equal partners with separate roles. These citizen structures should serve a range of purposes, not only giving people political opportunities but social and cultural ones as well. "We sometimes forget that people are desperate for social connections," says Lois Giess, the Rochester city council president. "They make time for things like NBN because these experiences fill a void in their lives."[67]

There are also the legal aspects to consider. It may be a mistake to create neighborhood structures that look like mini-governments, as in Los Angeles; it is clear from that example that the open meetings laws and other measures enacted to bolster citizen participation decades ago are no longer up to the task. At the same time, establishing structures and processes that have no laws whatsoever to protect them may be just as futile. We need a new legal framework for democratic governance, one that allows for flexibility, transparency, and permanence.[68]

Inside government, mayors and city department heads need to design organizational structures that can interface more easily with people and groups outside City Hall. In some instances, this means creating teams of employees from different departments who can work with neighborhoods in a more holistic way. In other cases, it may require flattening the organizational hierarchies. In most places, it means giving all kinds of public employees—not just a handful of community relations specialists—more chances to work directly with citizens. Just as democratic governance forces public officials to rethink their most basic assumptions, it will also be a difficult shift for their employees. To help them adapt, smart local leaders will provide training, incentives, and opportunities for them to compare notes with their peers.

We seem to be on the cusp of the most dramatic changes in the structure of local government in the last hundred years. It is a prospect that is both thrilling and terrifying. It is likely to be a painful transition, as citizens and public servants negotiate new rules for their relationship. But it also represents the opportunity of a lifetime, as we shape and are shaped by these changes, to establish forms of governance that are efficient and egalitarian, deliberative and decisive. It is a chance to renovate and revitalize the level of government that most directly affects the lives of ordinary people, creating systems that will help citizens and public employees understand, from one situation to the next, what they want from each other. The "will of the people" is turning from an abstract theory into a daily force in local politics; the question is whether we can design institutions that can accommodate it.

Conclusion—Things to Come

In the last ten years, I have found myself in the same situation over and over again. The recurring scene is a planning meeting: the people in the room are talking about how to mobilize citizens around a key issue in their community. The composition of the group varies from place to place, but it is usually a mix of public officials, long-time volunteers, neighborhood activists, and directors of nonprofit organizations. I am there to listen, and to describe what other communities have done.

For the most part, the tone of the discussion is hopeful: these are capable, confident people, leaders who believe that they can make progress on an issue like education, crime prevention, or public finance. They are talking about the difficulties of getting citizens, public officials, and community organizations to work together. Suddenly, the conversation comes to a complete halt: someone turns to me and says, "You've got to understand—it's different here. It's political."

The response to this statement is invariably the same: people nod solemnly, sigh, sometimes laugh a little ruefully, and move on. They act as though there is nothing they can do about "politics." They seem to think their community has been infected by some unique, incurable virus.

There are two ironies here. First, I have watched this scene being enacted so many times that I can say, from firsthand experience, that the scourge of "politics" is not unique to any one community. People in very different cities and towns have very similar complaints; if they had the chance to talk it through, I suspect they would come to roughly the same conclusions about what is wrong with public decision-making and problem-solving.

Second, these leaders seldom realize that what they are doing, or planning to do, is changing the very nature of politics. They may be focused on improving the schools, ending racism, or balancing the city budget, but their work is about more than that: they are trying to transform the ways in which citizens and government interact. They are part of a shift that is broader and deeper than they know.

In fact, we are all sailing on this same sea. In communities throughout North America, the skills, capacities, and frustrations of ordinary people are spilling over into the political process. Despite their disgust with politics, or perhaps because of it, citizens have become a stronger, more vocal force in public decision-making than at any time in the last 100 years. Obviously, these generalizations gloss over class and cultural differences—as usual, the "haves" are more connected than the "have nots," raising the question of how changes in democracy may reinforce social inequalities—but even in economically impoverished neighborhoods like Southwest Delray Beach and Rochester's Sector 10, people are demonstrating both their capacity for action and their impatience with expert rule.

At the same time, local leaders are trying to solve daunting public problems without the same levels of funding, legitimacy, and public trust that they used to enjoy. Practitioners in planning, education, law enforcement, human relations, environmental protection, housing, economic development, and public health are realizing that they need more support if they are going to succeed. They are increasingly unwilling or unable to sidestep citizens by hiding behind financial data or scientific jargon. They seem more aware of the benefits and complications presented by cultural difference. Many of them, like Mark Linder and Tom Argust, have experience as community organizers or neighborhood activists, and so they have seen the citizen-government divide from both sides of the barricade.

These conditions have set the stage for the development of democratic governance. It is neither a "top-down" shift nor a sign of grassroots "bottom-up" change: it is the result of both, interconnected, happening at the same time. Though these pressures are most visible at the local level, they are increasingly evident in regional, state, and federal politics as well. Citizens and officials are becoming frustrated with each other, and trying to find new ways to work together, even on policy questions like homeland security and pandemic influenza. The ripples are extending far beyond local politics, into the realms of the media, the Internet, presidential campaigns, and foreign policy.

It may be a little misleading to call this transition an "evolution" of democracy, since that term implies that we are moving inevitably toward some higher, better, more advanced plane of public life. It is unclear what lies ahead. But to make the most of the changes, we need to move beyond the assumption that "It's different here." We're all in this together; we're all facing the question of how politics ought to function. At the beginning of the twenty-first century, it is different in a lot of places.

Troubled Waters

Though it is clear that public life is changing, it is hard to tell where the currents are taking us. Some observers may argue that, pushed from above and below, our political system is already embracing principles of democratic governance. Others would point out that while civic experiments are proliferating, these projects and structures can be found in only a small percentage of the vast number of neighborhoods, cities, and towns in this country.

Democratic governance may even founder of its own accord. The principles embodied in these efforts have been useful so far, but there are at least three main ways to misuse them:

1. Organizers might repeatedly underestimate the importance of proactive, broad-based recruitment, and fail to allow enough time or resources to do it well. The people who have been left out might begin to confront and undermine democratic governance efforts. Public officials would start to doubt whether these projects and systems can be even remotely representative, and cite their accountability to the larger electorate as a rationale for tuning out active citizens.

2. Organizers might repeatedly misjudge the time and effort it takes to move from dialogue to action in these projects. If they do not give participants a meaningful chance to work on action ideas or advocate for policy changes, people will become frustrated and democratic governance will become associated with empty talk rather than tangible improvements.

3. Officials and other leaders may repeatedly try to co-opt civic experiments, and manipulate them so that participants come to the "correct" conclusions. This would probably damage both the reputation of democratic governance and the political fortunes of the officials themselves: when people have the chance to analyze information together in small groups, it usually becomes quite apparent when an organizer is withholding key facts, excluding common viewpoints, or asking the facilitators to operate in a biased way.

The first two examples could be considered typical flaws of traditional citizen involvement, to go with the others mentioned in Chapter 2; the third is simply an attempt to manipulate people. As you might expect, there have already been instances where one or more of these scenarios have played out in a community, and they are bound to recur in other places. Each time this happens, organizers are probably increasing citizen alienation and eroding public trust. Democratic governance efforts can increase trust, but to get started, they require at least a basic level of goodwill—citizens and officials have to be willing to take the leap of faith that this experience will help them make a real impact.[1] This suggests a kind of basic arithmetic: the number of well-planned, well-organized, ethically sound projects will have to stay sufficiently ahead of the faulty few.

Bigger Targets

There are other, more direct challenges that democratic governance efforts will have to face. In fact, the very success of these civic experiments may make them more vulnerable: as they gain more visibility, it becomes more enticing for other public figures to try shooting them down.

Tulsa, Oklahoma, provides one example. In 2004, the president of the Tulsa school board, Paul Thomas, began promoting the idea of greater community involvement in issues facing the public schools. He secured the support of several local churches and an interfaith group called the Tulsa Metro Ministry (TMM). Thomas and his allies felt that these faith institutions could be the neutral "convening group" for a democratic governance effort that would bridge the schools and the community. They also won over the mayor, three university presidents, and the school superintendent, who was in the midst of launching his own internal school reform effort, the Baldrige Initiative, which was designed to get educators talking with each other about ways to improve the schools. The mayor's office and the YWCA gave in-kind staff support, the local campus of Oklahoma State University donated office space, and TMM and other groups provided enough funding to get the project going. It would be called "Tulsa Talks: A Community Dialogue for Public Education."

The ambitious goal of Tulsa Talks was to involve 10,000 people in democratic small-group sessions within its first few years of operation. Before the project could even begin, however, a local radio station began campaigning against it. "Standing Up For What's Right!" is the motto of KFAQ Radio. The station made "The Truth Behind Tulsa Talks" one of the top stories on its broadcasts and website. The host of the station's morning show led the charge, calling Tulsa Talks "anti-American, anti-faith, and anti-family." One of the show's regular callers claimed that the project was "a front for the promotion of homosexual lifestyles and the Islamic movement."[2] This was despite the fact that many Oklahoma conservatives, including the Christian Coalition in Weatherford, had supported and participated in the previous statewide democratic governance efforts sponsored by the League of Women Voters (see Chapter 5).

The radio personality predicted that the Tulsa Talks discussions would start out innocently enough, but that midway through the dialogue, the facilitators would begin driving the groups toward particular conclusions. He recruited some of his listeners to attend the sessions, either to disrupt the proceedings or to use hidden tape recorders. Several of the small groups had great difficulty setting ground rules and getting their conversations started. At least one listener brought her clandestine recording to the radio station, in violation of the ground rules on confidentiality she had agreed to with her fellow participants, and the host played parts of it on the air. Another listener, when interviewed by the host, made references to her group's "lesbian-loving facilitator" on the air.

The mayor, superintendent, and other supporters of Tulsa Talks chose not to respond to these attacks, and they weren't mentioned in the *Tulsa World,* the city's major newspaper. Paul Thomas felt that any response would only give credence to KFAQ; he hoped that the station would "milk us for ratings and then move on to other topics." But while KFAQ did eventually move on, the radio assault was damaging to Tulsa Talks. The project had great difficulty raising enough money to stay afloat. Thomas said later that "it took a lot of the wind out of our sails. I felt like some of the main funding sources stayed away from us because they thought we were 'tainted' by the radio attacks."[3] In the next school board election, Thomas was defeated, to loud applause at KFAQ. (Because Thomas's district is primarily Democratic and African American, however, the KFAQ opposition probably didn't play a key role in the outcome.)

In retrospect, Thomas and his allies might have made a mistake by not attracting enough early supporters from the right of the political spectrum. The original convening group included synagogues, mosques, and mainstream Protestant and Catholic churches, but not evangelical churches. Other Tulsa observers, however, say that KFAQ would have attacked Tulsa Talks no matter how broad its base of support had been.[4]

On the other hand, Tulsa Talks seemed to have an effect on some of the KFAQ listeners who took part in the sessions. After the initial arguments about ground rules, most of the groups went fairly smoothly. Over 350 people participated in early 2005, and "some of the KFAQ people turned out to be very productive group members," says Thomas.[5]

So far, the saga of Tulsa Talks is by far the most extreme example of opposition to a democratic governance effort. It may be a harbinger of things to come: right-wing radio stations in other communities may react similarly to democratic governance. While "left-wing radio" is not quite the same cultural phenomenon, critics on that end of the spectrum may also find that they have a lot to gain by opposing these civic experiments.

Some of these criticisms may turn out to be justified and constructive. The KFAQ claims about "homosexual lifestyles and the Islamic movement" don't seem plausible or productive, but other challenges from the right or the left may be more on point. In fact, critics who urge their supporters to participate skeptically in a project—in order to keep the facilitators impartial and the organizers honest—are probably making a positive contribution to the development of democratic governance. Hidden tape recorders aside, KFAQ actually helped Tulsa Talks recruit right-wing evangelicals, an audience that Paul Thomas and his allies had definitely wanted to include.

As democratic governance comes up increasingly on the media radar, it will probably attract more attacks, both substantive and spurious. Elected officials and other public figures may also realize they can sometimes gain more by attacking democratic governance projects than supporting them. The experiment in Lakewood, Colorado, discussed in Chapters 3 and 8, came to an abrupt halt, in part for this reason. Mayor Steve Burkholder had assembled a politically diverse team of forty community leaders to plan a democratic governance effort focusing on the city's budget. The group met for nine months, designing a process that would help Lakewood residents decide whether a sales tax increase was necessary. A number of city council members who had been at odds over budget issues took part in these meetings. Finally, just before the project was to kick into high gear, one city councilman began publicly disputing the city's budget projections, attacking the plan to engage residents, and asking that the city manager resign or be dismissed. Tensions rose, and the pro-tax and anti-tax members of the planning group began to fall out with one another. Fundraising efforts faltered, and the group had to put their plans on hold.[6]

The Lakewood city councilman may have had valid concerns about the city manager and the incipient democratic governance effort. The point is that the project's high visibility gave him greater incentives to attack them. Especially if the issue being addressed is particularly divisive, or the people initiating the project are tilted toward one side of the political spectrum or the other, a public figure may have a lot to gain by throwing down the gauntlet.

As Paul Thomas and Steve Burkholder can attest, developing new forms of governance is arduous and sometimes painful work. Having weathered the storms, Tulsa Talks and the Lakewood budget project may turn out to be even stronger than before. In fact, over 500 people have now been involved in Tulsa Talks; the Lakewood sales tax increase finally passed in November 2005, and Burkholder is now planning to reconvene his group to try involving citizens in other issues. As civic experiments multiply, communities will have to ride out these unremitting waves of success and failure.

Combining Democracy and Republicanism

It may be a mistake to dwell on whether democratic governance will survive these challenges: the question is probably too simplistic. After all, we are not talking about a distinct, coherent movement, complete with its own leaders, followers, and rhetoric. It would be more accurate to say that communities all across the country, in the face of some new and widespread challenges, have responded to those conditions by organizing projects and structures that embody democratic principles. The pioneers of democratic governance are isolated from one another by geography, issue, and profession. It would be an understatement to say that this is a work in progress: what we are witnessing, in fact, are hundreds of works in various stages of development. Given all of this variety and flux, perhaps the real question is not whether democratic governance will survive, but how it too will adapt and change.

So far, the new civic experiments have taken two main forms: temporary organizing efforts like Lee County Pulling Together, the Decatur Round Tables, and Balancing Justice in Oklahoma (described in Chapters 3, 4, and 5), and permanent decision-making systems like the Chicago school councils and the Los Angeles neighborhood councils (Chapters 7 and 8). The short-term efforts have generally been more participatory and democratic: they use proactive, network-based recruitment to attract people who don't normally get involved, and they emphasize the importance of deliberative group processes, with facilitators, ground rules, and discussion materials that allow all voices to be heard.[7] The long-term structures tend to have more representative, republican elements, such as bylaws, elected officers, and an official role in public decision-making. These differences may be due to the fact that the temporary projects were driven by the need for dialogue and collaboration between citizens, whereas most of the permanent structures were intended to serve as arenas for neighborhood leaders, and were designed in imitation of traditional public institutions. There are however, exceptions: some of the most successful long-term projects, such as the Strong Neighborhoods Initiative in San José (Chapter 3), Kuna ACT (Chapter 5), the Plainfield Accountability Plan (Chapter 7), and Neighbors Building Neighborhoods in Rochester (Chapter 8), seem to embody a mix of democracy and republicanism. In other words, they have elected leaders who are charged with representing their constituents, but they also have regular, official, meaningful opportunities for all kinds of citizens to participate in powerful ways.

It seems safe to say that organizers will continue to use both short-term and long-term strategies. Temporary projects will be necessary to deal with crises, time-sensitive policy decisions, and the input-gathering needs of state and federal decision-makers. Permanent structures will arise from the desire to keep citizens mobilized, and to give neighborhood leaders and parent activists a more established role in local politics.

On the other hand, it remains to be seen how the dynamic between democracy and republicanism will play out. An historian might argue that large-scale democratic movements have a tendency to produce institutional republican reforms. In other words, when large numbers of citizens mobilize for discussion and action around a particular issue or cause, one common result is that new councils, commissions, and organizations are set up to protect their rights, provide them with power or official authority, and continue advocating for their interests. These new or reformed institutions are usually republican systems, however, with room for only a few citizens who have been elected to represent the rest. Once the victory is won, most of the people go home.[8] This, then, is one plausible possibility: democratic organizing efforts will lead to purely republican structures like school and neighborhood councils. (Some observers might argue that this is basically what happened in Chicago and Los Angeles.)

Another possibility is that democratic governance efforts, of both the temporary and permanent varieties, will continue proliferating without resulting in any other new institutions or types of reforms. Some of the people who promote this vision hold the view that civil society should be separate and distinct from the regular functioning of government. Others would say that the lines between government and civil society are already blurred, but have trouble envisioning any reforms that would make it easier for citizens, public officials, and public employees to work together on a permanent basis. Still others shy away from any outcome that includes the word "institution." "To institutionalize something is to kill it," seems to be a favorite pronouncement among people of the Baby Boom generation, who lived through the great institution-shaking decade of the 1960s.

The third major possibility is that more communities will follow the lead of Kuna, Plainfield, San José, and Rochester, and create new public processes and institutions that combine republican and democratic elements. This seems to be the most promising course. "Even when civil society is active, engaged and energized, there must be a framework that entrenches their engagement in the governing and decision making institutions of their lands," say the civic researchers Miriam Wyman and David Shulman. "Only with changes in the ways that citizen involvement is institutionalized will democracy be strong."[9] As Paul Thomas puts it, "We spend a lot of time doing public engagement, but if we don't change the organizations that we're engaging people in, we're just 'putting new wine into old wineskins.' "[10] Public institutions are the organizations which deal with public problems and make public decisions, and the way we structure them makes a critical difference. Like it or not, institutions matter—and if they are going to work for us, they must be both democratic and republican.

Building Better Boats

It is one thing to decide we need public institutions that combine democracy and republicanism; it is another thing to build them. In his book *The Democratic Wish,* the political scientist James Morone warns us about a disturbing historical phenomenon: the institutions that were intended to draw in the public often became more Byzantine, bureaucratic, and expert-dominated than the institutions they replaced.[11] When we wish for a democratic republic, we are imagining a ship of state that has not yet been built.

This doesn't mean we shouldn't try. Even Morone says that "the present challenge is to infuse our institutions with broad, workable forms of popular participation; rather than pursuing the ideal on the fringes, linking it directly to the institutions that govern the political economy: the people indoors."[12] It does mean that we need to pay careful attention to the experiences of existing democratic governance efforts. These programs suggest a whole new set of better practices.

Perhaps the most significant task is to build new citizen structures, or renovate the existing ones, at the school and neighborhood level. These school councils, neighborhood councils, priority boards, and other groups are promising for a number of reasons. They have the capacity to involve a wide variety of people, partly because they focus on the issues that are closest to home. They can give citizens the chance to affect citywide policies, formulate plans for their schools and neighborhoods, and take action themselves. They serve as springboards for new leaders. They give people access to community networks, cultural opportunities, and chances to connect with young people and senior citizens. They can confer a sense of political legitimacy on citizen efforts, emboldening residents to move forward with their ideas. Finally, they can give people the kind of "public happiness" that comes with belonging to a community where everyone is respected and heard.

In order to fulfill this potential, however, citizen structures need some basic prerequisites:

1. They need a clear sense of the extent and limitations of their authority. It may not matter so much whether these councils and associations have their own decision-making powers or are simply advisors to government: both can be influential roles.[13] The important thing is that people know what kinds of benefits and responsibilities come with their participation in this institution. "You have to make it clear to citizens that you aren't just asking for their input," says Roger Stancil, city manager of Fayetteville, North Carolina. "You want them to contribute their own time and effort to solving problems in their neighborhood and community."[14] Citizens must be given the message that they are legitimate actors.

2. They should use proactive, network-based recruitment strategies along with meeting agendas that allow room for deliberative small-group processes. But instead of mandating these procedures, city councils and school boards may be better off if they play a more advisory role, offering the kind of encouragement, incentives, and staff support demonstrated in Rochester and San José. Citizen leaders need "how-to" materials, opportunities for training, chances to hear from their counterparts in other places, and technical assistance from professionals who can listen to their concerns and help them design organizing strategies.

3. They should acknowledge how school and neighborhood priorities overlap. In most places, school councils and neighborhood councils seem quite segregated from one another, even though the parents at a school meeting and the residents at the nearby neighborhood meeting probably have many issues and concerns in common. Both kinds of structures would be better if they forged stronger connections and worked together on certain issues—in some cases, school and neighborhood councils might even be merged. In addition, both types will be more successful if they maintain strong ties with other local institutions, like churches, workplaces, colleges and universities, service clubs, youth groups, and libraries. People who congregate at those other places can be recruited to take part in the work of school and neighborhood councils; the councils could also hold some of their meetings at those other locations.

4. Communities should create more sophisticated methods for tracking the numbers and diversity of participants. By quantifying and assessing the

size and representativeness of the turnout, decision-makers would get a better sense of how broadly supported a group's policy recommendations might be. The leaders of these groups would be encouraged to include more of their neighbors and peers; they could establish benchmarks for turnout like the ones used by the Leadership, Innovation and Change Councils in the Plainfield Public Schools. A basic measure of the effectiveness of a group is whether people continue to participate in it—in that sense, they are "voting with their feet"—and so tracking turnout is one key way to gauge whether a citizen structure is being responsive to its constituency.

5.   Citizen structures may require their own staffing. It takes time and skills to perform all of the functions necessary to make democratic governance work, and many of these tasks are things that can't be done by people working out of City Hall, the planning department, or the school district office. Funding for these positions wouldn't necessarily have to come from government; indeed, one of the lessons of the recent wave of civic experiments is that nonprofit organizations, foundations, civic associations, and other groups are capable of funding and leading efforts to involve citizens in public life. But whatever its source, financial support for these positions must be steady and secure, so that staffers are not constantly searching for grants and donations in order to stay in their jobs.[15]

Citizen structures don't have to be the only political avenue for ordinary people. When important issues or policy decisions emerge, local officials should reach out to participants through other kinds of organizations: chambers of commerce, racial and ethnic organizations, environmental groups, historic preservation organizations, immigrant service groups, and political parties and clubs, churches, workplaces, universities, service clubs, youth groups, and libraries. In some situations, groups like the League of Women Voters or Springfield's Race Relations Task Force may even begin to resemble citizen structures themselves—attracting large numbers of members and regularly engaging them in discussion and action on a range of issues.

As the political culture of a community becomes an increasingly complex stew of different interconnected groups, conflicts and rivalries are bound to emerge. (In places like Dayton and Los Angeles, for example, neighborhood councils and priority boards are sometimes at odds with other groups in those neighborhoods). This will be a continuing challenge, and communities need procedures and meeting formats to help different sets of citizens come together to address these conflicts. Local officials, who will usually have the final say in these matters, will be better off if citizens can bargain face-to-face, as they did in Eugene and Sacramento Decisions (Chapter 8).

Public Meetings That Work for the Public

Another way we might refit our ship of state is by changing the way public meetings are run. City councils, school boards, land use commissions, and other public entities function in ways that are increasingly out of step with the larger changes in the citizen-government relationship. It may be tempting to think that if we can establish better school and neighborhood governance—creating a better "ground floor" for democracy, so to speak— then no further changes will be necessary. However, the more that citizens become active in addressing public problems, the more frustrated they become when they encounter governmental bodies that don't acknowledge their need to be heard. Stronger democracy at the grass roots may simply seed more conflict between citizens and government, and make it harder to handle disputes between different schools and neighborhoods.

The two main bywords for public meetings are efficiency (making decisions quickly, fairly, and well) and openness (in this case, meaning advance notice of meetings, opportunities for public comment, no confidential discussions, and published minutes or records). Both of these criteria are clearly compatible with democratic governance, but by themselves they do not guarantee successful meetings, and some of the methods for achieving them are out of date. For example, "comment periods" where people may approach an open microphone to ask questions or give their opinions, as they did at the Buffalo action forum (Chapter 8), are seldom satisfactory to either the citizens or the public officials. That time, which can be quite lengthy, would be better spent in facilitated small-group discussions with the officials mingling with the audience members. On particularly important questions, the board or council members should allow time for a separate session where they could deliberate with the public; this is essentially what happens when the Kuna school board or city council turns an issue over to Kuna ACT. This strategy tends to weed out spurious individual opinions and helps valid "minority" views gain broader support.

As they pioneer new processes, officials will have to negotiate the balance between openness and confidentiality. Small-group sessions are most successful when the participants can set their own ground rules, and confidentiality is one of the most common rules. When elected officials are part of the discussion, this practice may be in conflict with the letter, if not the intent, of open meetings laws. However, it is possible to hold these conversations in a way that is both workable and legal; one approach is to allow individual comments to be confidential as long as the small group makes some kind of consensual public report. In any case, local, state, and federal open meeting laws should be re-examined, and in some cases redesigned, so that they support rather than hinder democratic governance.[16]

When officials foresee that an upcoming agenda is likely to generate some controversy, they could recruit proactively for that meeting rather than relying on the standard advance notice procedures—a routine drill that tends to reach only the most government-focused citizens. In order to attract a wider array of people, officials should maintain strong coalitions of citizen structures and other community groups that can help them recruit, both by reaching people directly and by lending their credibility to government's call for participation. In some cases, third parties like Kuna ACT might be a more credible and legitimate host for such a forum than the government body itself. Other coalitions that link city councils with neighborhood leaders, like the Decatur Neighborhood Alliance, the Hampton Neighborhood Commission, and Rochester's Priority Council, demonstrate the ability of these groups to help officials foresee the issues that are emerging in the neighborhoods; Plainfield's district and school council system fulfills a similar role for that school system.

By using these tactics for recruitment, deliberation, and coalition-building, public boards and councils would add a third criterion—participation—to the traditional standards of openness and efficiency. Rather than having to sit through meetings where the public is either angry or absent, elected officials would enjoy a system that allows them to probe and comprehend how people feel about important issues. Citizens would not only get more opportunities to provide input to the policymaking process, they would gain new allies and a deeper understanding of how to make those policies work.

All Hands on Deck

Pioneers of democratic governance often focus on citizens and public officials, only to learn that government employees are also a critical part of the equation. Public employees need to be reoriented so that they are able to work more closely with the public. This is not simply a matter of asking public servants to be more approachable and eager to please. It also should not be confused with the common practice of "constituent service," where staffers of elected officials run around replying to hundreds of questions and requests from individual citizens—*How do I get a building permit?*

How can I get assistance for paying my heating bill? Where is city hall located?[17]

Rather than fulfilling requests, public employees need the skills, training, and organizational framework that will change their sense of accountability. As Harvard's Xavier Briggs puts it, "There are many ideas about how institutions should become more *responsive* to what we tell them we want—to our feedback, that is. But there is little recognition of the fact that the institutions themselves need new skills and capacities to engage with citizens in a new kind of problem-solving where expertise, resources, and decisions are all shared more widely."[18] It is not enough to say that government alone cannot solve all public problems: we have to follow up on that realization by giving public employees the tools they need to get help, advice, and support from citizens and community organizations.

In this transition, we need to enlarge the concept of planning, because it is the most proactive way for public employees to put their democratic skills to work. Planning should not be limited to land use questions: more cities should follow the lead of Decatur, Georgia (Chapter 3), and develop community plans that focus on social issues as well. These plans can help citizens, public employees, and elected officials set the goals and benchmarks they need to measure their progress and performance. "Planning is an essential act of democratic citizenship," says William Shutkin, president of the Orton Foundation.[19]

Reorienting public employees will require a fundamental change in the philosophy of public administration. "The employees usually look to the elected officials—it can be a big shift for them to think that the citizens are their main constituency," says Kevin Frazell, who works for the League of Minnesota Cities.[20] This may be particularly true for mid-level public employees, who are often more insulated from citizens than elected officials or rank-and-file employees like police officers or teachers. Making this shift work will require a comprehensive approach that reinforces the principles of democratic governance at different points in the career of a public employee. The first step is changing the orientation of the professional schools, a shift that is already occurring in some of the graduate programs in public policy and public administration (see Chapter 2). Instead of indoctrinating students to believe that their expertise will be enough to solve public problems, some professors are asking them to adopt the mindset that public administration is about helping people to govern themselves. Once they have entered the workforce, public employees need training programs, like the ones in San José and Rochester, which introduce or sharpen democratic governance skills like coalition-building, recruitment, facilitation, participatory land use planning, and participatory budgeting. And like the public officials, whose changing attitude towards citizens is evident at the meetings of the National League of Cities, staffers need opportunities to compare notes with their peers in other parts of the city and the country.

It may be difficult for public employees to interact more democratically with citizens if the departments and agencies they work in are old-fashioned, command-and-control environments. If civil servants feel that they do not have the freedom to make changes, they will not react well to suggestions made by citizens. In the private sector, many businesses have adopted management systems that give employees more control over the way they work; over the last fifteen years, many public-sector employers have followed suit. Efforts to engage citizens should go hand-in-hand with changes in the internal workings of City Hall or the school district office. This is evident in places like Kansas City, Kansas (Chapter 2), where the democratic governance initiative was paralleled by a process that helped educators decide how they might improve the schools.

Finally, public employees need strong relationships with organized groups of citizens, rather than having to respond to the questions and complaints of disconnected individuals. Connecting with citizen structures, as the planners in Kalamazoo, Hampton, and Delray Beach have done, can give staffers a clearer, more gratifying sense of who their true constituents are.

Each community will approach this work differently. As local leaders reorient their public employees and find other ways to strengthen democratic governance—rebuilding citizen structures, redesigning public meetings—they will undoubtedly construct their own unique models. There is no need for all these ships to be identical. As long as they combine elements of democracy and republicanism, they will be better able to link up with one another, connecting citizen voices to regional, state, and federal decision making. Legislators, other state and federal officials, and national civic groups can use the local structures to gather input on policies and gain support for implementing them. This will make projects like Balancing Justice in Oklahoma, Oregon Health Decisions, and the Canadian Immigration Review (Chapter 5) somewhat easier to organize.[21] To capitalize on these opportunities, state and federal officials must heed the same lessons about public employees and public meetings, and make changes that complement what is happening at the local level.

For people who are eager to effect change in national politics, this may seem like a long and arduous process. It is tempting to think that by holding some kind of national convention or Internet event, we can galvanize democracy overnight. But while the local work may appear gradual or even glacial, it isn't: communities have already made dramatic changes in a relatively short period of time. The best statewide democratic governance efforts—"Speak Up! Arkansas" is one example—have proved it is possible to organize across wide geographic expanses in ways that strengthen local democracy as well as affect state policy. Public officials are beginning to grasp these possibilities. "We believe that the processes of democratic governance work on any level: local, regional, state, and national," says Robin Beltramini, a city councilwoman from Troy, Michigan.[22] In any case, the local work cannot be ignored: without it, most attempts to get people involved in federal issues will not seem safe enough to get the support of public officials, or powerful enough to attract citizens. To construct a truly democratic republic, you have to build from the ground up.

Shaping the Future of Politics

Regardless of how communities fare as they try to create shared governance, the tide of change in local politics will affect other aspects of our lives. The way in which citizens and government interact has an impact on elections, polling, lobbying, the media, the Internet, and our attitudes toward democracy in other parts of the world. The shifts in that relationship—whether they are harmonious, acrimonious, or some combination of the two—are bound to produce other changes, both positive and negative.

The "small politics" of local decision-making and neighborhood problem-solving are usually drowned out by the "big politics" of elections, sound bites, and television ads. It is only a matter of time, however, before smart candidates take some of the concerns propelling democratic governance and convert them into the next generation of campaign issues. The most likely flashpoints seem to be land use, taxation, and education, partly because these concerns are most evident in the segment of the electorate that candidates are always trying to reach: middle-class homeowners with children.[23]

Each of these three issues provides fertile ground for new political rhetoric. To describe their positions on land use, candidates may adopt more forceful language, like "homeowner protection" or "neighborhood rule." They may try to paint their opponents as elitists, claiming that traditional zoning processes put the control of land firmly in the hands of government and developers. On questions of public finance, candidates may promise voters more control over their tax revenues, invoking slogans like "citizen-directed budgets" or "no taxation without authorization." By taking this stand, they can claim that their opponents support spending by politicians and lobbyists. When it comes to education, candidates may advocate "family-driven" or "parent-directed schools." They may promise voters a more permanent, official role in school decision-making, and accuse their opponents of supporting the status quo in education.

As officials invent or expand the language of democratic governance in order to get elected, this may in turn produce more democratic governance in practice. On the other hand, some candidates may only pay lip service to these ideas, using them to demonize developers, superintendents, and lobbyists without actually adopting new ways of governing. Making these issues "political" will probably also make it harder to mobilize citizens across party lines.

Because they focus on local issues, these kinds of election tactics will presumably emerge first in local campaigns—in fact, some observers will tell you that they already have. However, they won't necessarily stop there: even presidential campaigns often turn on concerns that first germinated in races for mayor, school board, or city council. Smart candidates speak to what people care about; the latest trends in land use, public finance, and education suggest new possibilities for state and federal policy, and new ways of appealing to voters.

If these issues do have an impact on state and federal elections, the consequences could be far-reaching. We are probably due for another tectonic shift in the balance of party politics: every decade or so, a new set of political ideas bursts onto the campaign scene, sending one major party into dominance, the other into the doldrums. The last major shift was the 1994 election, which shocked and awed the Democrats and gave the Republicans control of Congress. Perhaps the Democrats will use democratic governance to turn the tables.

But do these ideas actually belong to the left wing of the political spectrum, or to the right? The answer is probably neither. Some of the issues tackled by democratic governance efforts—like race, or sprawl—are nearer to liberal hearts than conservative ones. However, the outcomes of these projects can't be easily categorized as serving right-wing or left-wing interests. Liberals are excited by the passage of school bond issues in places like Kuna or Inglewood, but examples like Eugene Decisions are victories for fiscal conservatism. For every new economic development project backed by government funds, like the Strong Neighborhoods Initiative in San José, there are examples like the Village Academy in Delray Beach, where the private and philanthropic sectors bore most of the costs. Balancing Justice in Oklahoma yielded two major policy recommendations: one embraced by conservatives (truth-in-sentencing) and one which, at the time, was the sole domain of liberals (community corrections). If the experiences of these communities are any guide, active citizens cannot be stereotyped as supporters of big government nor as advocates of independent volunteerism—they seem to pick whatever philosophy suits their circumstances.[24]

Among the elected officials who have been advocates of democratic governance, there are Democrats like Kalamazoo's Hannah McKinney and Rochester's William Johnson, as well as Republicans like Karen Hasara in Springfield and Steve Burkholder in Lakewood. Pundits and commentators across the political spectrum, from Lani Guinier to Ralph Reed, have all tried to stake out the civic turf, establishing their own claims to the principles of citizenship and democracy. Presidential candidates from both parties, including Bill Bradley and Lamar Alexander, have used populist language about increasing the role of citizens in decision-making; Alexander's 1996 campaign slogan was "the people know what to do." These messages have not yet been effective in a presidential campaign, probably because the language has been too abstract: candidates will need to connect the rhetoric to more tangible issues like land use or education, so voters can understand what these new powers might allow them to do.

The latest developments in the citizen-government relationship challenge the credos of both liberals and conservatives. Many Democrats still seem to believe that the public sector could eradicate injustice, provide all necessary services, and solve all our problems if we only gave it enough funding to do the job. This blind faith in government even comes across in conversations about citizenship; many liberals seem to assume either that public officials are already as "responsive" as they need to be, or that avenues for dissent are already adequate and open to those with the commitment to use them. Many conservatives, on the other hand, cling to the belief that democracy is nothing more than a tool for the defense of liberty. They seem to advocate not only limited government but limited governance. Both parties will need to rethink their core assumptions in order to understand the changes now emerging at the local level.

Ultimately, both major parties may miss the boat. In East Hampton, Connecticut, participants in a democratic governance effort on town budget issues decided to form the Chatham Party (Chatham had been the name of the town many years before). The party assembled a city council slate that included both former Democrats and former Republicans; the main message of their platform was to give citizens a stronger role in town decisions. In the 2005 municipal election, in which voter turnout was nearly 50%, the

Chatham Party took most of the city council seats and became the main political force in town.[25]

The rise of democratic governance may also affect two other aspects of "big politics": polling and lobbying. There is an underlying contrast between the way that pollsters approach input-gathering and the way that the newer projects operate. Pollsters select people randomly in order to ask them questions, usually by phone or mail; they do not expect anything further from them. Democratic organizers recruit participants to be active citizens, to study an issue in a more intensive way and discuss it with their peers; they then expect the participants to help do something about it. Given this difference, some pollsters may see democratic governance as a threat to their philosophy and their work opportunities. They may attack the more deliberative, broad-based kinds of input-gathering projects as being unscientific or unrepresentative. Other pollsters will probably follow examples like Eugene and Sacramento Decisions and find ways to build polling exercises into democratic governance efforts. In fact, if polling became a standard practice in these projects, it might allay the fears about representation, produce better input, and even complement the more interactive work by raising awareness and enhancing the legitimacy of the project.

Lobbyists may also react in both confrontational and opportunistic ways. In Los Angeles, many businesses opposed the development of the new neighborhood council system. They feared that it would give residents more power to oppose new development and curtail business activity in their neighborhoods. But in the case of the police department's proposed policy on burglar alarms, the alarm company showed how businesses could react to the new system: by sending lobbyists to the neighborhood council meetings and working directly with residents. If decision-making becomes more decentralized, businesses will assuredly send their lobbyists and other representatives to the arenas where decisions are being made. Many neighborhood or school councils will be unprepared for this kind of intrusion and will not know how to handle it. The way that the Oklahoma League of Women Voters welcomed the sheriffs and police officers, who came to the Balancing Justice meetings armed with pamphlets about their campaign for a pay raise, may be the best response: asking the visitors to pile their material on a resource table, then inviting them to take part in the discussions like any other participant. The design of new citizen structures and their support systems will have to take these kinds of possibilities into account.

Reporting, Exporting, and E-mailing Democracy

Decision-making arenas aren't just magnets for lobbyists: they are sources of news as well. So if communities pass some policymaking authority down to neighborhood structures and other kinds of citizen groups, reporters are likely to follow. Just who those reporters will be working for is difficult to predict, however, since readership of local newspapers is dropping steadily, and ratings for local news broadcasts on television and radio are declining as well.

A renewed focus on "neighborhood news" might help reinvigorate the dailies, but perhaps the new generation of weekly newspapers will fill the void instead. Most of the weeklies started out by covering music, the arts, and other cultural events, but have since added a news component. Because the stories emanating from citizen structures are likely to be less time-sensitive (since neighborhood and school councils don't meet every day), the shelf life of the stories might give the weeklies an advantage. As the media industry consolidates at the top, upstarts like the new weeklies will have more room to grow at the bottom.[26]

On the other hand, the most likely reporters of neighborhood news might be the neighbors themselves. Many of the planning sectors in Rochester now have their own citizen-run newspapers—not the little newsletters often produced by neighborhood associations, but thicker, glossier publications that look more like the local dailies.

These different media might blend together in new ways. Ben Eason, a newspaper publisher and civic entrepreneur, says that "the most promising trend in media is the fusion between print publications, which can help to frame the debate on important issues, and then some sort of an Internet platform that can help to facilitate the dialogue among citizens."[27]

The Internet is probably the form of media that is most in tune with the latest changes in democracy.[28] The nature of online publishing and communication, which costs very little and is open to almost anyone with a basic level of computer skills, is an obvious fit for democratic governance, in which citizens are the producers, reporters, and consumers of the news. Because it is interactive, the Internet can provide not only a source of information, but a venue in which citizens can continue their dialogues, conduct research, and attract new allies for their action plans. Some democratic organizers already rely heavily on e-mail as a recruitment tool. Neighborhood websites, now common in many places, are probably more likely to dominate the future media landscape than neighborhood newspapers.

As a complement to traditional political processes, the Internet is a time-saving device and a quick source of information, but it has not transformed democracy by itself.[29] However, as a complement to democratic governance, it offers all kinds of capacities for citizens to tap into. The town of Winona, Minnesota, gives us glimpses of this potential. A project called "Winona Online Democracy," the brainchild of civic entrepreneurs Randy Schenkat and Steve Kranz, gave residents the chance to share views and opinions on issues like school reform and substance abuse prevention. That input was then used to craft a discussion guide for a series of face-to-face discussions on those topics, attracting large numbers of people. The participants in the small groups were then able to share their action plans and find allies for their efforts by using the project's website.[30] Schenkat and Kranz used the face-to-face meetings to build empathy, trust, and accountability; they used the Internet to catalyze and support action efforts. IBM and Microsoft are both developing software that could be adapted for use in these kinds of projects.[31]

As public officials use democratic principles more frequently to engage citizens, they may find that the practice of blogging helps them sustain and intensify that communication. Blogging is inexpensive and interactive—it allows leaders to convey a great deal of information in a way that is also personal and heartfelt. Mayor Bill Gentes, who calls himself the "Blogging Mayor" of Round Lake, Illinois, gets 600 hits a day on his blog.[32] In communities where much larger numbers of people take part in decision making, the Internet is likely to come into its own.[33]

Finally, changes in democracy at home may also have an impact on the way we think about democracy abroad. In the last twenty years, the United States has ramped up its efforts to "export" democracy—the first wave of work was initiated in response to the fall of communism, and the second wave was prompted by the threat of Islamic militancy. But though the democratization techniques vary from the philanthropic approach of George Soros to the more aggressive stance of George W. Bush, there is generally only one vision of democracy being promoted: republican systems of government that preside over free market economies. It is ironic that as we urge people in other countries to embrace voting, our own citizens are becoming less and less likely to vote. Our message to citizens and public officials in other countries does not reflect the latest developments and civic experiments in our own communities: we are encouraging them to build ships that don't have engines, life rafts, or radar.

In fact, some observers have argued that North Americans could learn a lot from successful democratic practices in other places—not just developed nations like Britain, Germany, and Denmark, but countries like Brazil, Nigeria, and Bangladesh.[34] In fact, the participatory budgeting process in the Brazilian province of Porto Alegre has become such a popular case study that it almost seems like a civic researcher must own a vacation home there in order to have any credibility.[35] By continuing to export an outdated brand of politics, we may be pushing aside existing political cultures and traditions that might actually be more democratic.

As North American communities struggle to establish a better relationship between citizens and government, the inconsistencies between our own democratic turmoil and our simplistic message to the rest of the world may become more apparent. If the U. S. cannot export a more compelling brand of politics, or at least give a candid account of our own struggles with citizenship, we risk being transformed from the world's leading democracy into the world's least credible one.

Who Is Governing Whom? (A Rebalancing Act)

It is difficult to foresee how communities will handle the changes in local politics, and even harder to tell what the fallout will be at home and abroad. We will manage this transition more successfully if we realize that we are in the midst of a rebalancing act, as active citizens assume a more central role in public life. We are searching for a new equilibrium between residents and public employees, between the empowered and the disempowered, and between active citizens and the larger electorate.

The negotiations between citizens and government will continue in every major field. We have many different names for these opposing roles: parents and educators, residents and police officers, low-income people and social service agencies, taxpayers and public officials, residents and planners. In each area, people on both sides will have to decide:

- how they will communicate;
- how they will address cultural differences;
- how policy decisions will be made;
- how they will divide responsibilities for action; and
- whether they will work together regularly or only when the need arises.

In some cases, citizens and government will battle it out—in the courts, in the media, on the campaign trail, and in packed meeting rooms. In other cases, they will arrive quickly at shrewd and amicable agreements.

The outcomes of these negotiations and confrontations will surely have an effect on social equality. In recruiting people to participate in governance, it is harder to attract those who are less educated, have lower incomes, or are newer to this country. It may be that traditional forms of protest become less effective because the voices of the disempowered are co-opted or drowned out by newly empowered middle-class citizens. There could be other angles too: the deepening of the digital divide, or the fact that suburbs that have reaffirmed their own sense of community may become less likely to support regional collaboration.

There could be positive effects on social equality as well. First and foremost, attempts to involve citizens in governance can establish new arenas in which the disempowered can find allies and articulate their interests. As people connect policy issues to their own experiences, listen to the views of others, and find ways to work together, they become aware of the cultural differences that have historically divided many of the "haves" from many of the "have-nots." Asking citizens to take a closer look at the challenges facing their communities can convince them—when nothing else can—that public work on behalf of the disadvantaged is something that benefits us all.[36]

The concern for social equality is part of a larger question about the balance between active citizens and the electorate as a whole. Dealing with this challenge may become increasingly difficult for elected officials, both on the campaign trail and when they are in office. Many citizens vote for candidates because they feel a strong emotional connection to that person, even though they may have never met him or her. Involving more people in decision-making, even if it is done openly, fairly, and deliberatively, may weaken the image of an elected official as a strong, fearless, independent leader. Passive citizens may begin to feel that their community is being run by a nameless, faceless mob, rather than that single personality who seems so vivid and familiar.

The fact that people educate themselves, and often change their opinions, when they are involved in addressing public problems is a positive attribute—but it is also another source of friction between active and passive citizens. Even if the participants in a democratic governance effort are a perfect microcosm of the community and perfectly reflect the political opinions of their neighbors, their policy recommendations may still not be representative because they will change in the course of their discussions.[37] The will of the people is never a static quality: it evolves in every civic experiment. Public officials will have to decide whether to follow the recommendations of active citizens or adhere to what they believe to be the views of their passive neighbors.

All of this confusion about who is in charge, and whether policy decisions reflect the will of the people, may cause passive citizens to distrust democratic governance efforts, and vote against the public officials who support them. Whether local leaders can walk this tightrope will depend on their ability to communicate their approach to the larger electorate: explaining how decisions are being made, demonstrating that they have involved a diverse array of people in policy making, and touting their own individual qualities of strength, decisiveness, and integrity. On the campaign trail as well as in office, public officials may have to appeal to two different audiences: to the active citizens, they may have to show how they can be collaborative and facilitative; to the passive citizens, they may have to seem independent and strong-willed.

"Democracy Is Good for Your Health"

These kinds of divisions will be more common and more severe if we continue to separate politics from the rest of community life. If local leaders focus too narrowly on their own goals, and do not consider the wider range of reasons why citizens might participate, they will limit the scope and power of their organizing efforts. The only core constituency for their efforts will be the people who are the most educated, passionate, and engaged in public life. Passive citizens will become increasingly distrustful of active citizens, who may start to seem like a passel of altruists, office-seekers, and busybodies.

To avoid this scenario, we should emulate the best examples of democratic governance, which increase the number of active citizens and strengthen their connections to the rest of the community. They "bring politics to the people" by giving every participant a chance to be heard, by helping citizens take action as well as make recommendations, by making their gatherings social occasions as well as political ones, and by holding meetings in living rooms, firehouses, and church basements as well as city hall.

This approach reflects the main motivations behind the shifting citizen-government relationship. Residents and public officials alike are tired of the emotional grind of land use hearings and school board meetings; they are trying to interact in ways that are less tense and more mutually validating. When they enter into the public sphere, citizens are constantly asking government to legitimize their words and actions. When they finally find situations where they feel heard and honored by the people around them, citizens value this sense of public happiness and try to sustain it. The current transition in democracy is not just a political phenomenon: it is a change driven by social, cultural, and psychological factors as well.

Pioneers of democratic governance might capitalize on these motivations more effectively by making some simple changes. First, local leaders who want to reach citizens need to work together to combine their goals and resources. They tout collaboration as one of their most prized values, but they rarely collaborate with one another when they try to engage citizens. Instead, educators launch public engagement efforts, law enforcement officials start crime watch groups, mayors and managers ask residents about budget priorities, state or federal officials convene forums or focus groups on hot legislative topics, and so on. Organizers would be more effective if they combined issues, joined forces, and went where the people are.

Second, organizers should put an even stronger emphasis on food, music, and local traditions. The cultural exchanges at the Jane Addams School for Democracy, and the songs and parades of ¿Oíste?, have much to teach us about how to combine politics with social and cultural functions (see Chapter 5).

Third, children and young people should be involved and highlighted to an even greater degree. Parents, grandparents, aunts, and uncles are far more likely to participate if the experience will allow them to focus on, brag about, show off to, and make things better for, their kids. As the students of Kuna (Idaho) and Hudson (Massachusetts) High Schools have shown, teenagers and young adults should be given key organizing roles in democratic governance efforts, not only because they are the leaders of the future but because they are sometimes the most effective leaders in the present.

Finally, leaders should rethink the architecture of our public spaces. By establishing "hubs" like the Village Academy in Delray Beach, neighborhoods and communities can create compelling physical centers that can house and attract all the different activities that make up public life.

By moving forward in these ways, local leaders would be bringing politics back in line with the other aspects of community life. They would combine the philosophy of temporary organizing efforts, which constantly ask "What's in it for citizens?," and the constancy of permanent citizen structures, which provide meeting places that become more familiar and popular over time. Instead of simply finding better ways of making public decisions, they would be giving people a greater sense of community, efficacy, and belonging.

Roger Bernier, the official at the Centers for Disease Control, looks at these psychological benefits and relates them to his own field. "Democracy is good for your health," he says.[38] In this view, politics is not some far-off, specialized activity conducted by experts and representatives: it is a central function, a way for people to connect emotionally with the world around them.

A Swiftly Tilting Planet

It is impossible to see that the earth is rotating when you're standing on it; it is difficult to trace an evolution when you're part of it; it is hard to write a history when you're in it. No wonder that we tend not to see the changes happening in our political system, even though they are occurring all around us. It makes sense that we would treat our public institutions as if they were static, immutable objects. It shouldn't be surprising that we think of "politics" as an incurable malady.

We don't give ourselves—or our political tradition—enough credit. We may not feel like inherently democratic beings, but our chief characteristic may be our boundless determination to govern ourselves. Again and again, the changing tide of community conditions wears away at our public institutions; again and again, we keep devising new approaches to governance. This time, we are casting off the protective, stifling embrace of expert rule. We are compelled to do this by unworkable city budgets, instances of police misconduct, angry debates over school closures, landfills, or housing developments, and other signs of alienation and mistrust between citizens and government. We don't intend to reshape democracy: these immediate, practical problems force us into new feats of ingenuity, compelling us to design public structures that fit the needs and assets of the age.

Some of the great treatises on democracy contain beautiful descriptions of ideal communities where citizens interact in perfect ways. This book, however, is not about utopia. If you spend time in the places where people are pushing the frontiers of democratic governance, you do not emerge with ideal visions of their efforts or their end goals. These are sailors without compass or map, trying to reach a distant shore with only the occasional glimpse of the stars behind the clouds. We are destined to continue in this way, taking part in this struggle and being buffeted by it, reaching destinations that will usually be better but will never be perfect. The next form of democracy may not be the best form of government, but it surely won't be the worst: it will carry all the thorny problems and thrilling potential of shared governance.

Notes

Notes to Introduction

1. An earlier version of this introduction appeared as "The Recent Evolution of Democracy," *National Civic Review,* Spring 2005. For more on the state of democracy, see Benjamin Barber, *A Place for Us: How to Make Society Civil and Democracy Strong* (New York: Hill and Wang, 1998); Stephen Coleman, *Direct Representation: Towards a Conversational Democracy* (London: Institute for Public Policy Research, 2005); Robert Dahl, *On Democracy* (New Haven, CT: Yale University Press, 1998); Jean Bethke Elshtain, *Democracy on Trial* (New York: Basic Books, 1996); Archon Fung, *Empowered Participation: Reinventing Urban Democracy* (Princeton, NJ: Princeton University Press, 2004); John Gastil, *By Popular Demand* (Berkeley: University of California Press, 2000); Amy Gutmann and Dennis Thompson, *Democracy and Disagreement* (Cambridge, MA: Belknap Press, 1998); John R. Hibbing and Elizabeth Theiss-Morse, *Stealth Democracy* (Cambridge, UK: Cambridge University Press, 2002); Paul Hirst, *Associative Democracy* (Amherst: University of Massachusetts Press, 1994); David Mathews, *Politics for People* (Champaign-Urbana: University of Illinois Press, 1999); James Morone, *The Democratic Wish* (New York: Basic Books, 1992); Robert Putnam, *Bowling Alone* (New York: Simon & Schuster, 2000); and Theda Skocpol, *Diminished Democracy* (Norman: University of Oklahoma Press, 2003). I think it is safe to say that all of these books were influenced by three earlier works: Benjamin Barber, *Strong Democracy: Participatory Politics for a New Age* (Berkeley: University of California Press, 1984); Harry Boyte, *CommonWealth: A Return to Citizen Politics* (New York: The Free Press, 1989); and Jane Mansbridge, *Beyond Adversary Democracy* (Chicago: University of Chicago Press, 1983).

2. I worked as an employee of the Study Circles Resource Center (SCRC) from 1994–2001, providing free technical assistance to local citizen involvement projects, and since then as a consultant to SCRC, the National League of Cities, the League of Women Voters, the Centers for Disease Control, and other groups. SCRC is the primary project of the Paul J. Aicher Foundation, a national, nonpartisan, nonprofit organization; it "helps communities develop their own ability to solve problems by bringing lots of people together in dialogue across divides of race, income, age, and political viewpoints" (www.studycircles.org).

3. Steve Burkholder, "Is Representative Democracy Obsolete?" *Listening to Lakewood,* December 2004.

4. See Carmen Sirianni and Lewis Friedland, *Civic Innovation in America: Community Empowerment, Public Policy, and the Movement for Civic Renewal* (Berkeley: University of California Press, 2001); John Gastil and Todd Kelshaw, *Public Meetings: A Sampler of Deliberative Forums That Bring Officeholders and Citizens Together* (report drafted for the Kettering Foundation, May 2000); Gwen Wright, Lena Delchad, and Matt Leighninger, *The Rise of Democratic Governance* (Washington, DC: National League of Cities, 2004); Martha L. McCoy and Patrick L. Scully, "Deliberative Dialogue to Expand Civic Engagement: What Kind of Talk Does Democracy Need?" *National Civic Review,* Summer 2002; "Speak Up! Engaging Policymakers with Educators and Communities in Deliberative Dialogue," *Insights on Education Policy, Practice, and Research,* October 1999; Edward C. Weeks, "The Practice of Deliberative Democracy: Results from Four Large-Scale Trials," *Public Administration Review* 60:360–72; Katherine Cramer Walsh, *Talking about Politics: Informal Groups and Social Identity in American Life* (Chicago: University of Chicago Press, 2004); Walsh, *Listening to Difference: Race, Community, and the Place of Dialogue in Civic Life* (Chicago: University of Chicago Press, 2007); and Simone Chambers, "Deliberative Democratic Theory," *Annual Review of Political Science* 6 (2003): 316.

5. For more on the earlier examples, see Jeffrey Berry, Kent Portney, and Ken Thomson, *The Rebirth of Urban Democracy* (Washington, DC: Brookings Institution, 1993), 47–53. On the more recent examples, see Terry L. Cooper and Pradeep Chandra Kathi, "Neighborhood Councils and City Agencies: A Model of Collaborative Coproduction," *National Civic Review* 93 (2004): 43–53; and Ken Thomson, *Neighborhood to Nation* (Hanover, NH: University Press of New England, 2001).

6. See Harlon L. Dalton, *Racial Healing* (New York: Doubleday, 1995), and Maggie Potapchuk, *Steps Toward an Inclusive Community* (Washington, DC: Joint Center for Political & Economic Studies, 2001).

7. See Walsh, "The Democratic Potential of Civic Dialogue" (paper presented at the annual meeting of the Midwest Political Science Association, Chicago, April 3–6, 2003); Ilana Shapiro, *Training for Racial Equity and Inclusion: A Guide to Selected Programs* (Washington, DC: The Aspen Institute, 2002); President's Initiative on Race, *Pathways to One America in the 21st Century: Promising Practices for Racial Reconciliation* (Washington, DC: Government Printing Office, 1999); Paul DuBois and Jonathan Hutson, *Bridging the Racial Divide: A Report on Interracial Dialogue in America* (Brattleboro, VT: Center for Living Democracy, 1997); and Patricia Reichler and Polly B. Dredge, *Governing Diverse Communities: A Focus on Race and Ethnic Relations* (Washington, DC: National League of Cities, 1997).

8. See Iris Marion Young, *Inclusion and Democracy* (Oxford: Oxford University Press, 2000), and Nicola Thompson and Derek R. Bell, "The Deliberative Fix: The Role of Staged Deliberation in a Deliberative Democracy" (paper presented at the Political Studies Association conference, University of Lincoln, UK, April 2004).

9. Kristina Smock, "Building Effective Partnerships: The Process of Structure and Collaboration," *Shelterforce Online,* May/June 1999; John Gastil, *Democracy in*

Small Groups: Participation, Decision Making, and Communication (Philadelphia: New Society, 1993); and Mansbridge, *Beyond Adversary Democracy.*

10. See Francesca Polletta, *Freedom is an Endless Meeting* (Chicago: University of Chicago Press, 2002); Sara Evans, *Born For Liberty* (New York: The Free Press, 1997); and Hannah Fenichel Pitkin and Sara M. Shumer, "On Participation," *Journal of Democracy* 2 (1982): 43–54.

11. See Chambers, "Deliberative Democratic Theory," 320; Archon Fung, "Deliberation Before the Revolution," *Political Theory* 33, no. 2 (June 2005): 414; and Cass Sunstein, "The Law of Group Polarization," *Journal of Political Philosophy* 10:175–95.

12. For some examples, see Michael Resnick, *Communities Count: A School Board Guide to Public Engagement* (Alexandria, VA: National School Boards Association, 2000); Jeffrey Kimpton and Marcia Sharp, *Reasons for Hope, Voices for Change* (Providence, RI: Annenberg Institute for School Reform, 1998); Carolyn Lukensmeyer, Joe Goldman, and Steve Brigham, "A Town Meeting for the 21st Century," in *The Deliberative Democracy Handbook,* eds. John Gastil and Peter Levine (San Francisco: Jossey-Bass, 2005); Matt Leighninger and Shirley Ponomareff, *Building Communities: The ABCs of Public Dialogue* (Washington, DC: League of Women Voters, 2004); Wright et al., *The Rise of Democratic Governance;* and Sandy Heierbacher, Tonya Gonzalez, Bruce Feustel, and David E. Booher, "Deliberative Democracy Networks: A Resource Guide," *National Civic Review* 93 (2004): 64–67.

13. This was particularly true for people of color who participated in race dialogue programs. Projects that did not lead to visible outcomes or did a poor job of publicizing those outcomes created a great deal of frustration among participants. For an explanation of this view in the words of participants themselves, see Catherine Flavin-McDonald, Damon Higgins, Jennifer Necci Dineen, Martha L. McCoy, and Ruth Sokolowski, *Study Circles on Racism and Race Relations Year 1—1997: A Report on the Focus Groups* (Pomfret, CT: Study Circles Resource Center, 1998).

14. Sarah Campbell, Amy Malick, and Martha McCoy, eds., *Organizing Communitywide Dialogue for Action and Change* (Pomfret, CT: Study Circles Resource Center, 2001): 65.

15. Kristin Houlé and Rona Roberts, *Toward Competent Communities* (Lexington, KY: Roberts & Kay, 2000).

16. Gwen Wright, Christopher Hoene, and Matt Leighninger, *Making Progress Toward Issues of Race: Goals and Processes for Citizen Involvement* (Washington, DC: National League of Cities, 2003).

17. Pitkin and Shumer, "On Participation"; Gastil, *Democracy in Small Groups;* Polletta, *Freedom*; and also Lawrence Goodwyn, *The Populist Moment* (Oxford: Oxford University Press, 1978).

18. John P. Kretzmann and John L. McKnight, *Building Communities from the Inside Out* (Chicago: ACTA Publications, 1993).

19. David Ryfe says that "the theory of deliberative democracy needlessly remains removed from its practice" ("Does Deliberative Democracy Work?" *Annual Review of Political Science* 8 (2005): 49–71).

20. For a concise history of the input-gathering activities of federal agencies, see Hanna J. Cortner, "Reconciling Citizen, Analyst, and Manager Roles in Demo-

cratic Governance" (Washington, DC: U. S. Army Corps of Engineers Institute for Water Resources, 2003). Also see Daniel Patrick Moynihan's famous critique of the "maximum feasible participation" edict, *Maximum Feasible Misunderstanding: Community Action in the War on Poverty* (Toronto: Free Press, 1969), which is itself discussed in Berry et al., *Rebirth*.

21. The track record of input-gathering efforts in Europe and Canada seems to be similar to those in the United States. See Miriam Wyman and David Shulman, *Learning to Engage: Experiences with Civic Engagement in Canada* (Ottawa: Canadian Policy Research Networks, 2001), and Miriam Wyman and David Shulman, *From Venting to Inventing* (London: The Commonwealth Foundation, 2002).

22. See Ruth Ann Bramson, *The Deliberative Public Manager: Engaging Citizens in Productive Public Conversations* (unpublished manuscript, Sawyer School of Management, Suffolk University, Boston); also Lauri Boxer-Macomber, *Too Much Sun? Emerging Challenges Presented by California and Federal Open Meeting Legislation to Public Policy Consensus-Building Processes* (Sacramento, CA: Center for Collaborative Policy, September 2003).

23. Cheryl King, Kathryn M. Feltey, and Bridget O'Neill Susel, "The Question of Participation: Toward Authentic Public Participation in Public Administration," *Public Administration Review* 58 (1998): 317–26.

24. See Thomson, *Neighborhood to Nation*; also Robert Greene, "Not In My Neighborhood Council: What Can Save L. A.'s Broken Neighborhood Councils?" *LA Weekly*, August 25–September 2, 2004.

25. See Lars Hasselblad Torres, *The Deliberative Agency* (Washington, DC: Deliberative Democracy Consortium, 2004).

26. See Chambers, "Deliberative Democratic Theory," 317.

27. John Parr, "Chattanooga: The Sustainable City," in *Boundary Crossers: Case Studies of How Ten of America's Metropolitan Regions Work*, eds. Bruce Adams and John Parr (College Park, MD: Academy of Leadership, 1998).

28. See Paul Epstein, Paul Coates, and Lyle Wray, with David Swain, *Results That Matter* (San Francisco: Jossey-Bass, 2006).

29. See Ryfe, "Does Deliberative Democracy Work"; also Catherine Flavin and Regina Dougherty, "Science And Citizenship At the National Issues Convention," *The Public Perspective* 7, no. 3 (April/May 1996): 46–50.

30. Matt Leighninger, "Enlisting Citizens: Building Political Legitimacy," *National Civic Review*, Summer 2002.

31. Jim Cross, "County OKs Plan to Cut Trash Flow," *Wichita Eagle*, October 23, 1997.

32. For an excellent summary of online democratic governance efforts, see Carolyn Lukensmeyer and Lars Hasselblad Torres, *Public Deliberation: A Manager's Guide to Citizen Engagement* (Washington, DC: IBM Center for the Business of Government, 2006), 33–43. See also Patricia Bonner, Bob Carlitz, Laurie Maak, Rosemary Gunn, and Charles Ratliff, "Bringing the Public and the Government Together through Online Dialogues," in *The Deliberative Democracy Handbook*, eds. John Gastil and Peter Levine (San Francisco: Jossey-Bass, 2005).

33. Lukensmeyer et al., "A Town Meeting"; also Manny Fernandez, "Sounding Off on City Problems," *Washington Post*, November 16, 2003.

34. Caroline Hendrie, "Judge Ends Desegregation Case in Cleveland," *EdWeek*, April 8, 1998.

35. Leighninger, "Enlisting Citizens."
36. I have lived in Hamilton, Ontario, since 1999. Since that time, I have assisted communities in Ontario, Alberta, and British Columbia in addition to my work with communities and organizations in the U. S. It seems to me that while the tradition of governments "consulting" with the public is stronger in Canada, the American projects have a more advanced sense of citizens as public actors and problem-solvers. In the Canadian view, public officials have a greater responsibility to communicate with their constituents; in the American view, citizens have a greater responsibility to tackle public problems with their own effort and ideas.

Notes to Chapter 1

1. See Skocpol, *Diminished Democracy.* On voting, see M. Margaret Conway, "Political Mobilization in America," in *The State of Democracy in America,* ed. William J. Crotty (Washington, DC: Georgetown University Press, 2001). On the social capital debate, see Putnam, *Bowling Alone.*
2. This and all subsequent quotes from Lisa Giordano are from personal communication with the author, 1997–2000. The name has been changed to protect the privacy of the individual.
3. See Skocpol, who characterizes this idea as "doing for" rather than "doing with" (*Diminished Democracy,* 223); also Gastil, *By Popular Demand*; and Nina Eliasoph, *Avoiding Politics: How Americans Produce Apathy in Everyday Life* (Cambridge, UK: Cambridge University Press, 1998).
4. The political philosopher Hannah Arendt did the most to popularize this term in the twentieth century. See *On Revolution* (New York: Viking Press, 1963).
5. Ibid., 119.
6. For various arguments about this, see Michael Schudson, *The Good Citizen: A History of American Civic Life* (New York: The Free Press, 1998); Morone, *The Democratic Wish*; Herbert J. Storing, *The Anti-Federalist* (Chicago: University of Chicago Press, 1985); and Gordon Wood, *The Radicalism of the American Revolution* (New York: Knopf, 1992).
7. For a much more thorough and illuminating explanation of this phenomenon, see Walsh, *Talking about Politics.*
8. Economists call this the "free rider" problem: people will not help to achieve something if they think they can reap the benefits without helping. For the classic rendition of this argument, see Mancur Olson, *The Logic of Collective Action* (Cambridge, MA: Harvard University Press, 1971).
9. "True representation is a daunting task for stakeholders," says Bill Potapchuk, a consultant who helps city governments work with neighborhood leaders on neighborhood plans. "Checkpoint meetings are typical but the laborious task of talking to a broad base of neighbors throughout an emerging process is rarely done." See Bill Potapchuk, Cindy Carlson, and Joan Kennedy, "Growing Governance Deliberatively: Lessons and Inspiration from Hampton, Virginia," in *The Deliberative Democracy Handbook,* eds. John Gastil and Peter Levine (San Francisco: Jossey-Bass, 2005), 254–68.
10. See Bramson, *The Deliberative Public Manager*; Walsh, *Listening to Difference*; and also Xavier de Souza Briggs, *Planning Together: How (and How Not) to En-*

gage Stakeholders in Charting a Course (Cambridge, MA: The Art and Science of Community Problem-Solving Project at Harvard University, 2003), 21.

11. See King et al., "The Question of Participation," and B. C. Smith, "Participation without Power: Subterfuge or Development?" *Community Development Journal,* July 1998.

12. See Walsh, *Listening to Difference*; Gastil and Kelshaw, *Public Meetings*; and also Archon Fung, "Varieties of Participation in Democratic Governance" (paper presented at the Theorizing Democratic Renewal conference, Vancouver, June 10, 2005).

13. See Frank Benest, "Engaging Citizens in the Bottom Line," *American City and County,* December 1997.

14. Bramson, *The Deliberative Public Manager.*

15. See Bramson; also Young, *Inclusion and Democracy.*

16. See Xavier de Souza Briggs and E. R. Mueller, *From Neighborhood to Community* (New York: Community Development Research Center, New School for Social Research, 1997); Mark Chupp, "Investing in People through Place: The Role of Social Capital in Transforming Neighborhoods" (Baltimore: Annie E. Casey Foundation, 1999; R. Gittell and A. Vidal, *Community Organizing: Building Social Capital as a Development Strategy* (Thousand Oaks, CA: Sage, 1998); Kretzmann and McKnight, *Building Communities from the Inside Out*; and Frank Lord, "How SoDo Saved Itself," *Hartford Courant,* August 3, 2003.

17. See Joel Garreau, *Edge City* (New York: Doubleday, 1991); Richard Moe and Carter Wilkie, *Changing Places: Rebuilding Community in the Age of Sprawl* (New York: Henry Holt, 1997); and David Rusk, *Cities Without Suburbs* (Washington, DC: Woodrow Wilson Center Press, 1993).

18. See Weeks, "The Practice of Deliberative Democracy," 363.

19. See Clarence Stone, "Civic Capacity and Urban Education," *Urban Affairs Review,* May 2001; Kimpton and Sharp, *Reasons for Hope*; Diane Pan and Sue Mutchler, *Calling the Roll: Study Circles for Better Schools* (Austin, TX: Southwest Education Development Laboratory, 2000); Deborah Meier, "The Road to Trust," *American School Board Journal,* September 2003; Wendy Puriefoy, "Linking Communities and Effective Learning Environments," *Voices in Urban Education,* Fall 2003; "Campaigning: Citizens Boost School Funding," *St. Paul Pioneer Press,* October 27, 2003; Elizabeth Sullivan, *Civil Society and School Accountability* (New York: NYU Institute for Education and Social Policy, 2003); and Matt Leighninger, "Working with the Public on Big Decisions," *School Administrator,* November 2003.

20. Harvard researcher Felton Earls claims that the most important variable in crime reduction was "neighbors' willingness to act, when needed, for one another's benefit." See Dan Hurley, "On Crime as Science (A Neighbor at a Time)," *New York Times,* January 6, 2004.

21. See Jonathan Eig, "Eyes on the Street: Community Policing in Chicago," *The American Prospect* 29 (November-December 1996); James Hill, "For Black Cops, Trust Hard to Gain: Diversity Doesn't Close Credibility Gap," *Chicago Tribune,* July 19, 1999; R. J. Sampson, "What 'Community' Supplies," in *Urban Problems and Community Development,* eds. R. F. Ferguson and W. T. Dickens (Washington, DC: Brookings Institution, 1999); and R. J. Sampson, S. W. Raudenbush, and F. Earls, "Neighborhoods and Violent Crime," *Science* 277 (1997).

22. See Dalton, *Racial Healing*; Maggie Potapchuk, *Steps Toward an Inclusive Community*; DuBois and Hutson, *Bridging the Racial Divide*; and Wright et al., *Making Progress Toward Issues of Race.*

Notes to Chapter 2

1. See Kimpton and Sharp, *Reasons for Hope*; Heather Voke, *Engaging the Public in its Schools* (Alexandria, VA: Association for Supervision and Curriculum Development, July 2002).
2. Michelle Alberti Gambone, Adena M. Klem, William P. Moore, and Jean Ann Summers, *First Things First: Creating the Conditions and Capacity for Community-wide Reform in an Urban School District* (Philadelphia: Gambone & Associates, 2002).
3. "Study Circles: Reconnecting the Schools to the Community," www.kauffman.org (accessed July 27, 2004). For more on First Things First, see Gambone et al., *First Things First.*
4. Pers. comm., March 4, 2005. See also Roger Bernier and Karen Midthun, "Getting the Science Right and Doing the Right Science in Vaccine Safety," *American Journal of Public Health,* June 2004.
5. Pers. comm., February 12, 2002.
6. Parts of this section appeared in Matt Leighninger, "The Seven Deadly Citizens," *The Good Society* 13, no. 2 (2004).
7. Thomas E. Patterson, *The Vanishing Voter: Public Involvement in an Age of Uncertainty* (New York: Vintage Books, 2003), 4; Conway, "Political Mobilization."
8. Michael Schudson, "America's Ignorant Voters," *Wilson Quarterly* 24, no. 2 (2000): 20.
9. David Osborne and Ted Gaebler, *Reinventing Government: How the Entrepreneurial Spirit is Transforming the Public Sector* (Reading, MA: Addison-Wesley, 1992).
10. *Connecting Citizens and Their Government* (Washington, DC: National League of Cities, 1996).
11. Ed Weeks, a professor in the public policy school at the University of Oregon, wonders if "we have become carried away with the notion of viewing the public as our 'customers.' The public are not customers and our governments are not markets. These views demean the nature of citizenship and the responsibilities of government" ("The Practice of Deliberative Democracy," 371).
12. Putnam, *Bowling Alone.* See also Skocpol's contributions to this debate, such as *Diminished Democracy.*
13. Robert Putnam, "Tuning In, Tuning Out: The Strange Disappearance of Social Capital in America," *PS: Political Science & Politics* 28 (1995). More recent studies suggest that the television threat is overblown. See Patricia Moy, Dietram Scheufele, and Lance Holbert, "Television Use and Social Capital: Testing Putnam's Time Displacement Hypothesis." *Mass Communication & Society* 2 (1999): 25–43.
14. See Harry Boyte, "Reframing Democracy: Governance, Civic Agency, and Politics," *Public Administration Review* 65 (2005): 538.
15. Dana Milbank, "A Few Degrees Warmer for Bush," *Washington Post,* June 15, 2002.

16. M. Margaret Conway, *Political Participation in the United States,* 3rd ed. (Washington, DC: CQ Press, 2000).
17. See King et al., "The Question of Participation."
18. Sirianni and Friedland devote a chapter to traditional community organizing in their excellent *Civic Innovation in America,* 35–84.
19. The Kettering Foundation has been one of the leaders in this work. See Sirianni and Friedland, *Civic Innovation in America,* 256–58.
20. Pers. comm., August 16, 2004. FOCUS stands for "Forging Our Comprehensive Urban Strategy." See www.kcmo.org/planning.nsf/focus/home.
21. Pers. comm., August 16, 2004.
22. Mary Hamilton, "Focus for Success," *Public Administration Times,* November 2003.
23. The initiative began as part of the "Reinventing Government" efforts led by Vice President Gore in the late 1990s.
24. govinfo.library.unt.edu/npr/custserv/hassle.html (accessed July 6, 2004).
25. www.cco.org/index.htm (accessed August 22, 2004).
26. Pers. comm., August 24, 2004.
27. Pers. comm., July 16, 2004.
28. Pers. comm., July 16, 2004.
29. See James S. Fishkin, *Democracy and Deliberation: New Directions for Democratic Reform* (New Haven, CT: Yale University Press, 1991), and *The Voice of the People* (New Haven, CT: Yale University Press, 1995).
30. Rick Montgomery, "Forum Gathers KC Opinions for National Discussion," *Kansas City Star,* January 25, 2004.
31. For more on Swope Community Builders, see Epstein et al., *Results That Matter,* 180.
32. For example, though both the Community Conversations and the KCK Study Circles were attempts to apply the methodology promoted by the Connecticut-based Study Circles Resource Center, the first project faded away while the second continues to thrive.
33. Pers. comm., July 23, 2004.
34. Quoted in "Study Circles: Reconnecting the Schools to the Community," www.kauffman.org (accessed July 27, 2004).
35. Pers. comm., July 23, 2004.
36. Frances Frazier, Gloria Mengual, and Matt Leighninger, *Using Democratic Principles to Initiate and Build Neighborhood Revitalization Efforts* (Washington, DC: NeighborWorks America, 2005).
37. Pers. comm., July 23, 2004.
38. Email from Diane Hentges, August 31, 2004.
39. Fisher, pers. comm., July 23, 2004.
40. Julie Fanselow, *Kansas City, Kansas: Where Neighborhood Voices Lead to Better Solutions* (Pomfret, CT: Paul J. Aicher Foundation, 2004).
41. One example is the city of Chicago: the school board established a massive system of local school councils during the same time period that the city and the police department created a citywide network of neighborhood councils to work with the police on crime issues. The two networks were never linked. See Archon Fung and Erik Olin Wright, "Deepening Democracy: Innovations in Empowered Participatory Governance," *Politics & Society* 29, no. 1 (March 2001): 9.

42. Wendell Maddox, National League of Cities conference, Charlotte, NC, December 8, 2005.

43. Fisher, pers. comm., July 23, 2004.

44. Quoted in "Study Circles," www.kauffman.org (accessed July 27, 2004).

45. Gambone et al., *First Things First.*

46. "Test Scores Up Sharply in KCK School District," *Kansas City Star,* May 30, 2003.

47. Fisher, pers. comm., July 23, 2004.

48. See Bill Simonsen and Mark D. Robbins, "The Benefit Equity Principle and Willingness to Pay for City Services," *Public Budgeting & Finance,* Summer 1999, 91.

49. An important precursor to these efforts was the Alliance for National Renewal, a coalition that was initiated by the National Civic League. ANR generated a fair amount of excitement when it was founded in 1994, partly because it cast its net so wide: it included many mainstream organizations for which issues of citizenship and democracy were clearly secondary, and perhaps—at the time, at least—a novelty. Local democratic work was just beginning to proliferate, and the ANR members probably didn't have enough in common otherwise to sustain the initial enthusiasm. See John Gardner, "National Renewal" (Civic Practices Network, 1994; www.cpn.org).

50. A number of very helpful lists, charts, and matrices have been produced recently that compare and contrast different tools for democratic governance. See Fung, "Varieties of Participation"; Sandy Heierbacher and Tonya Gonzalez, *Beginner's Toolkit to Dialogue and Deliberation* (Boiling Springs, PA: National Coalition for Dialogue and Deliberation, 2006; www.ncdd.org); John Gastil and Peter Levine, eds., *The Deliberative Democracy Handbook* (San Francisco: Jossey-Bass, 2005).

51. Robert Carlitz, Executive Director of Information Renaissance (presentation before the National Vaccine Advisory Committee, Washington, DC, September 13, 2004).

52. Pers. comm. with Terry Amsler and William Potapchuk, December 14, 2004; see also William Potapchuk, "Building an Infrastructure of Community Collaboration," *National Civic Review* 88 (Fall 1999): 3.

Notes to Chapter 3

1. Pers. comm., June 11, 2004. The name has been changed to protect the privacy of the individual.

2. Pers. comm., April 25, 2005.

3. Marc Fisher, "It May Be a Sign: Foes of Growth Protest Too Much," *Washington Post,* August 31, 2000.

4. For an example, see Randy Brown, "City-County Cooperation: Let's Not Just Talk About It," *Wichita Eagle,* January 11, 1998. Also see Karen Paget, "Can Cities Escape Political Isolation?" *American Prospect* 9, no. 36 (January 1998).

5. Howard Husock, "Let's Break Up the Big Cities," *City Journal,* Winter 1998.

6. Rusk also argues that metro-wide governments are more equitable, because the tax revenues gained from wealthy suburban areas can then be used to support services for poorer city-dwellers. His claim that regional governments create greater economic growth overall is an integral part of his message. Localists like Howard

Husock disagree. See Rusk, *Cities Without Suburbs*, and Husock, "Let's Break Up the Big Cities."

7. See Nick Wates, *The Community Planning Handbook* (London: Earthscan, 2000), and Briggs, *Planning Together.*

8. "Where it works, more participatory planning and decision-making can produce better substantive ideas, useful problem-solving relationships and the trust needed to take action together in the future ('social capital'), stronger community institutions, new possibilities for forging agreement across old divides, and other tangible and intangible benefits," writes Xavier de Souza Briggs, a Harvard professor who has researched the successes and failures of these projects (*Planning Together*, 3).

9. Kalima Rose, "Beyond Gentrification: Tools for Equitable Development," *Shelterforce Online,* May/June 2001.

10. Potapchuk et al., "Growing Governance Deliberatively."

11. Pers. comm., March 17, 2005.

12. "The challenge looking forward," says Bill Barnes of the National League of Cities, "is to move toward a framework that enables governments to engage with each other in constructive and appropriate ways relative to the society and today's complex economy." Barnes, "Beyond Federal Urban Policy," *Urban Affairs Review* 41, no. 3 (January 2006). See also William R. Barnes and Larry Ledebur, *The New Regional Economies* (Thousand Oaks, CA: Sage, 1998).

13. Angela Glover Blackwell, "Building Policy from the Ground Up: Regionalism, Equitable Development, and Developing New Leaders," *National Civic Review,* Spring 2005: 29.

14. Pers. comm., February 25, 2005. Other planners have made the same realization: Briggs quotes a planner named John Shapiro who says, "There used to be planning by the community without the [professional] planners. And that didn't work so well. Ditto for planning by the planners without the community. The trick is engaging both" (*Planning Together*, 19).

15. Jane Jacobs, the renowned observer of cities, put it best when she wrote forty years ago that "cataclysmic money," directed by outsiders rather than residents, can be worse than no development funds at all. In *The Death and Life of Great American Cities* (New York: Random House, 1961), 291–316.

16. This and all subsequent quotes from Mark Linder are from personal communication with the author, June 7, 2004, and February 25, 2005.

17. Mike Zapler, "Is San José Blighted?" *San José Mercury News,* August 10, 2002.

18. Deb Marois, "Diverse Voices Transform San Jose's Neighborhoods" (report to the League of California Cities, Sacramento, CA, July 2005).

19. Jacobs, *The Death and Life of Great American Cities,* 271.

20. Rose, "Beyond Gentrification."

21. "Strong Neighborhoods Update: Quarterly Status Report," February 2005; www.strongneighborhoods.org.

22. Barnes and Ledebur, *The New Regional Economies.*

23. Pers. comm. with Joan Kennedy, Director of the Hampton Neighborhood Office, August 24, 2005.

24. Gastil and Kelshaw, *Public Meetings.*

25. For some examples, see Rob Gurwitt, "The Casparados," *Preservation,* November/December 2000, and Gloria F. Mengual, "Portsmouth, NH: Where Public Dialogue is a Hallmark of Community Life" (www.studycircles.org).

26. Quoted in Mengual, "Portsmouth, NH."
27. Planning meeting, March 26, 1998. Merriss and many other local officials, including city commissioners and the school superintendent, took part in the Round Tables.
28. Pers. comm., November 10, 2004.
29. See Gastil and Kelshaw; also Peggy Merriss and Jon Abercrombie, "Investing in a Community of Stakeholders" (paper presented at the Best Practices 2000 conference of the International City-County Managers Association, Savannah, GA, March 30–April 1, 2000). The Decatur strategic plan can be accessed at www.decatur-ga.gov.
30. Pers. comm., November 10, 2004.
31. Gastil and Kelshaw hypothesize that "the forums designed for bi-directional influence will prove the most successful in the long run."
32. "Community Voices: Kecia Cunningham," *Focus on Study Circles,* Spring 2001.
33. The populations of the cities mentioned in this section: Pittsford 27,000; Portsmouth 20,000; Hampton 146,000; Decatur 17,000.
34. Oakland residents claim, with good reason, that Stein's jab is unjust. However, it is a clever turn of phrase that does accurately describe many other places.
35. Eventually, the school board enacted a redistricting plan quite similar to the option devised by the participants, but their deliberations took almost two years. One reason for the delay was a transition in school district leadership: the board hired a new superintendent, and one of the small-group facilitators was elected to the school board and subsequently became the board chair. At the last minute, the board also voted to close down a different school than the one people had been expecting them to close, resulting in anger and lawsuits from parents. Pers. comm., February 18, 2005.
36. The Compact was adopted by a formal resolution at a joint public meeting of the boards of all three entities in 2003. See "Community Collaboration" at www.townofpittsford.gov/government.
37. Potapchuk et al., "Growing Governance Deliberatively."
38. Cindy Carlson, "A Rightful Place: Expanding the Role of Young People in a Democratic Society," *The Good Society* 13, no. 2 (2004): 40.
39. Potapchuk et al., "Growing Governance Deliberatively."
40. Pers. comm., September 9, 2004.
41. Jacobs, *The Death and Life of Great American Cities.*
42. Christopher Swope, "After the Mall: Suburbia Discovers Main Street," *Governing,* October 2002.
43. See "Ethnic Diversity Grows, But Not Immigration," *Christian Science Monitor,* March 14, 2001, and William Booth, "One Nation, Indivisible: Is it History?" *Washington Post,* February 22, 1998.
44. Portions of this section appeared in Matt Leighninger, "Shared Governance in Communities," *Public Organization Review* 2, no. 3 (September 2002).
45. Myrne Roe, "Story is Best Told by Citizens," *Wichita Eagle,* February 26, 1997.
46. Kristi Zukovich, *Community Discussions on Solid Waste* (Wichita, KS: Sedgwick County Government, 1996).
47. Ibid.
48. Bill Roy, "County Says it is Ready to Pay for Recycling Bins: Local Companies Sought to Reimburse the County's Expenses," *Wichita Eagle,* April 30, 1997.

49. Zukovich, *Community Discussions.*
50. Jim Cross, "County OKs Plan to Cut Trash Flow," *Wichita Eagle,* October 23, 1997.
51. Pers. comm., September 3, 2000.
52. Kiran Cunningham and Hannah McKinney, "Creating Systemic Change: Convening the Community for Land Use Action," *Practicing Anthropology* 25, no. 4 (2003): 9–14.
53. "The fact that this project did not have an ideological bias, and that people recognized that, was critical," says McKinney. Pers. comm., March 17, 2005.
54. See Davydd Greenwood and Morten Levin, *Introduction to Action Research: Social Research for Social Change* (Thousand Oaks, CA: Sage, 1998). The development of what is called "democratic evaluation" is another example of democratic principles being applied to social science. See Ernest House, "The Many Forms of Democratic Evaluation," *The Evaluation Exchange,* Fall 2005: 7.
55. See Kiran Cunningham and Hannah McKinney, *Smarter Growth for Kalamazoo County* (Kalamazoo, MI: Convening for Action Project and Kalamazoo College, January 2003).
56. Kiran Cunningham and Hannah McKinney, "Creating Systemic Change."
57. Pers. comm., March 17, 2005.
58. Pers. comm. with Kiran Cunningham, December 16, 2005.

Notes to Chapter 4

1. W. E. B. DuBois, *The Souls of Black Folk* (Chicago: A. C. McClurg & Co., 1903).
2. See Walsh, *Listening to Difference.*
3. They "gain a greater awareness of how race matters in everyday life," as Walsh puts it (*Listening to Difference,* 249).
4. Ibid., 211–13, 237.
5. Speech at the Fund for an Open Society conference, Cherry Hill, NJ, October 22, 2004.
6. Remarks to the Municipalities in Transition Equity and Opportunity Panel, National League of Cities, Nashville, TN, December 3, 2004.
7. Governor's "State of the State" address, 1991.
8. Martha McCoy and Robert Sherman, "Bridging the Divides of Race and Ethnicity," *National Civic Review,* Spring/Summer 1994.
9. Pers. comm., January 7, 2005.
10. Katherine Cramer Walsh, "The Democratic Potential of Civic Dialogue"; see also DuBois and Hutson, *Bridging the Racial Divide.*
11. See "Ethnic Diversity Grows"; Booth, "One Nation, Indivisible: Is it History?"; Daniel J. Losen and Gary Orfield, *Racial Inequity in Special Education* (Cambridge, MA: Civil Rights Project at Harvard University, Harvard Education Press, 2002); and *Punishment and Prejudice: Racial Disparities in the War on Drugs* (Washington, DC: Human Rights Watch, June 2000).
12. Beverly Daniels Tatum, *Why Are All the Black Kids Sitting Together in the Cafeteria? And Other Conversations About Race* (New York: Basic Books, 1999).
13. Maggie Potapchuk, *Steps Toward an Inclusive Community.*
14. "News From Community-wide Programs," *Focus on Study Circles,* Fall 2001; "Yonkers, New York," *Focus on Study Circles,* Summer 2004; and Julie Fanselow,

Vermont: Where Deep-rooted Democratic Traditions Open the Way for Study Circles (Pomfret, CT: Paul J. Aicher Foundation, 2005).

15. Pers. comm., October 6, 2004.
16. Lincoln drew the "house divided" phrase from the book of Matthew in the New Testament. Portions of this section appeared in Leighninger, "Shared Governance."
17. Amy Malick, "An Interview with Sandy Robinson II," *Focus on Study Circles,* Fall 1999.
18. A year later, Meek was convicted of a separate crime. Lisa Kernek, "Circles Aimed at Bringing City Around on Race Relations, *Springfield State Journal-Register,* July 8, 1999.
19. At this stage, Robinson contacted the Study Circles Resource Center and began receiving advice on how to organize the project.
20. Pers. comm., July 3, 2000.
21. Houlé and Roberts, *Toward Competent Communities,* 153.
22. Ibid., 158.
23. Pers. comm., July 3, 2000.
24. Malick, "An Interview with Sandy Robinson II."
25. Julie Fanselow, *Springfield, Illinois: Where Conversations About Race Foster Understanding and Action* (Pomfret, CT: Paul J. Aicher Foundation, 2004).
26. Jefferson Robbins, "Study Group Offers Ideas to Boost Local Race Relations," *Springfield State Journal-Register,* June 17, 1998.
27. Ibid.
28. The quotation in this paragraph and those following are from the report to the Springfield Community Relations Commission, 1998.
29. Robbins, "Study Group Offers Ideas"; also pers. comm. with Judy Yeager, June 12, 2000, pers. comm. with Brian McFadden, July 5, 2000.
30. Pers. comm., July 5, 2000.
31. Ibid.
32. "For the first time ever in Springfield, test-takers scoring higher than 70 percent on the April [2000] written exam became eligible for an oral interview. The written test then made up 30 percent of the final score, while the oral exam accounted for the other 70 percent." Sarah Antonacci, "Minorities, Women Get High Marks on Cop Test," *Springfield State Journal-Register,* June 8, 2000.
33. Report to the Springfield Community Relations Commission, 1998.
34. The Race Relations Task Force also created large signs that read "*Hate—Not in Our Homes, Not in Our Neighborhoods, Not in Our City!*" The signs are still posted at the city limits. Sarah Antonacci and Matt Buedel, "Diversity overshadows hate: focus on celebration as Hale speech passes with little incident," *Springfield State Journal-Register,* July 15, 2001.
35. Jason Piscia, "Police Focus on Neighborhood Involvement," *Springfield State Journal-Register,* March 28, 2004.
36. Jayette Bolinski, "Police Review Board Negotiated," *Springfield State Journal-Register,* May 5, 2004. See also "Applications Being Taken for Police Review Group," *Springfield State Journal-Register,* October 7, 2005.
37. See "Frazier case chronology," *Springfield State Journal-Register,* March 31, 2004, and Jayette Bolinski, "Black Guardians Complaint Seeks Outside Investigation," *Springfield State Journal-Register,* April 20, 2004.
38. " 'Banding' idea has merit," *Springfield State Journal-Register,* July 2, 2004.

39. Sandy Robinson, panel presentation, national conference of the Study Circles Resource Center, Chicago, October 7, 2005. See also Fanselow, *Springfield, Illinois*.

40. Pers. comm., June 12, 2000.

41. "Lee County Pulling Together," in President's Initiative on Race, *Pathways to One America in the 21st Century: Promising Practices for Racial Reconciliation* (Washington, DC: Government Printing Office, 1999).

42. Pers. comm., January 26, 1999.

43. Betty Parker, "Dunbar Dream Almost Reality," *Fort Myers News-Press,* November 24, 1999.

44. See Dahl, *On Democracy*.

45. Pers. comm., April 3, 2003.

46. Pers. comm., July 3, 2000.

47. See Walsh, *Listening to Difference*.

48. Two state agencies, the Ohio Department of Health and Human Services and the Delaware Department of Labor, have developed strategies that help employees address issues of race, both inside the department and in their relationships with the citizens they serve. See Houlé and Roberts, *Toward Competent Communities*, 245.

49. See "Ethnic Diversity Grows," and Booth, "One Nation, Indivisible."

50. Speech to the Montgomery County Business Roundtable for Education, March 15, 2004. For video, see www.mcps.k12.md.us/departments/studycircles.

51. See "Lima, Ohio" on the U. S. Conference of Mayors Best Practices Database (www.usmayors.org/uscm/best_practices/bp_volume_2/lima.htm).

52. Remarks to the Municipalities in Transition Equity and Opportunity Panel, National League of Cities, Nashville, TN, December 3, 2004.

Notes to Chapter 5

1. For an in-depth exploration of the attitudes of public officials about democratic governance, see Bramson, *The Deliberative Public Manager*.

2. See Matt Leighninger, *The "Potentially Concerned Public": A Report on the Citizen Involvement Activities of U. S. Federal Agencies* (Atlanta: Centers for Disease Control, 2002).

3. Portions of this section appeared in Leighninger, "Shared Governance"; see also Julie Fanselow, *Kuna, Idaho: Where a Community Pulls Together to Face Growth* (Pomfret, CT: Paul J. Aicher Foundation, 2004).

4. Arnette Johnson, Kuna ACT report, 1999.

5. Ibid.

6. Bramson, *The Deliberative Public Manager*.

7. National League of Cities Democratic Governance Panel, *The Rise of Democratic Governance* (Washington, DC: National League of Cities, 2004).

8. Pers. comm., December 1, 2004.

9. Welcoming remarks by Roger Bernier, national stakeholder meeting, Public Engagement Pilot Project on Pandemic Influenza, Washington, DC, July 13, 2005.

10. Pers. comm., July 23, 2003.

11. Pers. comm., July 23, 2003.

12. Pers. comm., June 10, 2000.

13. Arnette Johnson, report of the Kuna ACT, 1999.

14. Ibid.

15. Ibid.
16. Ibid.
17. Ibid.
18. Pers. comm., July 23, 2003.
19. Pers. comm., July 23, 2003.
20. The City Club of Portland, Oregon, has developed a similar routine: they hold "Friday Forums" that focus on key issues facing the city. The Forums regularly attract 200–400 people. Pers. comm. with Wendy Radmacher Willis, director of the City Club of Portland, September 27, 2005.
21. Pers. comm., June 10, 2000. Rutan has since left Kuna for a position in another school district.
22. Pers. comm., July 23, 2003.
23. Kuna ACT facilitator training, November 12, 2000.
24. Joe Goldman, "Kuna, Idaho" (report drafted for the Kettering and Hewlett Foundations, 2004), 18.
25. Pers. comm., July 22, 2003.
26. See Sirianni and Friedland, *Civic Innovation in America*, 96–97.
27. See Skocpol, *Diminished Democracy*, and Putnam, *Bowling Alone*.
28. Gastil, *By Popular Demand*, 177.
29. Pers. comm., February 15, 2001. Portions of this section appeared in Leighninger, "Enlisting Citizens."
30. Pers. comm., May 4, 1998.
31. Ibid.
32. See William DiMascio, *Seeking Justice: Crime and Punishment in America* (New York: The Edna McConnell Clark Foundation, 1997).
33. For an overview, see Marcus Nieto, *Community Correction Punishments: An Alternative To Incarceration for Nonviolent Offenders* (Sacramento, CA: California Research Board, California State Library, May 1996).
34. Gary Fields, "Lawmakers Plan for Bipartisan Measures After Report Offers Advice for Overhaul," *Wall Street Journal,* January 14, 2005.
35. Pers. comm. with Carol Scott, February 15, 2001.
36. Sheriffs turned out in force all across the state, partly because they were lobbying for a statewide pay increase at the time; some of them came armed with pamphlets explaining their rationale for a raise. Forewarned, the Leaguers invited them to stack their pamphlets on a resource table and join the discussions. Some of the law enforcement personnel were particularly enthusiastic participants: in Weatherford, the sheriff helped citizens get a closer look at the corrections system by organizing a field trip to the county jail. See Leighninger, "Enlisting Citizens."
37. The quotation in this paragraph and those following are from the Balancing Justice final report, May 1997.
38. Leighninger, "Enlisting Citizens."
39. Matt Leighninger, " 'Balancing Justice' in Oklahoma: Involving the Full Community in the Criminal Justice Dialogue," *Community Corrections Report,* 1997.
40. Balancing Justice final report, May 1997.
41. Foreword to Leighninger and Ponomareff, *Building Communities*.
42. Sara Evans argues eloquently that the active citizenship of women may actually have declined after the passage of the Nineteenth Amendment.

"With one stroke the 19th Amendment enfolded women into a particular version of the American political heritage defining citizenship as a relationship between the individual and the state, whose key expression was the act of voting. To win this right women had to organize together, to act as a group. But the right itself undermined collectivity. Indeed, throughout the nineteenth century, as male politics came to be associated more and more with voting, female politics had developed its own separate track outside the electoral arena. Women learned to create institutions, to demand that governments accept some responsibility for community life whether in the form of pure drinking water or of libraries and schools. Many of the leaders of the suffrage movement believed that once women had the right to vote they would, as individuals, express these female values through the electoral process and there would be no more need for collective organization" (*Born for Liberty*, 172).

43. Maria Alamo, panel at the Council on Foundations conference, Toronto, Ontario, April 27, 2004.
44. See www.oiste.net.
45. The West Side of St. Paul has been called the "Ellis Island of the Midwest" for its role in the history of immigration in the region. The current wave of immigrants in the neighborhood includes large numbers of Hmong, Latinos, and Somalis. The neighborhood is also near the University of Minnesota and the College of St. Catherine. See Nicholas Longo and John Wallace, "Creating Democratic Spaces: Jane Addams School for Democracy," *CURA Reporter,* June 2000.
46. "The Jane Addams School creates a non-hierarchical environment where everyone is both learner and teacher," says Kari. There are children's circles as well, which also provide "an environment where teaching and learning are reciprocal. This contrasts with the more typical models children experience in school or child care," Kari says. Pers. comm., June 17, 2005.
47. Bob San, "Jane Addams School for Democracy Honors New U. S. Citizens," *Hmong Times,* June 1, 2002.
48. See www.publicwork.org/jas; Margaret Post, "Building Relational Culture at the Jane Addams School for Democracy," *Family Involvement Network of Educators Forum* (Harvard Family Research Project, Fall 2002); and Ruth Ann Bramson and Matt Leighninger, "Engaging the Community in Productive Public Conversations about Immigration," *International Journal of Economic Development* 5, no. 4 (2004).
49. Pers. comm., July 1, 2002.
50. Pers. comm., July 2, 2002.
51. One notable exception to this is watershed preservation. See Sirianni and Friedland, *Civic Innovation in America*, 91–110.
52. Much of this work is subject to the Federal Advisory Committee Act (FACA), a law that was originally passed to enhance citizen involvement but which, ironically, has made it more difficult. FACA forces federal officials to adhere to a dizzying array of rules, administrative procedures, and requirements for judicial review. See Lukensmeyer and Torres, *Public Deliberation,* 13. Rebecca Long and Thomas Beierle say that FACA exerts a "chilling effect" on public participation, in *The Federal Advisory Committee Act and Public Participation in Environmental Policy* (Washington, DC: Resources For the Future, 1999), 9.

53. Julie Hoover, "Major Investment Studies: An ISTEA Legacy with Promise," in *ISTEA Planner's Workbook*, ed. Margaret Franko (Washington, DC: Surface Transportation Policy Project, 1995).

54. Hanna J. Cortner, *Reconciling Citizen, Analyst, and Manager Roles in Democratic Governance* (Washington, DC: U. S. Army Corps of Engineers Institute for Water Resources, 2003).

55. NIH eventually adopted a new compromise plan that saved scores of other trees that had been scheduled for removal. However, the oak that began the controversy was felled. The U. S. Navy claimed a 35-foot segment of the tree, which was estimated to be 175–300 years old, for use in the restoration of "Old Ironsides," the *U. S. S. Constitution*. Rich McManus, "Not So Ancient After All: Trees Recycled for Navy, Parks Restoration Projects," *NIH Record,* March 10, 1998.

56. Remarks by Jan Hedetniemi at a meeting of the National Vaccine Advisory Committee, Washington, DC, September 13, 2004.

57. Sirianni and Friedland, *Civic Innovation in America*, 91–110.

58. Pers. comm., July 24, 2002.

59. Harris L. Coulter and Barbara Loe Fisher, *DTP, A Shot in the Dark* (San Diego: Harcourt Brace, 1985).

60. See www.nvic.org/About.htm.

61. Quoted in Lorraine Fraser, "Autism Study Prompts Fears Over Mystery Environmental Factor," *Sunday Telegraph,* May 18, 2003.

62. Epidemiologists refer to this as "herd immunity." See Bruce Taylor Seeman, "Texas Flu Researchers Test 'Herd Immunity' Theory," *Newhouse News Service,* October 26, 2004.

63. Roger Bernier, opening remarks to the Wingspread Conference on "Exploring Public Engagement within the U. S. Immunization Program," Racine, Wisconsin, July 31, 2002.

64. The participation in the project seems to have been skewed toward health care workers, however. See Archon Fung, "Recipes for Public Spheres: Eight Institutional Design Choices and Their Consequences," *Journal of Political Philosophy* 11, no. 3 (September 2003): 338–67.

65. Sirianni and Friedland, *Civic Innovation in America*, 152–62; Peter Wong, "State of Health Care Troubles Oregon's Ex-governor," *Statesman-Journal,* July 18, 2004; and Ellen Pinney, "Oregon Health Plan: Boon or Bust?" *Alternatives,* Winter 1997.

66. In Alread, roughly 100 people took part in a 1998 project—a percentage of the community that is unlikely to be matched. In the sessions, the school board was able to resolve an issue that had caused contention for years: whether to allow parents and other citizens to use the gym and other facilities after school hours. Participants also put on a school-community play, revised the student handbook, and raised the funds to build a computer center at the school which students use during the day and is open to the public after school hours.

67. Pers. comm. with Heather Gage-Detherow, Arkansas School Boards Association, May 7, 2005; also University of Arkansas at Little Rock, Institute of Government, *Arkansans Speak Up! on Education* (report to the Arkansas Blue Ribbon Commission on Public Education, April 17, 2002).

68. In the early 1990s, the Canadian government faced a public crisis over its federal immigration policy. The country was mired in one of the most extended economic

downturns in its history while levels of immigration were at an all-time high. Meanwhile, funding for social programs that supported recent immigrants had been cut. In response, the federal government announced plans to limit immigration to 1% of the population. But that did little to diminish the concern over competition for jobs, charges that immigration led to higher crime levels, scandals relating to supposed mismanagement by the Immigration and Refugee Board, confusion over laws and terms such as "refugee," and anger over the budget cuts for social programs, along with direct accusations of racism. See Bramson and Leighninger, "Engaging the Community"; also Wyman et al., *Learning to Engage.*

69. Wyman et al., *Learning to Engage,* 17.
70. See "Going Beyond the 'Up or Down' Vote: Research Sheds New Light on Public Deliberation," www.americaspeaks.org.
71. Thomas C. Beierle, "Democracy Online: An Evaluation of the National Dialogue on Public Involvement in EPA Decisions," *Resources For the Future (RFF) Report,* January 2002.
72. Matt Leighninger, "Enlisting Citizens."
73. Wong, "State of Health," and Pinney, "Oregon Health Plan."
74. Leighninger, "Enlisting Citizens."
75. See "Citizen Voices on Pandemic Flu Choices" (report of the Public Engagement Pilot Project on Pandemic Influenza, 2005).
76. See *Local Voices: Citizen Conversations on Civil Liberties and Secure Communities* (Washington, DC: League of Women Voters, 2005).

Notes to Chapter 6

1. Told by Sharon Hogarth at a Delray Beach action forum, April 29, 2000.
2. See Amie Parnes, "MAD DADS Succeed: Delray Group Patrols Streets," *Fort Lauderdale Sun-Sentinel,* February 7, 1999.
3. Kristina Smock identifies five major categories of organizing being practiced today: the power-based model, the community-building model, the civic model, the women-centered model, and the transformative model. See Smock, *Democracy in Action: Community Organizing and Urban Change* (New York: Columbia University Press, 2004).
4. This and all other quotes from Chuck Ridley are from personal communication with the author, October 2, 2002.
5. In this planning phase, MAD DADS received advice and assistance from several groups outside Delray Beach. David Harris of the MacArthur Foundation and Sharvell Becton of the Community Foundation of Palm Beach and Martin Counties directed the three local leaders to resources and neighborhood success stories from around the country. Both foundations provided financial support to MAD DADS at various times. Gus Newport, a longtime community organizer and the former mayor of Berkeley, California, visited MAD DADS to conduct a training session in comprehensive planning techniques. The staff of the Study Circles Resource Center, a national nonprofit that aids local citizen involvement efforts, also provided free training and technical assistance. Hogarth and the Ridleys connected with many of these national resources by attending meetings of the National Community Building Network, which brings together practitioners in economic development, race relations, affordable housing, and job training from all over the country.

6. Lois Solomon, "Group Proposes an Academy for Underprivileged Students," *Fort Lauderdale Sun-Sentinel,* May 11, 1999.

7. Ibid. The Village Academy format was based in part on the "Beacon School" model developed by Albert Mamary of Renewal for Better Schools, an organization based in Binghamton, New York.

8. "Alinsky was all about building grassroots power through an adversarial approach," says Terry Cooper, a public administration professor and former community organizer. "He would say, 'You always have to have a devil to fight against.' You would raise latent anger to the surface, and you would direct it at the devil. And that might be City Hall." Quoted in Robert Greene, "Not In My Neighborhood Council."

9. Kristina Smock describes how this innovation has emerged in a number of settings in "Building Effective Partnerships."

10. Nirvi Shah, "Nearly 1 in 4 Third Graders May Fail," *Palm Beach Post,* April 20, 2004. See also www.delraybeach.com/aacity/all_america_city.htm.

11. This and all subsequent quotes from Sharon Hogarth and Cynthia Ridley are from personal communication with the author, October 2, 2002.

12. Pers. comm., October 2, 2002.

13. See Katie Mee, "MAD DADS Fix Homes for Elderly Owners," *Palm Beach Post,* May 16, 2001.

14. Pers. comm., October 1, 2002.

15. Smock, *Democracy in Action,* 11.

16. Richard Wood, *Faith in Action: Religion, Race and Democratic Organizing in America* (Chicago: University of Chicago Press, 2002); Sirianni and Friedland, *Civic Innovation in America,* 46–48.

17. Quoted in Michael Grinthal, "Activist Reactions to Deliberation" (report drafted for the Kettering and Hewlett Foundations, September 2003).

18. Pers. comm. with Warren Adams-Leavitt, August 24, 2004.

19. The Industrial Areas Foundation, which is perhaps the largest community organizing network, claims that the "iron rule" of organizing is, "Never do for others what they can do for themselves." See Sirianni and Friedland, *Civic Innovation in America,* 49.

20. Michael Grinthal relates one story about a longtime community organizer who, after years of work, was invited to become part of the mayor's inner circle. The regular meeting place for this group was literally a "smoke-filled room" in a local restaurant.

21. Kim Bobo, Jackie Kendall, and Steve Max, *Organizing For Social Change* (Washington, DC: Seven Locks Press, 2001).

22. Pers. comm., August 24, 2004. Some observers characterize this change as a shift from "power over" to "power with." Sirianni and Friedland, *Civic Innovation in America,* 48.

23. See Robert Fisher, *Let the People Decide* (New York: Twayne Publishers, 1997); also Sirianni and Friedland, *Civic Innovation in America,* 54–55.

24. See William Gamson, "Civic Renewal and Inequality," *The Good Society* 12, no. 1 (2003).

25. Pers. comm., February 5, 2005.

26. William Traynor, "Community Building: Hope and Caution," *Shelterforce Online,* September/October 1995. See also Archon Fung, "Deliberation Before the Revolution," *Political Theory* 33, no. 3 (2005): 397–419.

27. See www.delraybeach.com/aacity/all_america_city.htm.

28. Sirianni and Friedland, *Civic Innovation in America*, 50–56.

29. "[CDCs] recognized they could not maintain thousands of units of housing without simultaneously addressing such issues as drugs and crime," note Sirianni and Friedland, ibid. See also Jane Knitzer and Fida Adely, "The Role of Community Development Corporations in Promoting the Well-Being of Young Children" (report to the National Center on Children in Poverty, 2002); and Pablo Eisenberg, "Time to Remove the Rose-Colored Glasses," *Shelterforce Online,* March/April 2000.

30. Anne C. Kubisch, Patricia Auspos, Prudence Brown, Robert Chaskin, Karen Fulbright-Anderson, and Ralph Hamilton, *Voices From the Field II: Reflections on Comprehensive Community Change* (Washington, DC: The Aspen Institute, 2002).

31. "Good planners and administrators said, 'What we have here is a bull's-eye. Let's see how much we can hit it with,' and they began adding day care, crime programs, small-business incubators, job training, tax-exempt bond financing.' " Richard Cowden, quoted in Carl Vogel, "Open for Business," *The Neighborhood Works* 20, no.1 (January/February 1997). See also Marilyn Gittell, Kathe Newman, and Francois Pierre-Louis, *Empowerment Zones: An Opportunity Missed* (New York: Howard Samuels State Policy and Management Center, City University of New York, 2001); Sirianni and Friedland, *Civic Innovation in America*, 64–68; and Winton Pitcoff, "EZ'er Said Than Done," *Shelterforce Online,* July/August 2000.

32. Kubisch et al., *Voices From the Field II*, 13.

33. See Anne Kubisch, "Comprehensive Community Initiatives: Lessons in Neighborhood Transformation," *Shelterforce Online,* January/February 1996; and Lisbeth Schorr, *Common Purpose: Strengthening Families and Neighborhoods to Rebuild America* (New York: Doubleday, 1997).

34. Lewis D. Solomon, *In God We Trust? Faith-Based Organizations and the Quest to Solve America's Social Ills* (Lanham, MD: Lexington Books, 2003), 83–87. See also Hurley, "On Crime as Science."

35. Meghan Meyer, "Foundation Accepts Delray Activist's Resignation," *Palm Beach Post,* April 24, 2003.

36. Traynor, "Community Building." Pablo Eisenberg claims that, in the last twenty years, "community accountability lost its cachet with CDC directors and staff" ("Time to Remove the Rose-Colored Glasses").

37. William Traynor, *Reflections on Community Organizing and Resident Engagement in the Rebuilding Communities Initiative* (Baltimore: Annie E. Casey Foundation, 2002): 23–24; Rebecca Stone and Benjamin Butler, *Core Issues in Comprehensive Community-Building Initiatives: Exploring Power and Race* (Chicago: Chapin Hall Center for Children, 2000), 64.

38. Leon Fooksman, "Village Foundation to Cease Operations," *Fort Lauderdale Sun-Sentinel,* July 16, 2004.

39. Meghan Meyer, "Delray Agency's Director Resigns," *Palm Beach Post,* April 22, 2003.

40. Quoted in Kubisch et al., *Voices from the Field II*, 56.

41. Pitcoff, "EZ'er Said Than Done."

42. Pers. comm., October 8, 2004. Xavier de Souza Briggs makes the same claim about nonprofit community development organizations:

Some years back, two colleagues and I, in a study of the social effects of community development in U. S. cities, found that this organizational capacity to manage in a more participatory way was underdeveloped even in respected "community-based" nonprofit organizations that interacted regularly with resident clients and held community participation as a core commitment or ethos. Managers reacted tensely to "gripe and grievance" sessions with their clients—sessions that might have been structured differently—while residents participated unevenly, expecting that important decisions had already been made. (*Planning Together*, 3)

43. Stone and Butler, "Core Issues," 131; see also Andrew Mott, "Twenty-Five Years of Building Power and Capacity," *Shelterforce Online,* March/April 2000.
44. Fooksman, "Village Foundation To Cease Operations," and Shah, "Nearly 1 in 4 Third Graders May Fail."

Notes to Chapter 7

1. Pers. comm., March 3, 1995.
2. "In any effort to make democracy more deliberative, the single most important institution outside government is the education system," say the political theorists Amy Gutmann and Dennis Thompson in *Democracy and Disagreement* (Cambridge, MA: Belknap Press of Harvard University Press, 1996), 359–61. See also their *Why Deliberative Democracy?* (Princeton, NJ: Princeton University Press, 2004).
3. Mathews, *Is There a Public for the Public Schools?* (Dayton, OH: Kettering Foundation, 1997). See also Clarence Stone, Jeffrey Henig, Bryan Jones, and Carol Pierannunzi, *Building Civic Capacity: The Politics of Reforming Urban Schools* (Lawrence: University Press of Kansas, 2001), and Henry Giroux, *The Abandoned Generation* (New York: Palgrave Macmillan, 2003).
4. See Kimpton and Sharp, *Reasons for Hope*; and Heather Voke, *Engaging the Public in its Schools.*
5. See James Comer, "Parent Participation in the Schools," *Phi Delta Kappan,* February 1986; Joyce Epstein and Lori Connors, *Trust Fund: School, Family, and Community Partnerships in High Schools* (Boston: Center on Families, Communities, Schools, and Children's Learning, 1992); Tony Wagner, *How Schools Change* (Boston: Beacon Press, 1994); and Deborah Meier, "The Road to Trust," *American School Board Journal,* September 2003.
6. For one typical example, see Marc Hansen, "School Board vs. The World," *Des Moines Register,* July 16, 2005.
7. Jeffrey S. Kimpton and Jonathan Considine, "The Tough Sledding of District-led Engagement," *School Administrator,* September 1999, and Leighninger, "Working with the Public."
8. Judy Molland, "Parents Are Going Beyond Bake Sales to Help Support Public Education," *Parenthood.com,* January 2004. See also "Poll: Most Parents Raise, Spend Money for Schools," www.cnn.com//2004/EDUCATION/02/25/parents.school. supplies.ap/index.html (accessed February 25, 2004).

9. Karen Kleinz, "Engaging the Public in the Public Schools," *Focus on Study Circles,* Spring 2000.

10. Pers. comm. with Paul Thomas, October 20, 2005; pers. comm. with Anne Bryant, November 3, 2005; see also "Small Groups Produce Big Changes in Westminster, Colorado," www.nsba.org (accessed November 4, 2005); and Resnick, *Communities Count.*

11. Leighninger, "Working with the Public." See also Caroline Hendrie, "In U. S. Schools, Race Still Counts," *EdWeek,* January 21, 2004.

12. While laws like No Child Left Behind require schools to divulge more information, they give little guidance on how parents and educators ought to use this information. Critics say that while legislators endorse the idea of public engagement, they don't give much support for schools that want to make it happen. See Wendy Puriefoy, "Why the Public is Losing Faith in the 'No Child' Law," *EdWeek,* June 8, 2005.

13. School Accountability for Learning and Teaching (SALT) Leadership Team, *Conducting School Report Night* (Providence: Rhode Island Department of Education, 1997).

14. See Martha McCoy, Biren Nagda, and Molly Barrett, "Mix It Up: Crossing Social Boundaries as a Pathway to Youth Civic Engagement," *National Civic Review,* April 2006. Pers. comm., Amy Malick, June 7, 2005. See *Reaching Across Boundaries: Talk to Create Change* (Pomfret, CT: Southern Poverty Law Center and the Study Circles Resource Center, 2003).

15. See Jean Johnson and Will Friedman, "Dear Public: Can We Talk?" *School Administrator*, February 2006.

16. National Education Association Foundation for the Improvement of Education, "Engaging Public Support for Teachers' Professional Development," Fall 2000 (www.neafoundation.org/publications/engaging.htm).

17. Jeanne Jehl, Martin J. Blank, and Barbara McCloud, *Education and Community Building: Connecting Two Worlds* (Washington, DC: Institute for Educational Leadership, 2001), 23–24.

18. See Donald Borut, Anne Bryant, and Paul Houston, "Conflict or Consensus? Why Collaboration Between Cities and Schools Is the Key to Reform," *EdWeek,* September 21, 2005.

19. Portions of this section appeared in Leighninger, "Shared Governance."

20. There are obvious parallels between processes like Total Quality Management, which engage employees in small-group discussions of how to improve workplace practices, and democratic governance efforts that involve citizens in discussions of how to improve the community. See Randy Schenkat, *Quality Connections: Transforming Schools Through Total Quality Management* (Alexandria, VA: Association for Supervision and Curriculum Development, 1993).

21. Biren Nagda, "Description of Inglewood, California" (report to the Study Circles Best Practices Project, Pomfret, CT, 2000).

22. Ibid.

23. Duke Helfand, "Inglewood Writes the Book on Success," *Los Angeles Times,* April 30, 2000.

24. Ibid.

25. Pers. comm. with Andrea Bobbitt, June 7, 2005.

26. Portions of this section appeared in Matt Leighninger, "Marrying Citizens and Educators in Decision Making," *School Administrator,* October 2005.

27. The Public Education Fund Network represents Local Education Funds (LEFs) in thirty-four states. See Elizabeth Useem, "From the Margins to the Center of School Reform: A Look at the Work of Local Education Funds in Seventeen Communities," *Public Education Network Research Series,* Number 1 (1999).

28. Pers. comm., March 22, 2004.

29. Ibid.

30. Pers. comm., May 27, 2004.

31. Pers. comm., May 27, 2004.

32. Pers. comm., March 22, 2004.

33. Clarence Stone, "Civic Capacity and Urban Education," *Urban Affairs Review,* May 2001.

34. These dynamics are explored more thoroughly in Jehl et al., *Education and Community Building.*

35. "In a society where we have pushed for greater citizen involvement and responsibility and pushed the devolution of government responsibility and decision making ever deeper into the community, public engagement represents the natural redistribution of both the responsibility and the accountability for public education. In successful engagement, the word 'power' is replaced with responsibility and accountability." Kimpton and Considine, "The Tough Sledding," 10.

36. See Archon Fung, *Empowered Participation: Reinventing Urban Democracy* (Princeton, NJ: Princeton University Press, 2004).

37. Donald R. Moore and Gail Merritt, *Chicago's Local School Councils: What the Research Says* (Chicago: Designs for Change, 2002).

38. Archon Fung, "Deliberation Where You Least Expect It: Citizen Participation in Government," *Connections,* Fall 2003: 30–33. See also Fung, "Recipes for Public Spheres: Eight Institutional Design Choices and their Consequences," *Journal of Political Philosophy* 11, no. 3 (2003).

39. "Chicago Local School Councils Run Short of Candidates," *IASB School Board News Bulletin,* April 2004.

40. Amanda Paulson, "Chicago Hope: Maybe *This* Will Work," *Christian Science Monitor,* September 21, 2004.

41. Archon Fung, "Can Social Movements Save Democracy?" *Boston Review,* February/March 2003.

42. Sheldon H. Berman, "Teaching Civics: A Call to Action," *Principal Leadership,* September 2004.

43. Ibid.

44. Plainfield Accountability Task Force, *Plainfield Public School District Accountability System,* 2001.

45. Pers. comm., September 27, 1995. See also Larry Leverett, "Connecting the Disconnected," *School Administrator,* September 1999.

46. Pamela Coumbe, "Reach Out, Bring In, Work Together: Parent Involvement Is Recognized as a Key Ingredient in any School Reform Effort," *School Leader,* September/October 1998.

47. Kimpton and Sharp, *Reasons for Hope.*

48. Leverett, "Connecting the Disconnected."

49. R. F. Elmore, *Building a New Structure for School Leadership* (Washington, DC: Albert Shanker Institute, 2000).

50. Larry Leverett, "Warriors to Advance Equity: An Argument for Distributing Leadership," *Spotlight on Student Success,* 2002.

Notes to Chapter 8

1. Portions of this section appeared in Leighninger, "Smart Democracy: How to Engage Citizens," *IQ Report* 36, no. 9 (September 2004).

2. Weeks, "The Practice of Deliberative Democracy," 363.

3. For one exploration of this question, see Janet M. Kelly, "The Dilemma of the Unsatisfied Customer in a Market Model of Public Administration," *Public Administration Review* 65, no.1 (January 2005).

4. Frank Benest, "Engaging Citizens in the Bottom Line," *American City and County,* December 1997.

5. See Sirianni and Friedland, *Civic Innovation in America*; Epstein et al., *Results That Matter,* 76-122; and Jonathan Rauch, "Volunteer Nation," *National Journal,* November 23, 2002.

6. Pers. comm., December 14, 2004.

7. See Weeks, "The Practice of Deliberative Democracy," 363–64; also Simonsen and Robbins, "The Benefit Equity Principle," 93.

8. Weeks, "The Practice of Deliberative Democracy," 364.

9. Ibid., 365.

10. Jessica Flintoft, "Participatory Budgeting" (report to the Hewlett Foundation, Menlo Park, CA, May 21, 2004).

11. "Public Space Management in Downtown Eugene," www.downtowneugene.com (accessed June 20, 2005).

12. Weeks, "The Practice of Deliberative Democracy," 366.

13. Weeks also points out that the questionnaires were significantly more complex than most surveys, and that they were mailed out over the holidays. Weeks, "The Practice of Deliberative Democracy," 366.

14. Ibid., 370.

15. Ibid., 370. See also Simonsen and Robbins, "The Benefit Equity Principle."

16. Comments at a meeting in Lakewood, CO, September 9, 2004.

17. See Sydney Cresswell, Jordan Wishy, and Terrence Maxwell, *Fostering Social Equity and Economic Opportunity Through Citizen Participation: An Innovative Approach to Municipal Service Delivery* (Albany: Intergovernmental Solutions Program, State University of New York, 2003); Howard Chernick and Andrew Reschovsky, *Lost in the Balance: How State Policies Affect the Fiscal Health of Cities* (Washington, DC: The Brookings Institution on Urban and Metropolitan Policy, 2001).

18. Benest, "Engaging Citizens."

19. Pers. comm. with Pamela Beal, August 30, 2005.

20. Pers. comm., February 12, 2002.

21. Quoted in Hurley, "On Crime as Science." See also Sampson et al., "Neighborhoods and Violent Crime."

22. Pers. comm., February 12, 2002.

23. Pers. comm., February 6, 2001.
24. The author is an authority on this subject.
25. Pers. comm., May 10, 2001.
26. Pamela Beal and Jacqueline Housel, *Promoting Cooperative Strategies to Reduce Racial Profiling* (Washington, DC: U. S. Dept. of Justice Community Oriented Policing Services office, December 2003).
27. Pers. comm., February 12, 2002.
28. Pers. comm. with Terry Amsler and William Potapchuk, December 14, 2004; See also William Potapchuk, "Building an Infrastructure."
29. "Seeking a Deli Truce," *Buffalo News,* July 8, 2003. See also Beal and Housel, *Promoting Cooperative Strategies.*
30. Pers. comm. with Angela Jones, February 3, 2004. Pers. comm. with Pamela Beal, February 4, 2004.
31. Pers. comm., July 12, 2005.
32. See Berry et al., *Rebirth.*
33. See Bill Potapchuk et al., "Growing Governance Deliberatively."
34. See Cooper and Kathi, "Neighborhood Councils and City Agencies," 43–53, and Thomson, *Neighborhood to Nation.*
35. Ninety-five neighborhoods have applied for certification and eighty-three have been certified, according to the website of the Los Angeles Citywide Alliance of Neighborhood Councils (www.allncs.org; accessed July 12, 2005).
36. Robert Greene, "Not in My Neighborhood Council."
37. Attempts are being made to exempt the neighborhood councils from the open meetings requirements, or at least to clarify and streamline these procedures. For a comprehensive look at the status of the L. A. councils, see Juliet Musso, Christopher Weare, and Terry Cooper, *Neighborhood Councils in Los Angeles: A Midterm Report* (Los Angeles: University of Southern California Neighborhood Participation Project, June 7, 2004), 16, 47.
38. Greene, "Not In My Neighborhood Council."
39. Ken Thomson has defended the L. A. stakeholder policy, saying that "the importance of the 'stakeholder' concept that has been developed in Los Angeles cannot be overstated. By basing all issues of eligibility on this concept, and using it in every discussion of neighborhood council formation, everyone involved in the council process has the occasion to ask themselves, 'Who *does* have a stake in this community?' " Thomson, "Los Angeles Participation: The Vision and the Reality" (paper presented at "Civic Engagement Through Neighborhood Empowerment: The L.A. Experiment and Beyond," a conference of the Neighborhood Participation Project at the University of Southern California, January 25, 2002).
40. Ibid.
41. Musso, 24
42. Musso, 48.
43. Greene, "Not In My Neighborhood."
44. The diverse character of Los Angeles is reflected in the great variety of projects pursued by the neighborhood councils: Coastal San Pedro, near the harbor, is creating a freshwater marsh; in Mid City West, the council established a Crime Alert Network that helped to apprehend a serial burglar; and suburban Chatsworth established "Equestrian Safety Month." *Neighborhood Councils' Accomplishments.* City

of Los Angeles Department of Neighborhood Empowerment, May 27, 2005 (www. lacityneighborhoods.com).

45. Robert Greene, "Grasping for the Ring of Power," *LA Weekly*, June 30, 2005.

46. Ibid. Work is already underway on this front: DONE is clarifying the election system for neighborhood councils, and trying to streamline the open meeting procedures.

47. Quoted in Cresswell et al., "Fostering Social Equity," 6.

48. In other cities, attempts like this to redraw boundaries have been somewhat controversial, but in Rochester the neighborhood association presidents seem to have been fairly amenable to the NBN sector plan. It probably helped that Argust gave the neighborhood leaders a chance to give input on the boundaries, and followed their recommendations. See Rick Armon, "Time to ID Your Sector," *Rochester Democrat and Chronicle*, February 9, 2003; also Berry et al., *Rebirth*.

49. Pers. comm., July 13, 2005.

50. Cresswell et al.,"Fostering Social Equity," 12.

51. See *Building on the Fruits of our Neighbors: Neighbors Building Neighborhoods Progress Report* (Rochester, NY: City of Rochester Department of Community Development Bureau of Neighborhood Initiatives, 2001), and John Melville, Joe Brooks, Doug Henton, and John Parr, *Inclusive Stewardship: Emerging Collaborations Between Neighborhoods and Regions* (Denver, CO: Alliance for Regional Stewardship, 2003), 21–22.

52. William Johnson, "Revitalization and Equity in a Weak-Market City" (speech to the Community Development Partnership Network, Atlanta, May 5, 2004).

53. Lara Becker, "Neighbors Program Takes Stock of Itself," *Rochester Democrat and Chronicle,* June 22, 1999.

54. Cresswell et al., "Fostering Social Equity," 9.

55. Cresswell et al., "Fostering Social Equity," 11–13.

56. Pers. comm. with Tom Argust, July 13, 2005.

57. Dibya Sarkar, "Government at the Grass Roots," *Government E-Business,* September 2001.

58. Pers. comm. with Lois Giess, June 8, 2004.

59. Pers. comm., July 13, 2005.

60. Pers. comm., July 13, 2005.

61. Pers. comm., December 9, 2005.

62. Lara Becker Liu, " 'State of the City' to Sound Warning," *Rochester Democrat and Chronicle,* March 1, 2004.

63. Pers. comm., July 13, 2005.

64. Lara Becker, "Neighborhood Groups Redefine Power," *Rochester Democrat and Chronicle,* January 7, 2000.

65. As Ken Thomson puts it, "The success of information flow in a participation system is not the quantity of information provided to stakeholders, but the ability of the system to distill down that quantity into meaningful packets of value to community stakeholders in making their own decisions and having input into the decisions of government" ("Los Angeles Participation").

66. There are other similarly innovative networks, like the one maintained by the Jacksonville Community Council in Florida and the Citizen's League in Minnesota. See Epstein et al., *Results That Matter,* 40, 102–14.

67. Quoted in Leighninger, *The Rise of Democratic Governance*, 9.

68. See Boxer-Macomber, "Too Much Sun?"; also Chambers, "Deliberative Democratic Theory."

Notes to Conclusion

1. Research also suggests that public officials must be willing to trust citizens in order to be supportive of citizen involvement efforts. See Kaifeng Yang, "Public Administrators' Trust in Citizens: A Missing Link in Citizen Involvement Efforts," *Public Administration Review,* May/June 2005.
2. *The Michael DelGiorno Show*, KFAQ broadcast, January 27, 2005.
3. Pers. comm., October 20, 2005.
4. Pers. comm. with Carol McGowen, coordinator of Tulsa Talks, October 7, 2005.
5. Pers. comm., October 20, 2005.
6. Pers. comm. with Steve Burkholder, September 14, 2005.
7. There are some temporary projects that are more republican in nature, such as citizen's juries and Deliberative Polls®. These initiatives aim to recruit a small, representative sampling of citizens who will impress public officials with the quality of their insights. At best, these projects are inspiring demonstrations of how citizens can grapple with tough policy choices. At worst, they seem like sporadic, unrealistic deliberations—sort of a civic *Brigadoon*—that aren't sustainable enough to be a regular part of public life. See Ryfe, "Does Deliberative Democracy Work?" 49–71; Flavin and Dougherty, "Science And Citizenship," 46–50; Arthur Lupia, "The Wrong Tack," *Legal Affairs,* January/February 2004; and Richard Posner, "Smooth Sailing," *Legal Affairs,* January/February 2004.
8. Sara Evans makes this argument about the democratic movement for suffrage leading to purely republican reforms in *Born for Liberty,* 172.
9. Wyman and Shulman, *From Venting to Inventing*, 5.
10. Pers. comm., October 20, 2005.
11. The examples Morone deals with include the two national political parties, the major labor unions, and the public service agencies set up during the Progressive Era.
12. Morone, *Democratic Wish*, 336.
13. Ken Thomson, who has been studying neighborhood councils for twenty years, says that "technically and legally in almost every case, they are 'merely' advisory. But in practice they have real clout. They are recognized as the legitimate voice of the neighborhoods they serve" ("Los Angeles Participation").
14. Quoted in Wright et al., *Rise of Democratic Governance*, 4.
15. Berry, Portney, and Thomson discuss this problem in *The Rebirth of Urban Democracy*.
16. See Boxer-Macomber, "Too Much Sun?"
17. Some communities have set up ombudsman offices to bear the brunt of these requests, which range from complicated and politically sensitive petitions to simple questions that can be answered by reading the public service pages of a telephone book. Joe Moore, a Chicago alderman, claims that his office fields thousands of these requests every year (pers. comm., June 11, 2004). Even members of Congress are inundated with them; many legislators feel that this kind of constituent service is the key to being reelected.
18. Briggs, *Planning Together*, 18.

19. Meeting at the Study Circles Resource Center, April 5, 2005. The Orton Foundation provides technical assistance to communities on different kinds of planning efforts.
20. Quoted in Wright et al., *Rise of Democratic Governance,* 4.
21. Though they are closer to the "ground floor" of democracy, efforts to affect regional policy may still be the most uncommon, simply because there are so few regional policies. Organizers at that level will continue to face the challenge of forming metro-wide coalitions in order to recruit participants and implement changes all across a region.
22. Pers. comm., February 16, 2006. Beltramini has mobilized her constituents to help make important land use decisions in Troy.
23. One rendition of this argument appeared in Matt Leighninger, "For Next Set of Campaign Issues, Think Locally," *Christian Science Monitor,* July 13, 2005.
24. See Sirianni and Friedland, *Civic Innovation in America,* 261.
25. The Chatham Party city council candidates spent dramatically less on their campaign than their Democratic and Republican rivals. See Gregory Seay, "A New Party Sprouts from the Grassroots," *Hartford Courant,* November 24, 2005.
26. Ben Eason, who runs several weekly newspapers, says that these free papers "are a healthy and growing segment of the industry. Their reporting includes more of the 'chicken dinner' news about things like school lunch menus, but this may give them a chance to play the broad democratic role that daily newspapers have traditionally played." Pers. comm., September 27, 2005.
27. Pers. comm., September 27, 2005.
28. See Lukensmeyer and Torres, *Public Deliberation,* 33–43.
29. Local governments currently conduct a fair amount of "e-business" (allowing residents to apply for permits, pay parking tickets, or file complaints online), political candidates and interest groups use mass emailing to gather supporters and donations, and political junkies who are technologically oriented use the online chatrooms and weblogs. The Internet has clearly become an important political tool, but so far it doesn't seem to have had the impact some observers predicted in the mid-1990s. See Michael Delli Carpini and Scott Keeter, "The Internet and an Informed Citizenry," in *The Civic Web,* eds. David Anderson and Michael Cornfield (Lanham, MD: Rowman & Littlefield, 2003). For a Canadian perspective on this, see *Citizens and Government in a Digital Era* (Ottawa: EKOS Associates, 2003).
30. See Leighninger, "Smart Democracy."
31. Curtis Clark of IBM and Terrance Herron of Microsoft Public Sector (presentation at the National League of Cities Congress of Cities, Charlotte, NC, December 8, 2005).
32. Presentation at the National League of Cities Congress of Cities, Charlotte, NC, December 9, 2005.
33. This in turn may reinforce the social and political inequalities apparent in the "digital divide"—the fact that low-income, less educated people are far less likely to have access to computers and the Internet. Concerns about the digital divide are already being voiced, but the situation will become far more difficult if the Internet suddenly becomes a full-fledged arena for public life. It may be that communities can bridge the gap by expanding access to the Internet at public libraries and other locations, as Rochester has done.

34. See Jeff Haynes, *Democracy and Civil Society in the Third World: Politics and New Political Movements* (Cambridge, UK: Polity Press, 1997).

35. For a description of the Porto Alegre model by the people who developed it, see Iain Bruce, ed. and tr., *The Porto Alegre Alternative: Direct Democracy in Action* (Ann Arbor, MI: Pluto Press, 2004).

36. For more thorough explorations of the effects of democratic governance on social equality, see Young, *Inclusion and Democracy*; Seyla Benhabib, ed., *Democracy and Difference: Contesting the Boundaries of the Political* (Princeton, NJ: Princeton University Press, 1996); and David Miller, "Is Deliberative Democracy Unfair to Disadvantaged Groups?" in *Democracy as Public Deliberation*, ed. Maurizio Passerin D'Entrèves (Manchester, UK: Manchester University Press, 2002).

37. David Ryfe, a journalism professor who has studied democratic governance, writes that, "To the extent that learning takes place [in a deliberative discussion], individuals cease to represent the community from which they were drawn" ("Does Deliberative Democracy Work?" 53).

38. Pers. comm., October 29, 2005.

Index